This book belongs to

17/7/1989.

GREAT WESTERN COACHES APPENDIX

Volume One

STANDARD PASSENGER STOCK

This photograph shows an end view of a third class Hawksworth corridor carriage No. 796, built in 1946 to Lot No. 1691.

GREAT WESTERN COACHES APPENDIX

Volume One
STANDARD PASSENGER STOCK

by J. H. Russell

Oxford Publishing Co.

SBN 86093 084 X

Set by Katerprint Co. Ltd.
Printed and Bound in the City of Oxford

This work is dedicated to the memory of Michael Longridge and his enthusiasm for the Great Western Railway Company.

Photographs in this work are by courtesy of British Rail, the late Michael Longridge collection and the author's collection.

The publishers wish to point out that several of the line illustrations are taken from official drawings and due to the age of these, the reproduction is not as clear as they would wish.

Published by Oxford Publishing Co.
8 The Roundway,
Headington,
Oxford.

INTRODUCTION

Having already completed two previous works dealing exclusively with the carriage rolling stock of the Great Western Railway, it was assumed that, with such a specialised subject as passenger coaches, a two volume coverage would more than satisfy the interest of the average enthusiast-cum-modeller.

In the event however, this was an erroneous assumption. *Coaches I* and *II** have actually stimulated a wider search for coach details, and rather than proving an end in themselves, these two books have engendered quite a new-found enthusiasm for the chocolate and cream vehicles, constructed and operated by the Great Western Railway.

Rather to my surprise, the main comments I received about the carriage books were, not so much about the vehicles I had put into volumes I and II, but about all those I had left out! In fact, it soon became apparent that if I was to keep my readers' good faith, I would have to search around for photographs and information about all those vehicles which had been omitted from the first two works.

Fortunately for me, my old friend and fellow modeller the late Michael Longridge, had, before his lamented death in 1954, energetically photographed a vast collection of Great Western coaches. Add to these, many of the official photographs taken for record purposes by the studio at Swindon factory, plus several of my own humble efforts, and I was pleased to find that nearly all the gaps left in my two previous works could be filled by this edition of *Great Western Coaches Appendix* and its second volume, to follow.

With such a mass of pictorial material, and being limited by size and costs, it has once again been necessary to divide this work into two volumes to give as great and final coverage as possible. Volume One deals with the standard passenger carrying stock, in other words those vehicles in which seated passengers normally travelled. These were the Firsts, Brake Thirds, and Composites. Volume Two will follow on with the specific duty vehicles, coaches such as Slips, Dining Cars, Sleepers, Mail Vans, Brake Vans, Saloons, etc., plus any of the other special stock which has not been illustrated before.

Limited again by space, the accent in this *Appendix* has had to rest on the photographs, only comparatively few drawings being added where it was thought the need arose, to make a design point clear to the reader. Modellers can, however, obtain any of the drawings through the BR/Oxford Publishing Co. Joint Venture by referring to the list of diagrams and code numbers on the back pages of each volume.

In order to show the spread over from Great Western to British Rail ownership, I have also included many of the purely British Rail carriage illustrations, which were after all, not only constructed, but also photographed at Swindon. My only hope now, is that modellers and enthusiasts alike will accept this collection for the reason which brought it into being, an earnest wish to make available to all those seeking more information, a further mass of detail which it has been my pleasure to assimilate over the years.

Jim Russell
June 1981

**A Pictorial Record of Great Western Coaches: Part One (1838–1913)* and *Part Two (1903–1948), published by The Oxford Publishing Co., Oxford.*

INDEX

INDEX

INDEX

INDEX

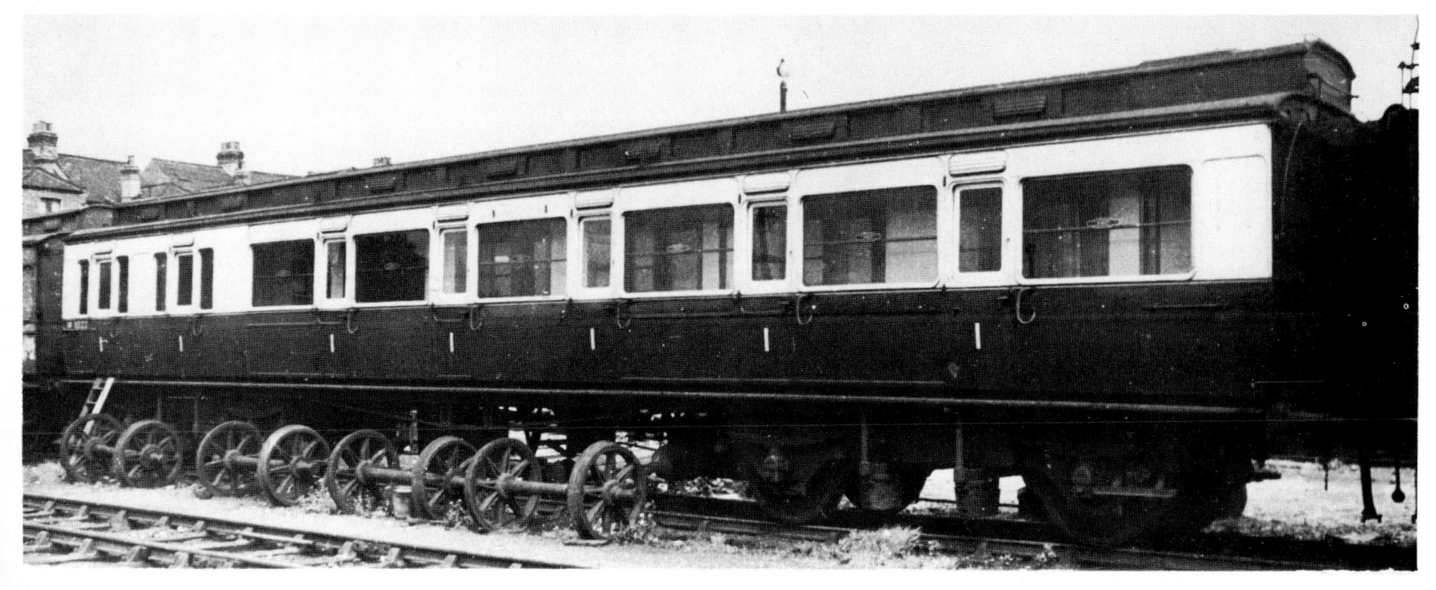

Fig. 1

DIAGRAM A7
FIRST Corridor Carriage
Clerestory Stock

Lot 1001 of 1902
Running numbers 314/5
After 1907 8314/5
Lot 1007 of 1903
Running numbers 319–22
After 1907 8319–22
Dimensions: 58′ 0¾″ x 8′ 6¾″

Shown on this page, No. 8322 is seen at Old Oak Common in 1951, painted in chocolate and cream livery. The corridor side is depicted in **Fig. 1** and the compartment side in **Fig. 2**.

Fig. 2

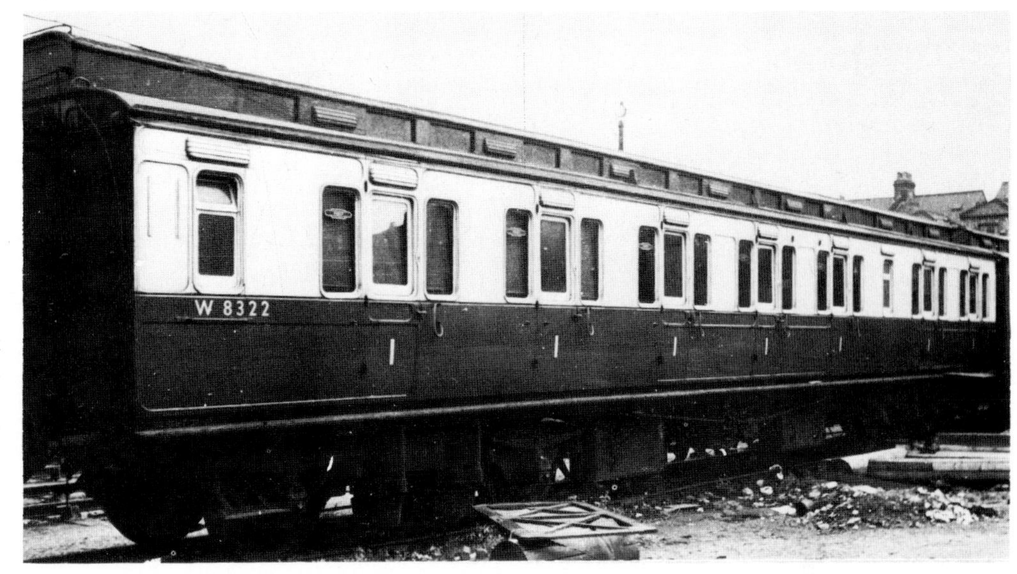

DIAGRAM A8
FIRST Corridor Carriage
Clerestory Stock

Lot 1021 of 1903
Running numbers 316–8
After 1907 8316–8
Dimensions: 58′ 0¾″ x 8′ 6¾″

Fig. 3 shows the compartment side of No. 8316 at Swindon in 1952, painted milk chocolate brown.

Fig. 3

Fig. 4

Fig.5

DIAGRAM A9
FIRST Non-Corridor Carriage
'Toplight' Stock, Bars I

Lot 1157 of 1908
Running numbers 8197–8216
Dimensions: 60′ 0″ x 9′ 0″

This series had only one toplight over the end compartment.

Fig. 4 No. 8201 in BR livery at Old Oak Common in 1950. **Fig. 5** Banbury is the location for this view of No. 8204, dating from 1951. **Fig. 6** No. 8199, photographed at Tyseley in 1950, is seen carrying GWR livery.

Fig. 6

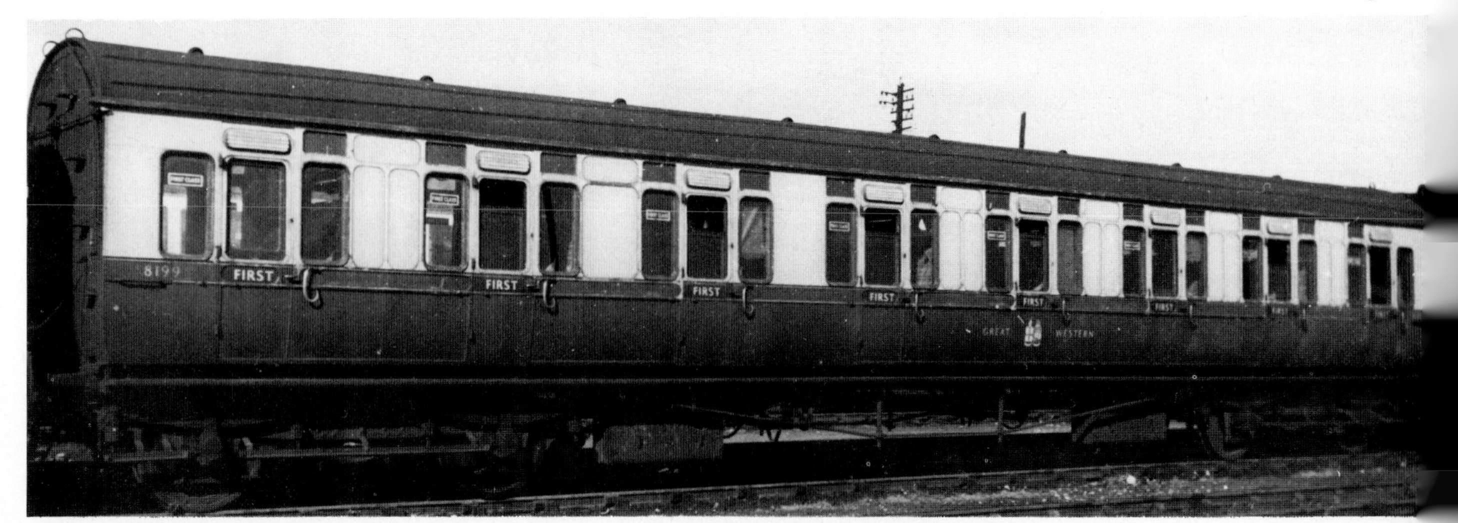

Fig. 7

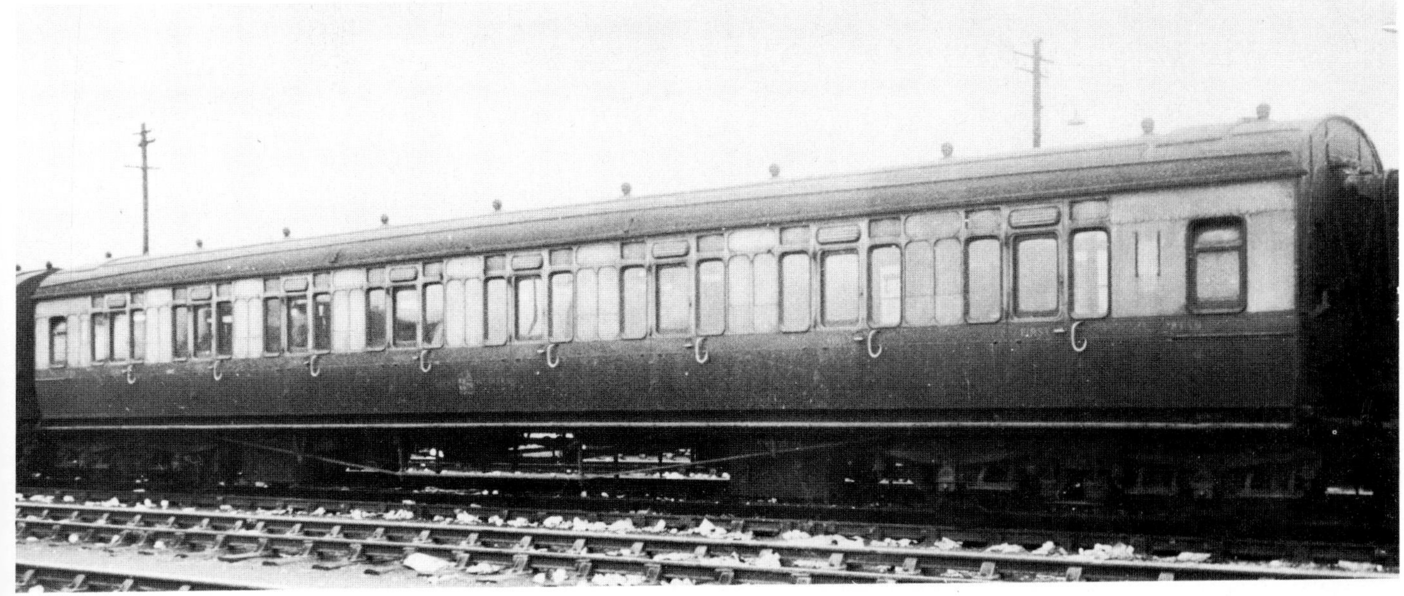

Fig. 8

DIAGRAM A10
FIRST Corridor Carriage
'Toplight' 'Fishguard Boat' Stock

Lot 1176 of 1910
Running numbers 8181–96
Dimensions: 70′ 0″ x 9′ 0″

Fig. 7 The corridor side of No. 8186 carries GWR livery in this photograph of 1950, taken at Old Oak Common. At the same location, the compartment side of No. 8189 is also seen in GWR livery (**Fig. 8**). The view is dated 1951, as is **Fig. 9**, showing No. 8194 at Old Oak Common and sporting GWR livery.

Fig. 9

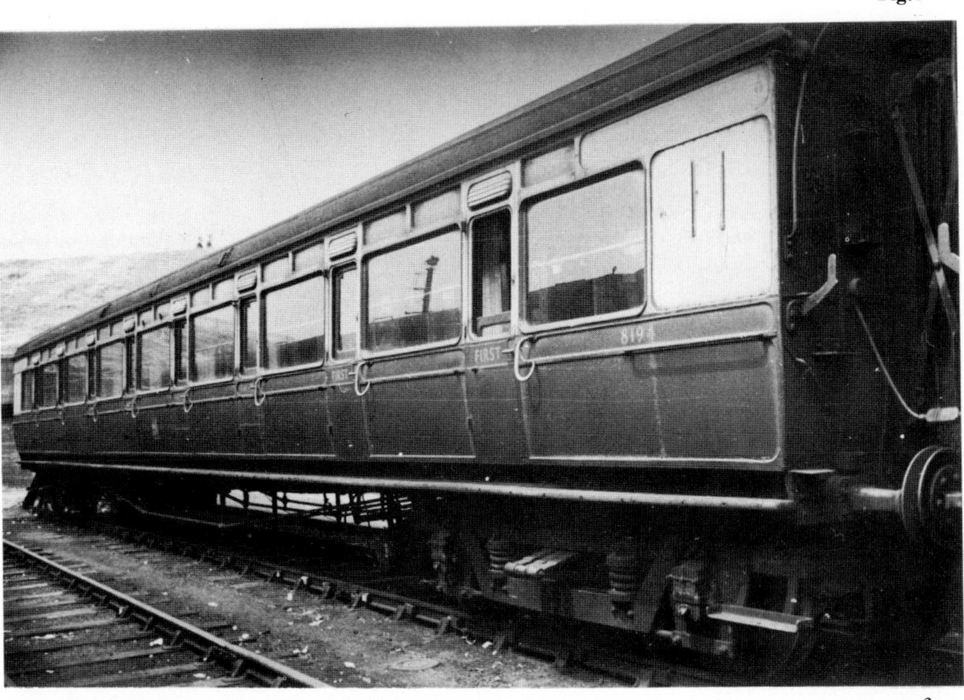

Fig. 10 A Swindon official photograph of No. 8178 dated 1920, illustrating the crimson livery with white roof and also the corridor side.

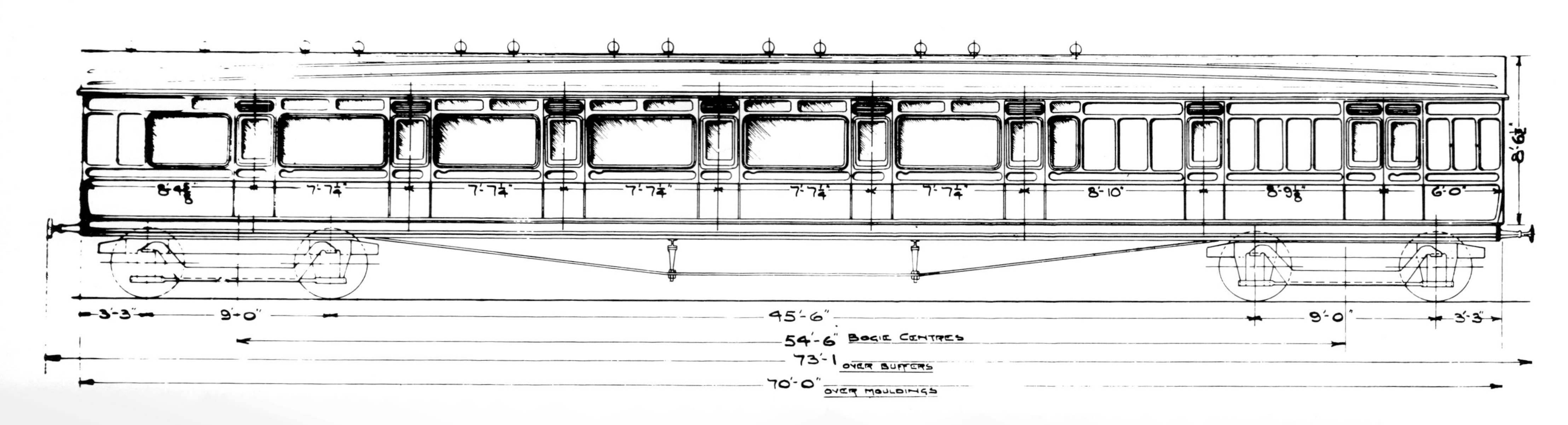

DIAGRAMS A10 and A11
BRAKE FIRST Corridor Carriage
'Fishguard Boat' Stock.

Fig. 10

Fig. 11

Fig. 12

DIAGRAM A11
BRAKE FIRST Corridor Carriage
'Fishguard Boat' Stock

Lot 1182 of 1910
Running numbers 8178–80
Dimensions: 70′ 0″ x 9′ 0″

Fig. 11 The corridor side of No. 8179, in BR livery at Old Oak Common in 1949. The compartment side of No. 8178 is shown in **Fig. 12**, wearing BR livery at Old Oak Common in 1951. Note that the air conditioning ducting has been removed from the roof.

Fig. 13 A close-up of the coupling, buffing, gangway and air-ducting connections between coaches. The carriages are Nos. 8187 (*A10*) and 8179 (*A11*) of the 'Cunard Ocean Special' train and are in 1922 crimson livery.

Fig. 13

DIAGRAMS A10 and *A11*
FIRST Corridor Carriage
'Fishguard Boat' Stock

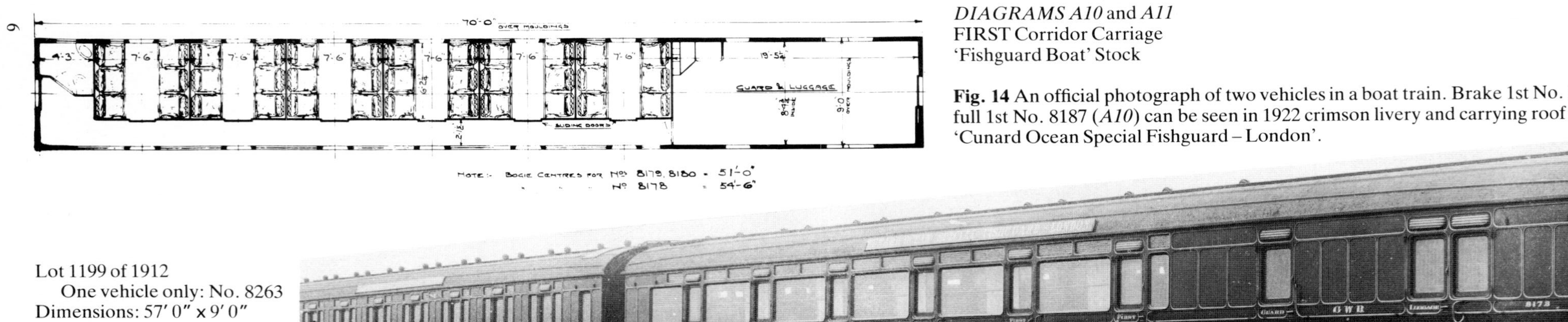

Fig. 14 An official photograph of two vehicles in a boat train. Brake 1st No. 8178 (*A11*) and full 1st No. 8187 (*A10*) can be seen in 1922 crimson livery and carrying roof boards reading 'Cunard Ocean Special Fishguard – London'.

Fig. 14

Lot 1199 of 1912
One vehicle only: No. 8263
Dimensions: 57' 0" x 9' 0"

DIAGRAM A12
FIRST Non-Corridor Carriage
'Toplight' Stock, Bars II

Fig. 15 Official photograph of No. 8263 in crimson livery with white roof.

Fig. 16

Fig. 17

DIAGRAM A13
FIRST Corridor Carriage
'Toplight' Stock, Multibar

Lot 1239 of 1914
Running numbers 8323–37
Dimensions: 69′ 11¼″ x 8′ 11¼″

Fig. 16 shows No. 8337 in this official Swindon record photograph displaying the crimson livery. **Fig. 17** depicts No. 8331 in the first BR livery at Old Oak Common in 1950. **Fig. 18** A three-quarter view of No. 8329, also at Old Oak Common and photographed in 1951.

Fig. 18

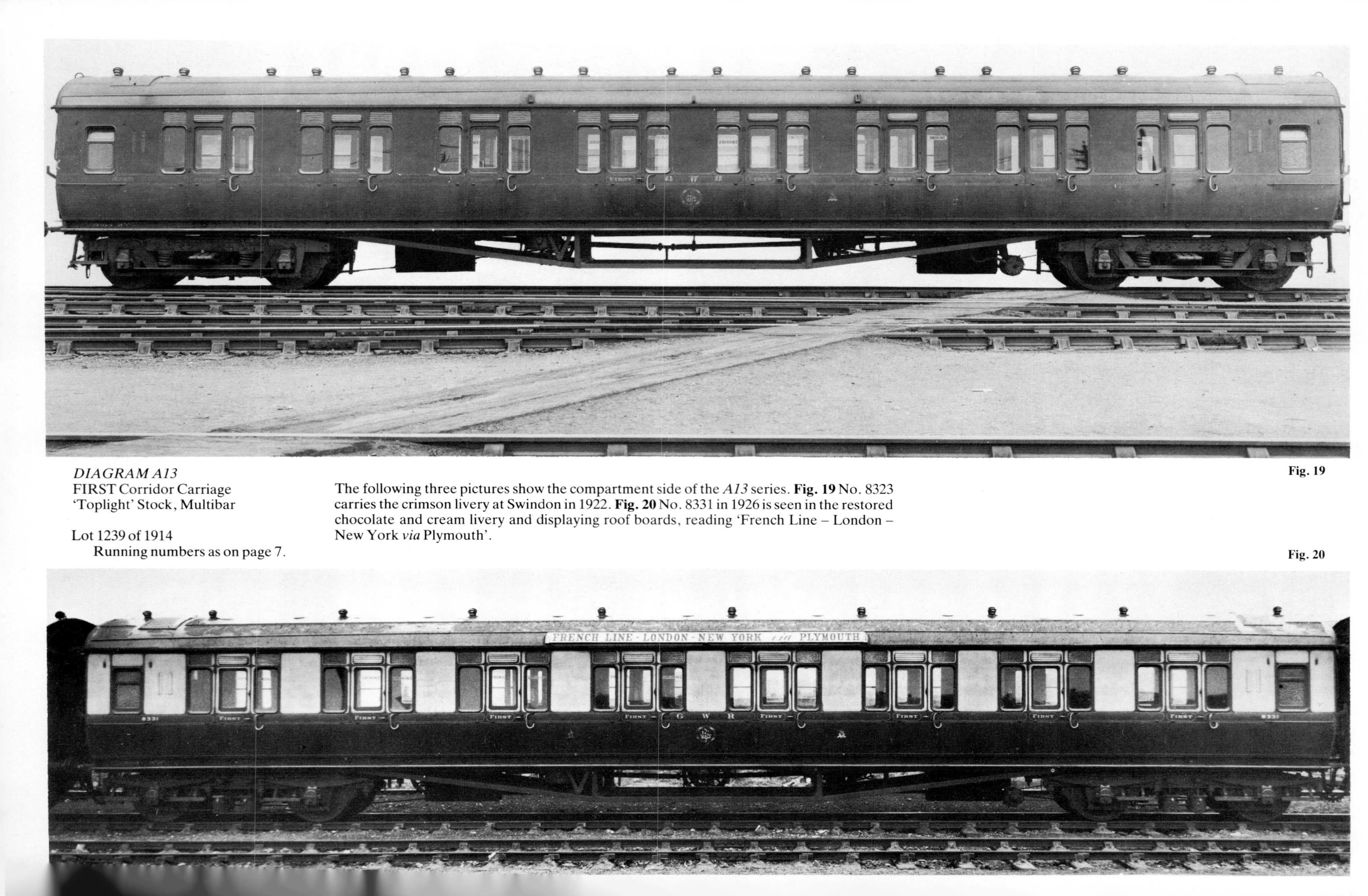

Fig. 19

DIAGRAM A13
FIRST Corridor Carriage
'Toplight' Stock, Multibar

Lot 1239 of 1914
Running numbers as on page 7.

The following three pictures show the compartment side of the *A13* series. **Fig. 19** No. 8323 carries the crimson livery at Swindon in 1922. **Fig. 20** No. 8331 in 1926 is seen in the restored chocolate and cream livery and displaying roof boards, reading 'French Line – London – New York *via* Plymouth'.

Fig. 20

Fig. 21 shows No. 8332 in the first BR livery at Old Oak Common in 1952.

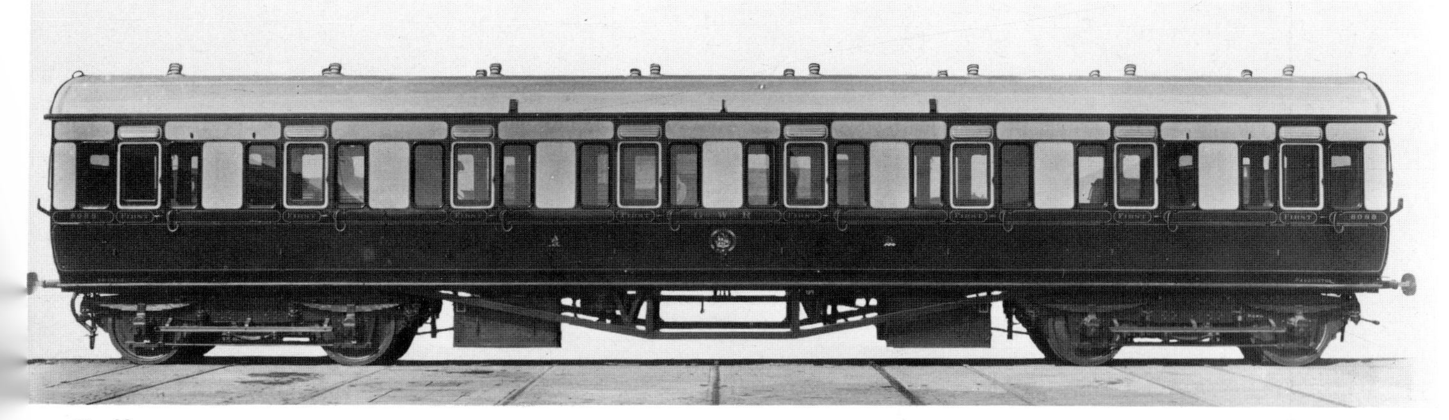

Fig. 22

DIAGRAM A15
FIRST Non-Corridor Carriage
Multibar Stock

Lot 1302 of 1922
Running numbers 8072–89
Dimensions: 56′ 11¼″ x 8′ 11¼″

Fig. 22 This official photograph shows No. 8088 in the GWR chocolate and cream livery with painted panels and is dated 1924. **Fig. 23** No. 8072 in the post-war GWR livery at Banbury in 1947. In **Fig. 24** No. 8080 is seen in the first BR livery at Old Oak Common in 1951.

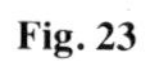

Fig. 23

Fig. 24

Fig. 25

DIAGRAM A16 (converted into A18)
FIRST Corridor Carriage
Bow-ended Ex-articulated Stock

Lot 1363 of 1925
Original running numbers 10001/9/17/25/33/41
Renumbered in 1936/7 8011–6
Rebuilt dimensions: 55′ 4¾″ x 9′ 0″
Rebuilt as separate vehicles in 1936/7

Fig. 25 No. 8011 at Old Oak Common in 1951.

DIAGRAM A17
FIRST BRAKE Corridor Carriage
Bow-ended Ex-articulated Stock

Lot 1364 of 1925
Original running numbers 10000/8/16/24/32/40
Renumbered in 1936/7 8017–9
Rebuilt dimensions: 58′ 3¾″ x 9′ 0″
Rebuilt as separate vehicles in 1936/7

No. 8017 at Old Oak Common in 1949. **Fig. 26** shows the compartment side, and **Fig. 27** illustrates the corridor side of the same vehicle. It will be noted that this is the left-hand van design.

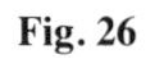

Fig. 26

Fig. 27

Fig. 28

DIAGRAM A18
FIRST Corridor Carriage
Bow-ended Ex-articulated Stock

Part of Lot 1363 of 1925
Renumbered in 1936 8014–6
Condemned April 1959

Fig. 28 Swindon record photograph, dated 1936, illustrating the 'roundel' livery. **Fig. 29** shows the compartment side of No. 8011 at Reading in 1947, sporting the post-war GWR livery. **Fig. 30** Vehicle No. 8015 standing in Reading station in 1947 with the corridor side towards the camera.

Fig. 29

Fig. 30

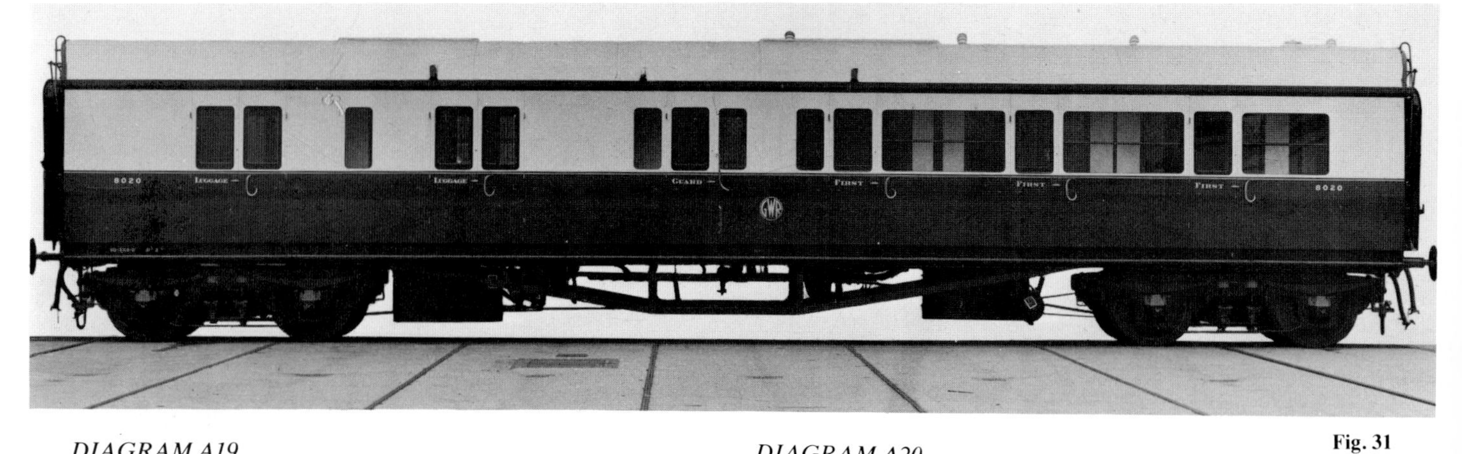

Fig. 31

DIAGRAM A19
BRAKE FIRST Corridor Carriage
Bow-ended Ex-articulated Stock

Part of Lot 1364 of 1925
Renumbered in 1937 8020–2
Condemned March 1962

Fig. 31 The corridor side of No. 8020 in 1937 livery with 'roundel'.

DIAGRAM A20
FIRST Corridor Carriage
Flat-ended Flush-sided Stock

Lot 1581 of 1937
Running numbers 8043–52
Dimensions: 60′ 1¼″ x 9′ 0″
Bogie centres: 44′ 7¼″
Provided with only one lavatory.

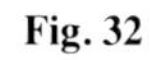
Fig. 32

Fig. 32 No. 8049, compartment side, at Old Oak Common in 1951.

Fig. 33 No. 8045, corridor side, also at Old Oak Common in 1951.

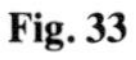
Fig. 33

DIAGRAM A22
FIRST Corridor Carriage
Flush-panelled Stock

Lot 1586 of 1938
Running numbers 8092-8111
Dimensions: 60′ 1¼″ x 8′ 11″
Bogie centres: 41′ 8″
Provided with 9′ pressed-steel bogies

Fig. 34 Corridor side of No. 8109 at Paddington in 1951 in strawberry and cream livery.

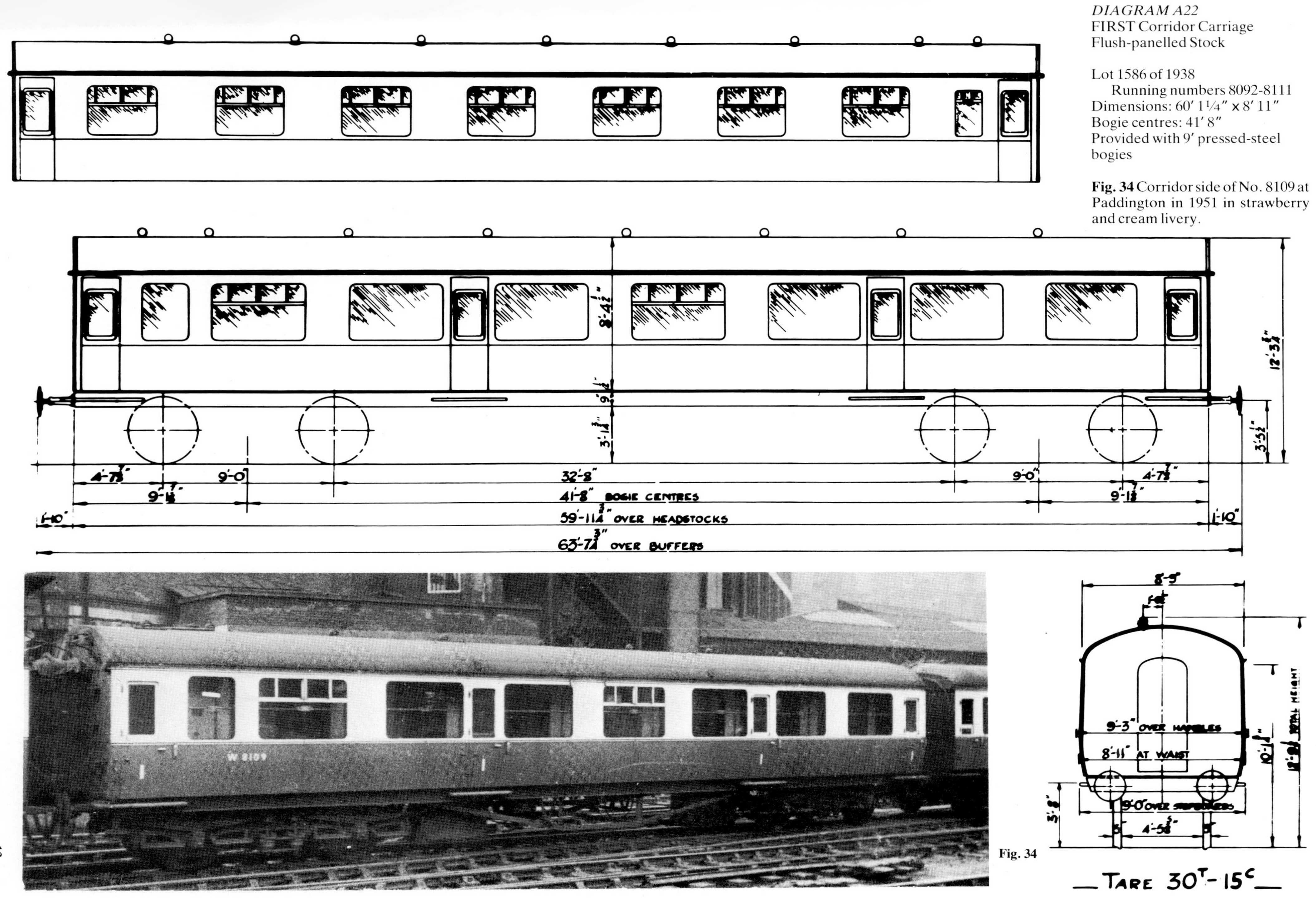

Fig. 34

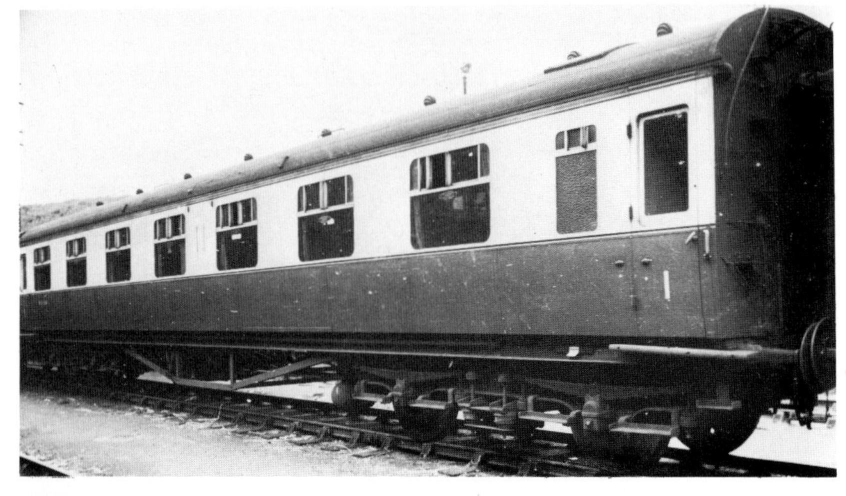

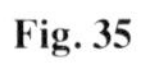

Fig. 35

DIAGRAM A23
FIRST Corridor Carriage
'Hawksworth' Stock

Lot 1688 of 1949
  Running numbers 8001–3
Lot 1703 of 1950
  Running numbers 8053–64
Lot 1734 of 1950
  Running numbers 8112–25
Dimensions: 64′ 0″ x 8′ 11″
Provided with only one lavatory.

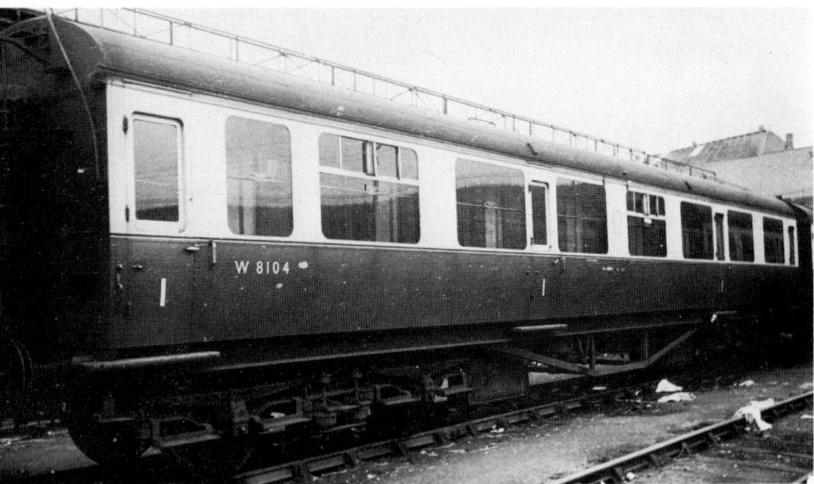

Fig. 35 No. 8104, compartment side, at Old Oak Common in 1951. **Fig. 36** The same vehicle but this time seen from the corridor side, photographed at the same location and date. **Fig. 37** shows the compartment side of No. 8057 at Old Oak Common in 1951, complete with 'Paddington and Bristol' roof boards. **Fig. 38** Corridor side of No. 8060 inside Old Oak Common carriage shed in 1951.

Fig. 36

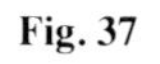

Fig. 37

Fig. 38

Fig. 39

FIRST Corridor Carriage
BR Mark 1 Standard Stock

Fig. 39 A 1951 vehicle, No. E13030, built to BR Lot 30019, with the corridor side facing the camera. **Fig. 40** shows the compartment side of No. W13077, constructed to BR Lot 30083 of 1953 (*Diagram BR116*). **Fig. 41** An example of a vehicle built to BR Lot 30147 of 1955, No. W13135, displays its compartment side to the camera.

Fig. 40

Fig. 41

FIRST Corridor Carriage
BR Mark 1 Standard Stock

BR Lot 30147 of 1955
Dimensions: 63′ 5″ x 9′ 0¾″

Fig. 42 No. W13135 in strawberry and cream livery.

Fig. 43

DIAGRAM C19
THIRD Non-Corridor Carriage
8-compartment Clerestory Stock

Lot 970 of 1901
Running numbers 5260–74
Renumbered in 1907 1351/3–5/9/61–4/6–9/71/3
Lot 971 of 1901
Running numbers 5231–40
Renumbered in 1907 1331/3/6–9/41–3/9
Lot 981 of 1901
Running numbers 5275–9
Renumbered in 1907 1375/6/9/82/3
Dimensions: 50′ 0¾″ x 8′ 6¾″
This series was originally second class.

Fig. 43 shows No. 1341 at Aberdovey in 1936.

DIAGRAM C23
THIRD Non-Corridor Carriage
10-compartment Clerestory Stock

Lots 1041, 1057, 1070, all of 1904
Running numbers 3248–72, 1001–5/9–28
Dimensions: 58′ 0¾″ x 8′ 6¾″
Condemned June 1957

Fig. 44

Fig. 44 No. 1017, photographed at Swindon in 1952.

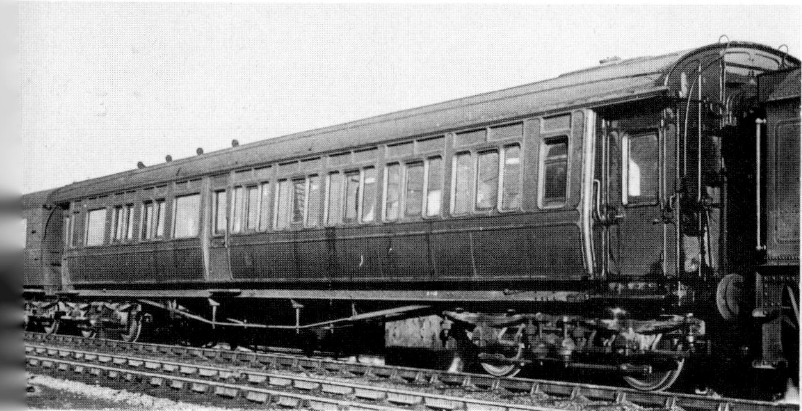

Fig. 45

DIAGRAM C24
THIRD Corridor Carriage
'Dreadnought' Stock

Lots 1069, 1084, 1098, all of 1905
Running numbers 2295–2300, 3277–90/91–3300
Dimensions: 69′ 0″ x 9′ 6″
Condemned July 1956

Fig. 45 No. 2299 at Banbury in 1948 as fitted with a 9′ plate bogie. **Fig. 46** No. 3299, seen at Reading in 1950, has '1914' pattern bogies and sheeted-over toplights.

Fig. 46

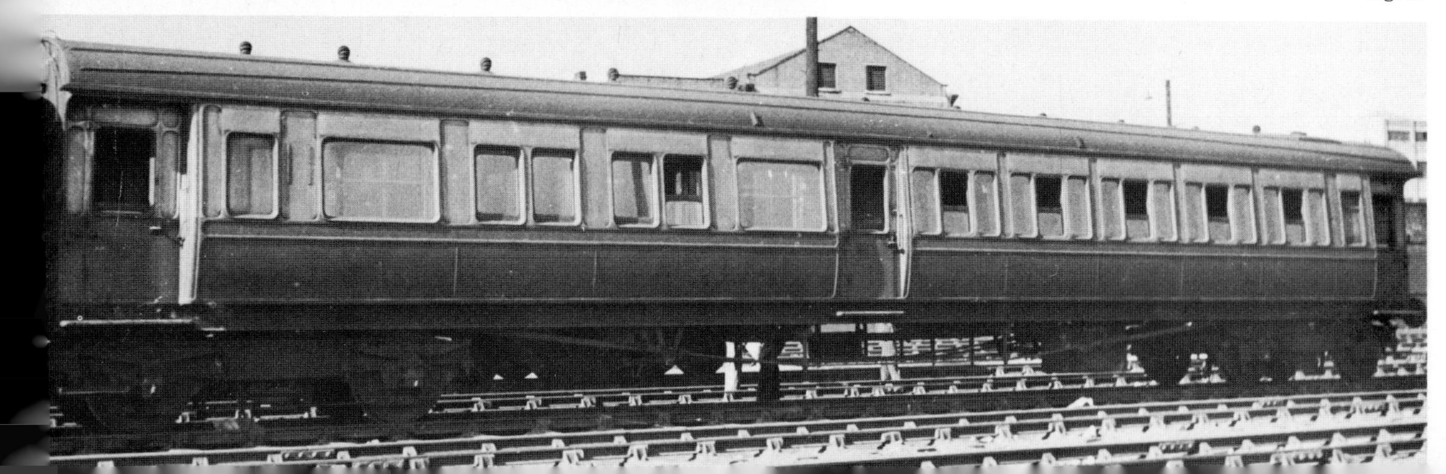

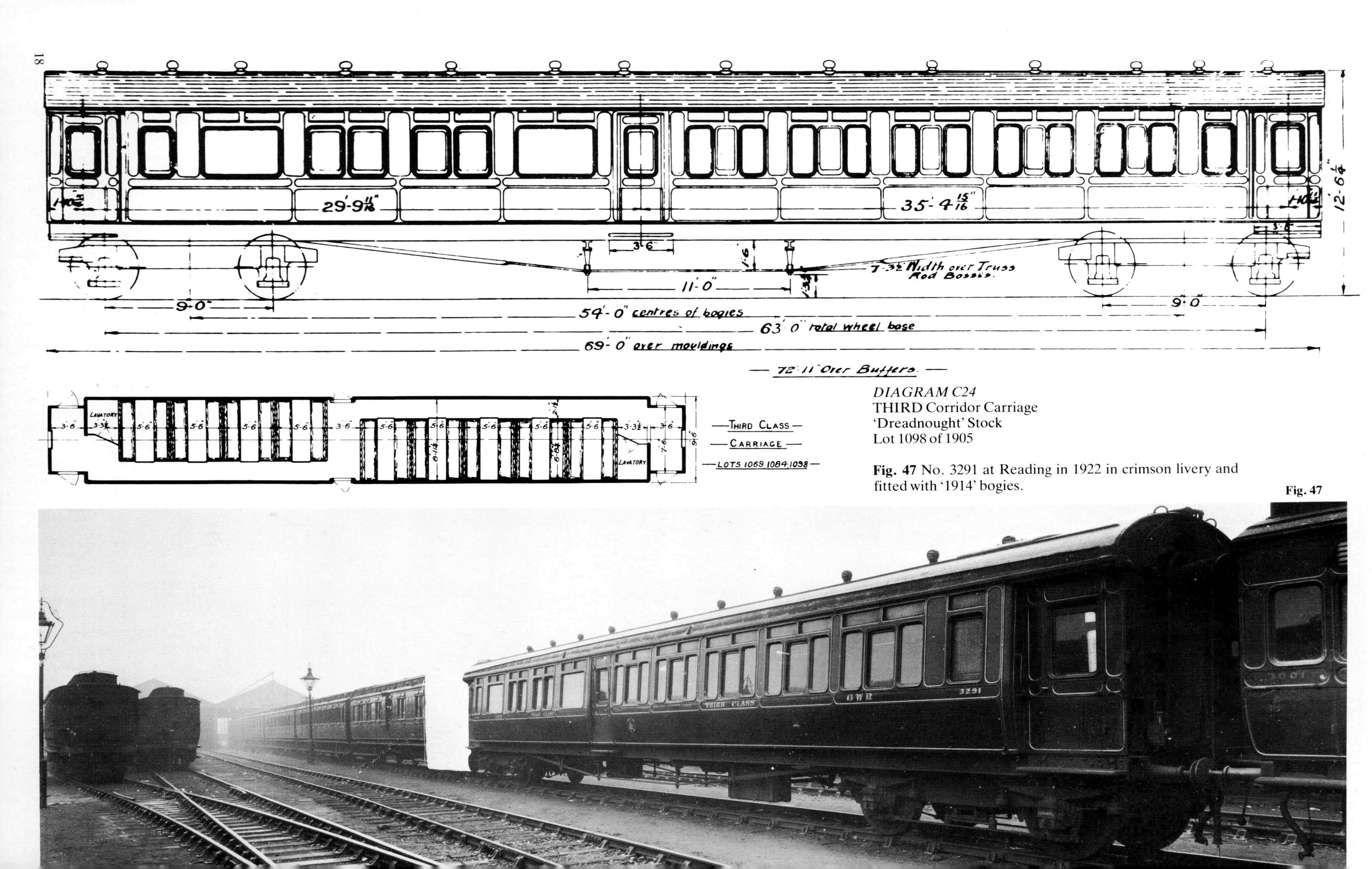

DIAGRAM C24
THIRD Corridor Carriage
'Dreadnought' Stock
Lot 1098 of 1905

Fig. 47 No. 3291 at Reading in 1922 in crimson livery and fitted with '1914' bogies.

Fig. 47

Fig. 48

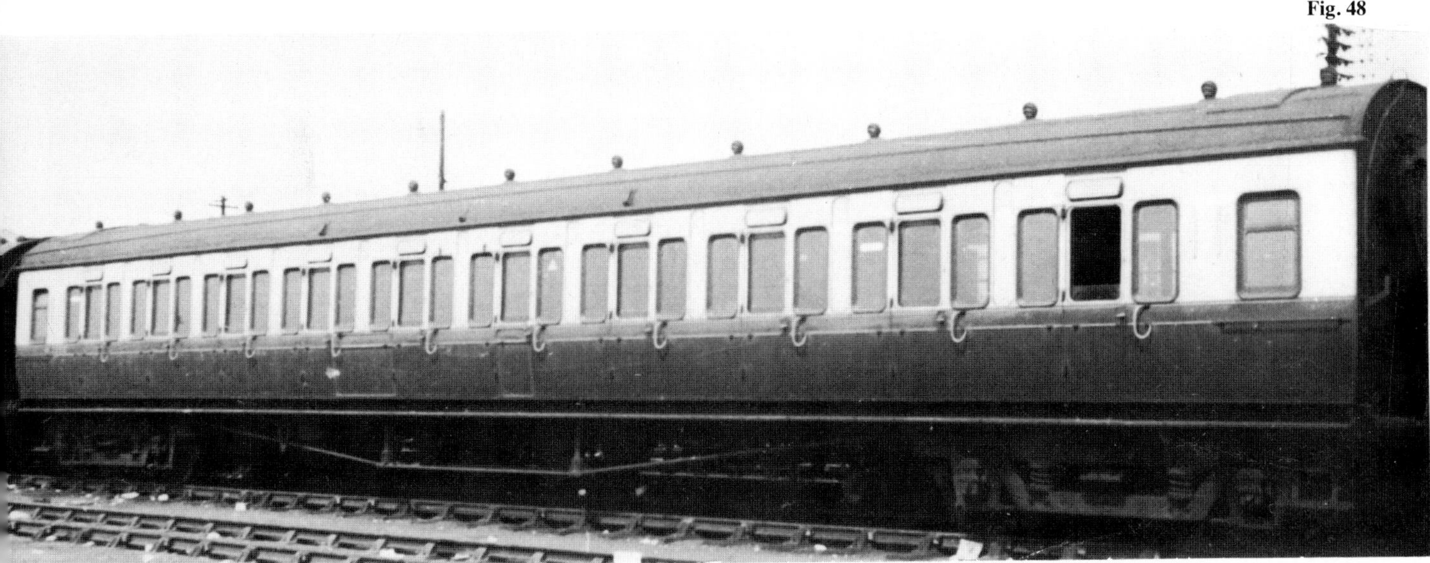

Fig. 49

DIAGRAM C25
THIRD Non-Corridor Carriage
10-compartment Elliptical-roof Stock

Lots 1077 and 1080 of 1905
Running numbers 1029–32/4–42/4–7/50–2
Dimensions: 58′ 0¾″ x 8′ 6¾″
Condemned June 1959

Fig. 48 shows No. 1045 fitted with 10′ bogies, at Old Oak Common in 1949.

DIAGRAM C29
THIRD Corridor Carriage
'Toplight' Stock, Bars I

Lot 1154 of 1909
Running numbers 3669–88
Lot 1208 of 1912
Running numbers 2539–48, Bars II
Lot 1214 of 1913
Running numbers 2549–68, Multibar with round bar trussing
Dimensions: 70′ 0″ x 9′ 0″
Condemned November 1957

Fig. 49, taken at Old Oak Common in 1950, shows the compartment side of No. 2552 with toplights blanked off. **Fig. 50** shows the corridor side of No. 3678, also at Old Oak Common in 1950, but complete with toplights.

Fig. 50

Fig. 51

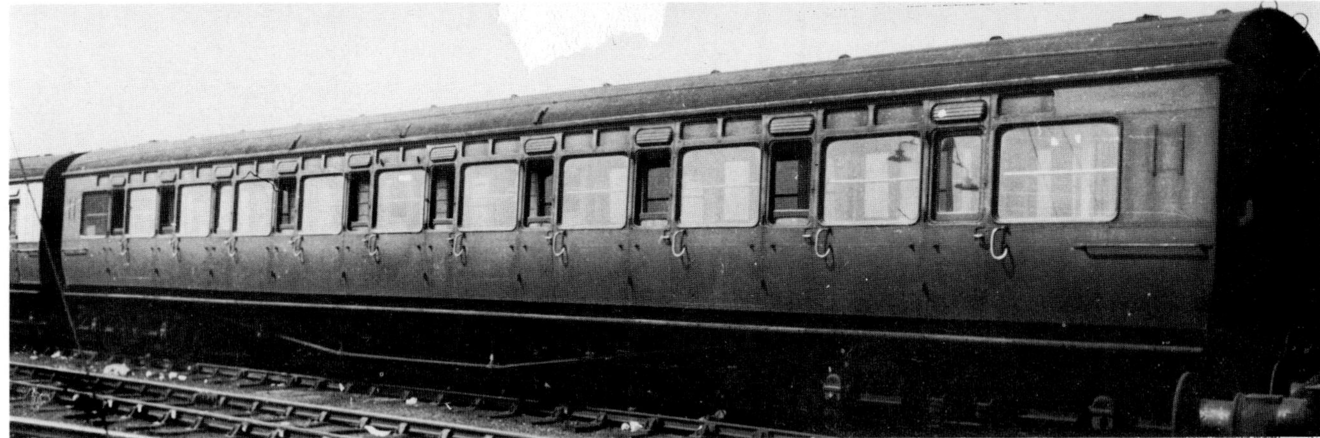

Fig. 52

Fig. 53

DIAGRAM C29
THIRD Corridor Carriage
'Toplight' Stock, Bars I

Fig. 53 illustrates the experimental 9′ plate bogie fitted with transverse springs on *C29* coach No. 2558, seen here at Old Oak Common in 1950.

Fig. 51 Old Oak Common is the location for this view of the corridor side of No. 3674 in 1950, fitted with American 9′ bogies. **Fig. 52** shows the corridor side of No. 3678, provided with 9′ plate bogies, at Old Oak Common in the same year.

DIAGRAM C30 ▷
THIRD Corridor Carriage
8-compartment 'Toplight' Stock, Bars I

Lot 1167 of 1910
Running numbers 2422–35
Dimensions: 56′ 0″ x 9′ 0″
Condemned October 1961

Fig. 54 No. 2425, showing the compartment side, at Tyseley in 1950. It is fitted with American 8′ bogies and is painted in BR strawberry and cream livery.

Fig. 54

Fig. 55

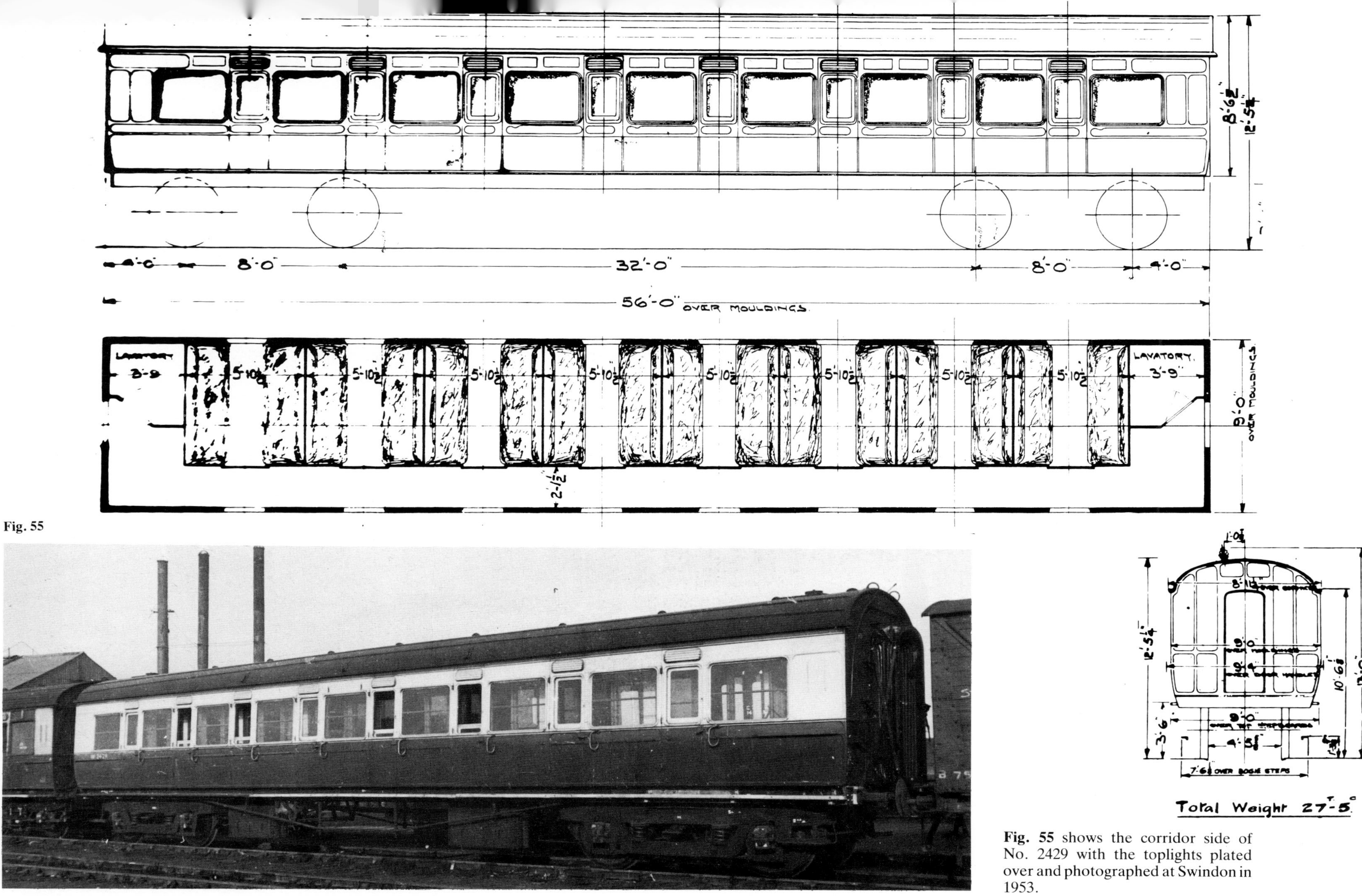

Fig. 55 shows the corridor side of No. 2429 with the toplights plated over and photographed at Swindon in 1953.

Fig. 56

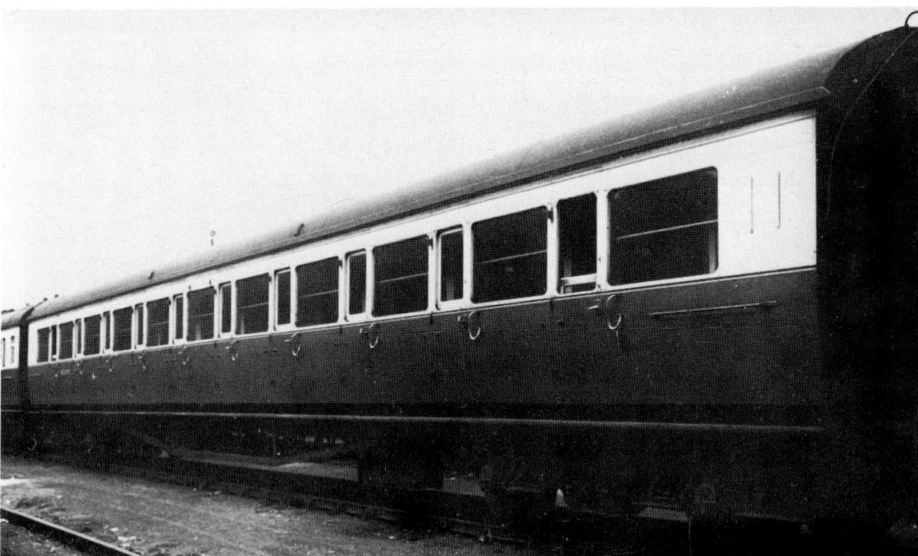

Fig. 57

DIAGRAM C32
THIRD Corridor Carriage
'Toplight' Stock, Multibar

As originally constructed, with angle-iron trusses, the series comprised the following:
Lot 1234 of 1914
 Running numbers 2569–80
Lot 1246 of 1915
 Running numbers 3913–47, of which 3929/39 were sold to WD

Various vehicles were re-purchased from the War Department and rebuilt to *Diagram C32* as follows:
Lot 1269 of 1920 (originally purpose-built ambulance stock)
 Running numbers 3879–3900
Lot 1286 of 1921 (originally *C32* and built as ambulance stock)
 Running number 3621
Lot 1312 of 1932 (originally built as ambulance stock)
 Running numbers 2463/4 (originally *C28*)
 Running number 2466 (originally *C32*)
 Running numbers 2467–71/6 (originally *C28*)

Dimensions: 57′ 0″ x 9′ 0″
Condemned June 1962
Differs from *C31* series in panelling and toplights.

DIAGRAM C31
THIRD Corridor Carriage
'Toplight' Stock, Bars I, Bars II, Multibar

As originally constructed the series comprised the following:
Lot 1172
 Running numbers 2436–55, of which 2452/5 were sold to WD
Lot 1179 of 1911
 Running numbers 2466–91
Lot 1194 of 1913
 Running numbers 2456–64
 Running numbers 2492–2532
Lot 1202 of 1912
 Running numbers 2533–38
(Lots 1179, 1194 and 1202: all sold to WD)

Various vehicles were re-purchased from the War Department and rebuilt to *Diagram C31* as follows:
Lot 1286 of 1921 (originally *C28* and built as ambulance stock)
 Running numbers 3629/30/2–5
Lot 1289 of 1921 (originally *C31* and built as ambulance stock)
 Running numbers 3636–44
Lot 1292 of 1921 (originally *C31*)
 Running numbers 3653–9
Lot 1294 of 1921 (originally *C31*)
 Running numbers 3660–1
Lot 1297 of 1921 (originally *C31*)
 Running number 2524
Lot 1311 of 1922 (originally *C28*)
 Running numbers 2452/5–62
Lot 1312 (originally *C31*)
 Running number 3630
Lot 1312 (originally *C28*)
 Running numbers 2467–71
Lot 1343 (originally *C31*)
 Running numbers 4541–4

Dimensions: 57′ 0″ x 9′ 0″
Condemned June 1960

Fig. 56 illustrates No. 3629, showing the corridor side, at Tyseley in 1950. **Fig. 57** No. 2475 at Old Oak Common in 1952, without door vents. **Fig. 58** No. 2466 at the same location, depicting the compartment side in post-war GWR livery.

Fig. 58

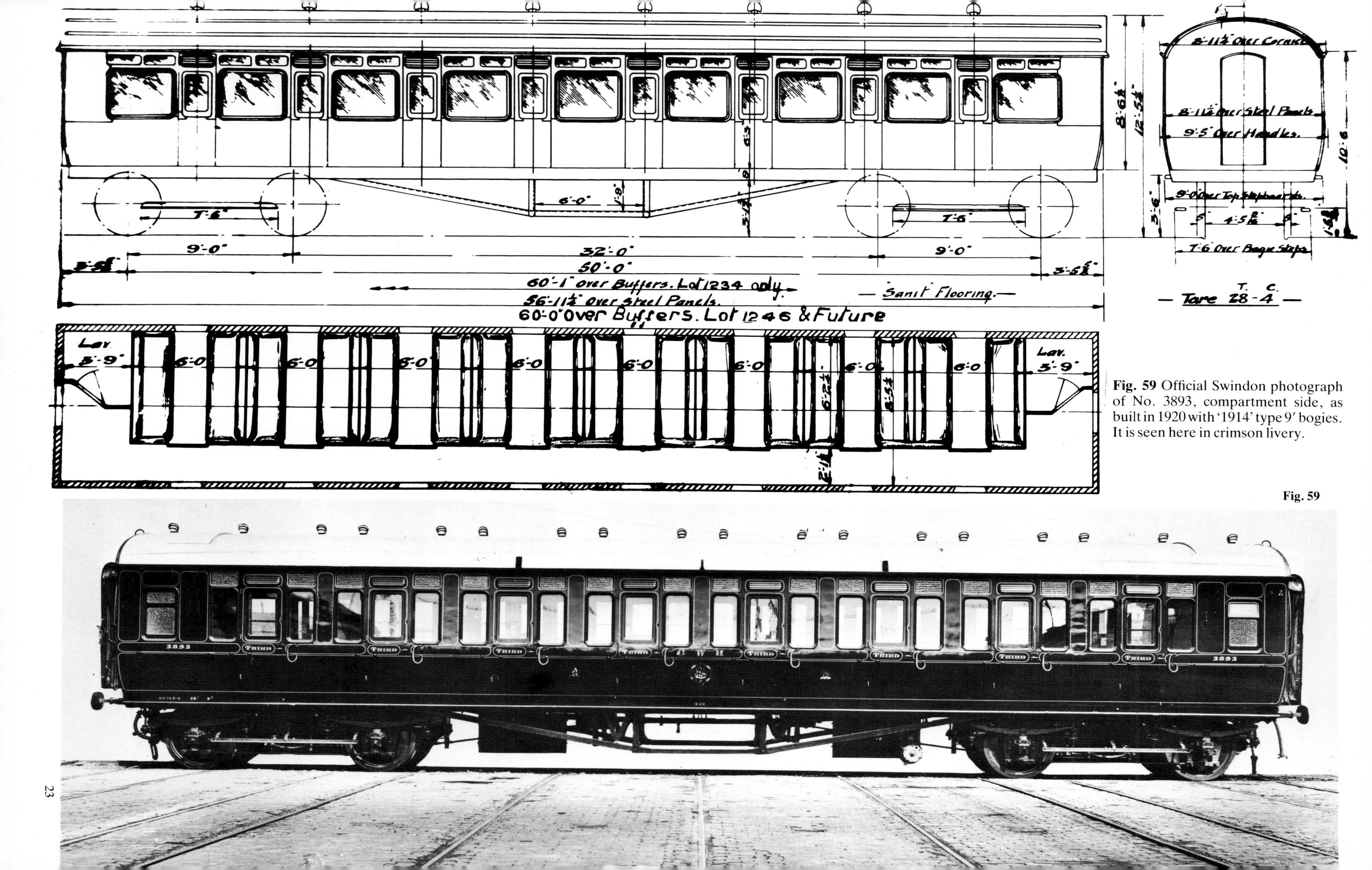

Fig. 59 Official Swindon photograph of No. 3893, compartment side, as built in 1920 with '1914' type 9' bogies. It is seen here in crimson livery.

Fig. 59

Fig. 60

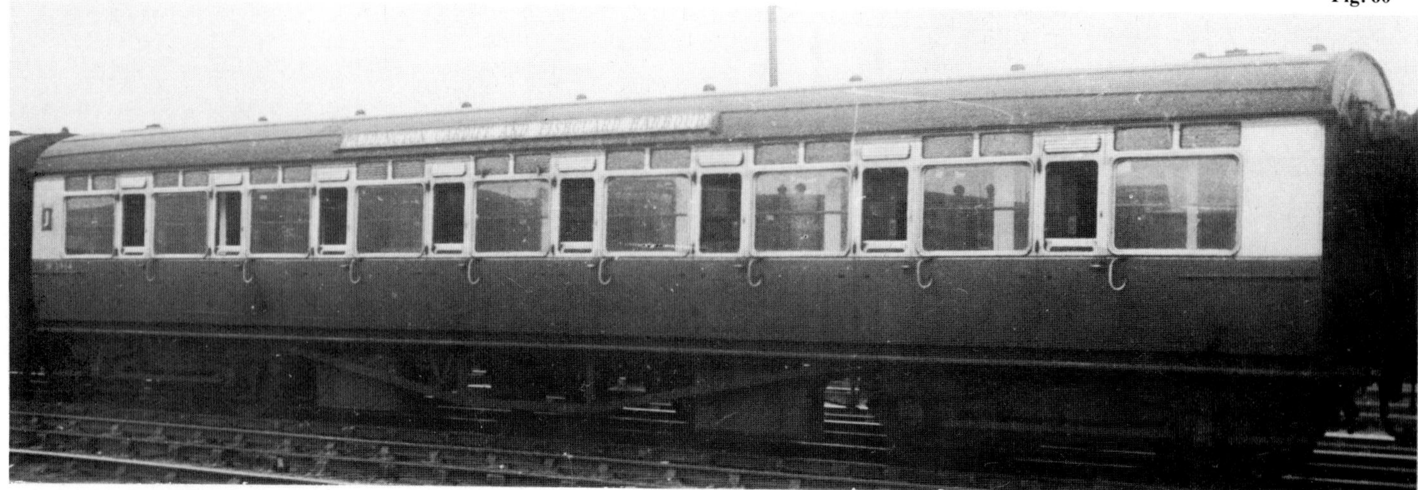

Fig. 61

DIAGRAM C32
THIRD Corridor Carriage
'Toplight' Stock, Multibar

Fig. 60 No. 3914, photographed at Old Oak Common in 1950, illustrates the corridor side of this series and carries roof boards 'Paddington, Cardiff and Fishguard Harbour'. **Fig. 61** The compartment side of No. 3892 with 9′ pressed-steel bogie, seen in Tyseley carriage sidings, 1950. **Fig. 62** No. 3941, compartment side, at Kingsbridge in 1950; this vehicle is fitted with '1914' type bogies. **Fig. 63** Corridor side of No. 3891 at Old Oak Common in 1950, painted in post-war GWR livery and fitted with 7′ plate bogies.

Fig. 62

Fig. 63

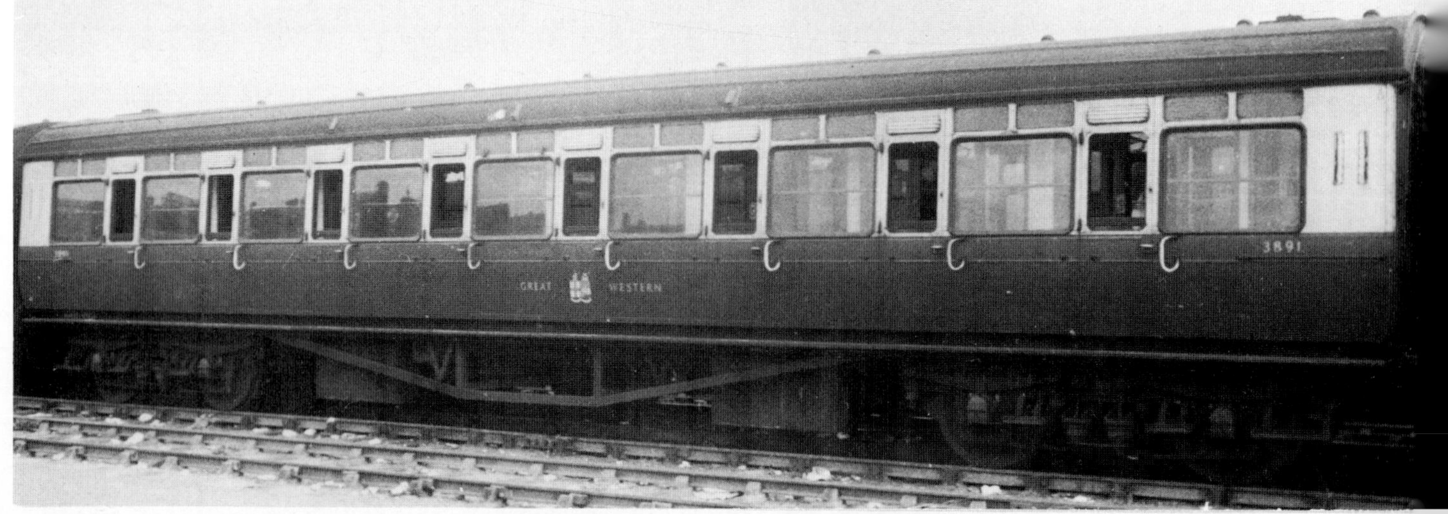

Fig. 64

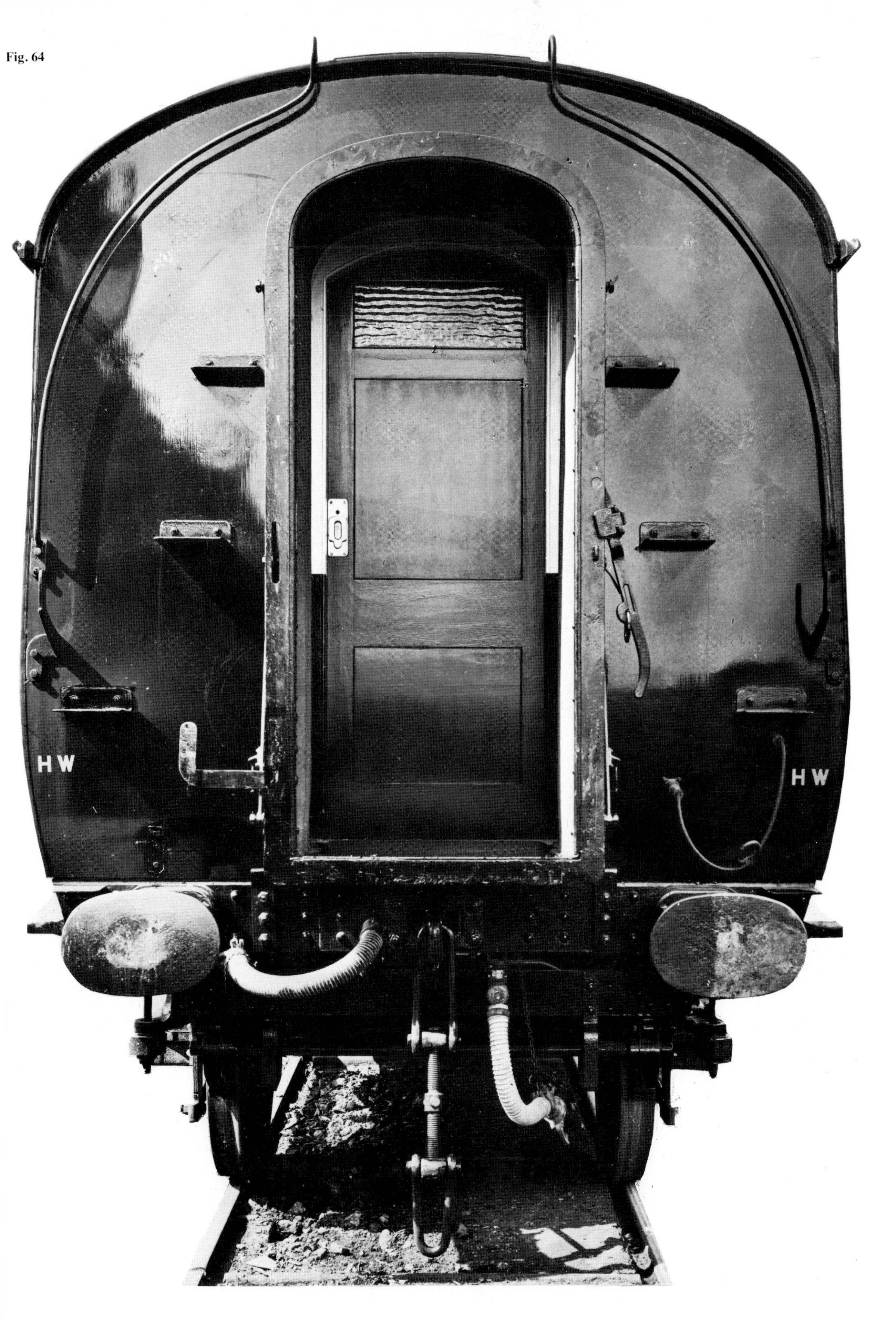

DIAGRAM C32
THIRD Corridor Carriage

Fig. 64 The rear of carriage No. 3893 is seen in this official Swindon photograph taken in 1920.

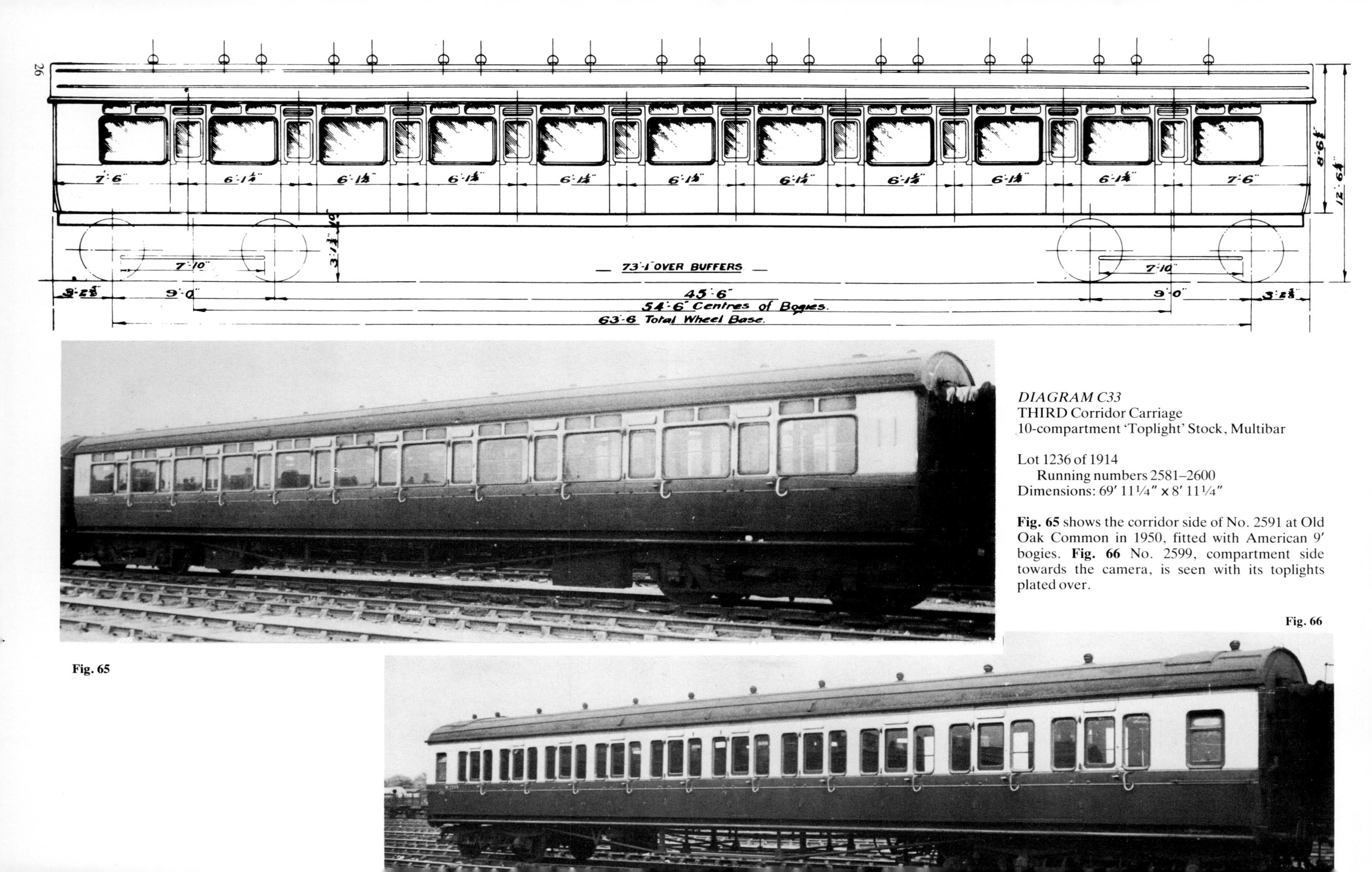

DIAGRAM C33
THIRD Corridor Carriage
10-compartment 'Toplight' Stock, Multibar

Lot 1236 of 1914
Running numbers 2581–2600
Dimensions: 69′ 11¼″ x 8′ 11¼″

Fig. 65 shows the corridor side of No. 2591 at Old Oak Common in 1950, fitted with American 9′ bogies. **Fig. 66** No. 2599, compartment side towards the camera, is seen with its toplights plated over.

Fig. 65

Fig. 66

Fig. 67

DIAGRAM C35
THIRD Corridor Carriage
'Toplight' Stock, Multibar

Lot 1256 of 1919
Running numbers 3949–57 (ordered 4/1915, built 1917)
Running numbers 3958–81
3952–4/7 sold to WD and replaced by similar vehicles under same serials
3958/9/65/6/8/74/9 sold to WD after use in traffic
3967/70–3/5/8 sold to WD after use in traffic

Various vehicles were re-purchased from WD and rebuilt to *Diagram C35* as follows:

Lot 1290 of 1921 (originally *C35*)
Running numbers 3645–52
Lot 1295 of 1921 (originally *C35*)
Running numbers 3662–7
Lot 1313 of 1922 (originally *C35*)
Running number 3666

Dimensions: 56′ 11¼″ x 8′ 11¼″
Condemned June 1963

Fig. 68

Fig. 67 Corridor side of No. 3977 at Old Oak Common in 1956. **Fig. 68** is a three-quarter view of No. 3977. **Fig. 69** No. 3980 at Old Oak Common in 1950, showing compartment side and fitted with 1914 pattern bogie.

Fig. 69

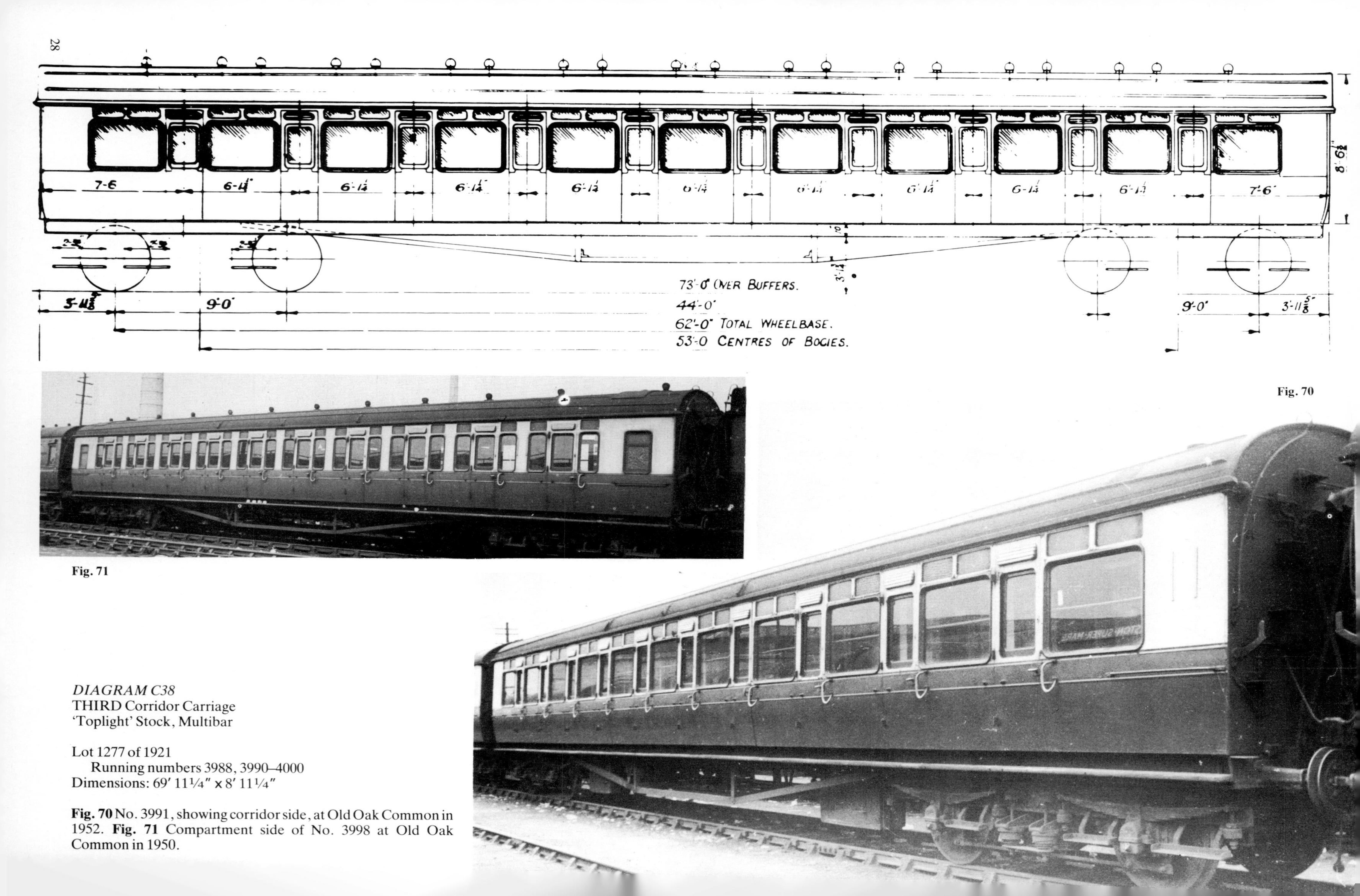

Fig. 71

Fig. 70

DIAGRAM C38
THIRD Corridor Carriage
'Toplight' Stock, Multibar

Lot 1277 of 1921
Running numbers 3988, 3990–4000
Dimensions: 69' 11¼" x 8' 11¼"

Fig. 70 No. 3991, showing corridor side, at Old Oak Common in 1952. **Fig. 71** Compartment side of No. 3998 at Old Oak Common in 1950.

Fig. 72

Fig. 73

DIAGRAM C39
THIRD Corridor Carriage
Experimental underframe

Lot 1248 of 1921
One vehicle only: No. 3948
Dimensions: 57′ 0″ x 9′ 0″
Condemned June 1958
Larger lavatories than *C35*

Fig. 72 Compartment side of No. 3948 at Old Oak Common in 1951. The roof boards read 'Paddington, Bristol and Weston-Super-Mare'.

DIAGRAM C43
THIRD Non-Corridor Carriage
Flat-ended Stock

Lot 1317 of 1924
Running numbers 4379–98
Lot 1328 of 1924
Running numbers 4409–33

Fig. 73 shows No. 4427 at Windsor in 1951 in BR red livery. **Fig. 74** illustrates No. 4379 as built in 1923 with painted panelling and white roof.

Fig. 74

Fig. 75

Fig. 76

DIAGRAM C45
THIRD Corridor Carriage
Each coach has one bow end and one flat end

Lot 1308 of 1923
Running numbers 2473–5
Lot 1320
Running numbers 4501/2
Dimensions: 70′ 8¼″ x 9′ 0″
Condemned February 1960
Originally built as trial vehicles for automatic coupler

Fig. 75 shows No. 2475, compartment side, at Henley on Thames in 1954.

DIAGRAM C46
THIRD Corridor Carriage
Flush-sided, Flat-ended Stock

Lot 1320 of 1924
Running numbers 4503–14
Lot 1337 of 1925
Running numbers 4706–50
Dimensions 70′ 0″ x 9′ 0″
Condemned June 1963

Fig. 76 illustrates No. 4717, corridor side, at Kingsbridge in 1950, painted in late GWR livery. **Fig. 77** The compartment side of No. 4709 at Old Oak Common in 1952.

Fig. 77

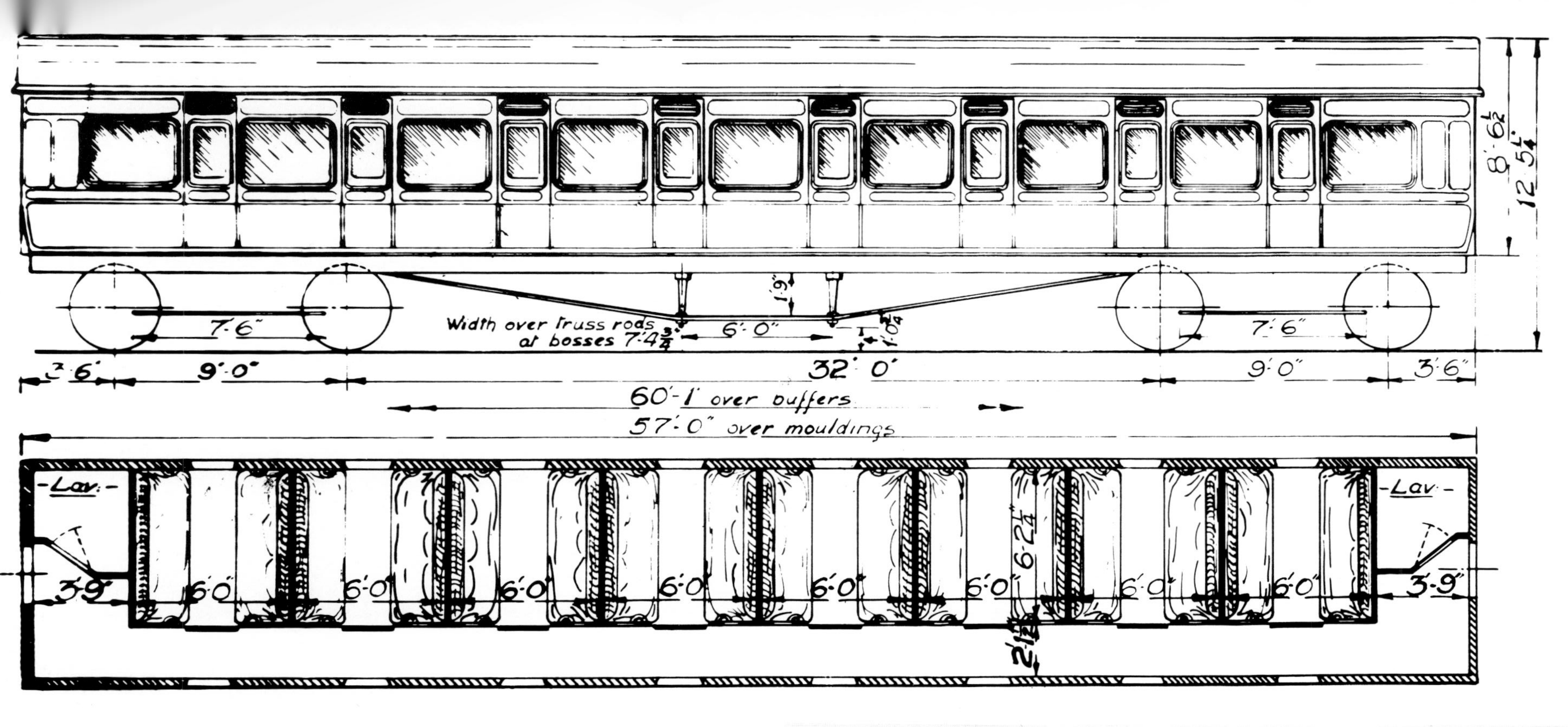

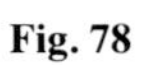
Fig. 78

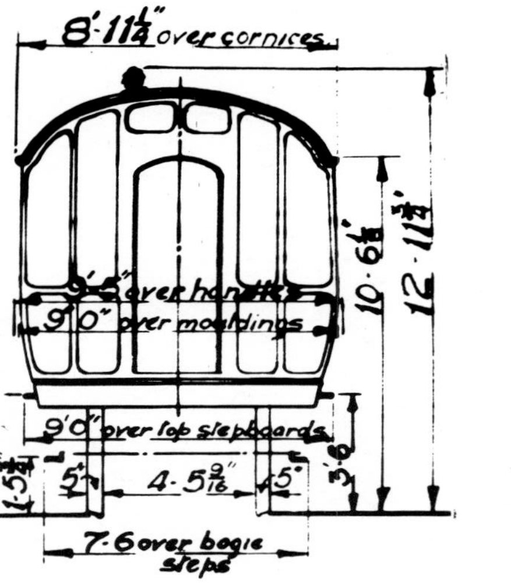

DIAGRAM C49
THIRD Corridor Carriage
Ex-Ambulance Stock

Lot 1325 of 1923
Running numbers 4521–40
Dimensions 57' 0" x 9' 0"
Condemned June 1959
Originally Bars I stock to *Diagram C31*

Fig. 78 No. 4533, seen in last GWR livery at Exeter in 1947, showing the corridor side.

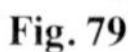

Fig. 79

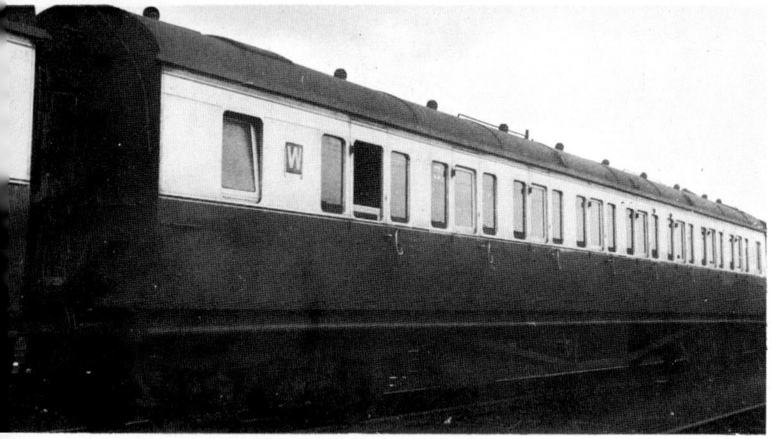

Fig. 80

DIAGRAM C50
THIRD Corridor Carriage
Bow-ended, Flush-panelled Stock

Lot 1320 of 1924
Running numbers 4515–20
Dimensions 71′ 4½″ x 9′ 0″
Condemned February 1959

Fig. 79 shows No. 4517, corridor side, at Henley on Thames in 1954 painted in BR livery.

DIAGRAM C52
THIRD Corridor Carriage
Ex-Articulated Stock

Lot 1362 of 1925
Original running numbers 10005/13/21/9/37/45
Rebuilt and renumbered in 1936: 4190–4201
Condemned December 1962
Later became *Diagram C72*

Fig. 80 is the compartment side of No. 4190 at Old Oak Common in 1954. Letter 'W' in bracket is for seat reservation purposes.

Fig. 81

Fig. 82

DIAGRAM C53
THIRD Non-Corridor Suburban Carriage
Main Line & City Articulated Stock

Lot 1341 of 1925
Running numbers 9802/5/8/11/4/7
Dimensions 48′ 0″ x 8′ 6″
Condemned July 1960

Fig. 81 No. 9811 at Swindon in 1953; BR maroon livery.

Fig. 82 Compartment side of No. 4789 (first series) at Reading in 'Great Western' livery in 1947.

Fig. 83

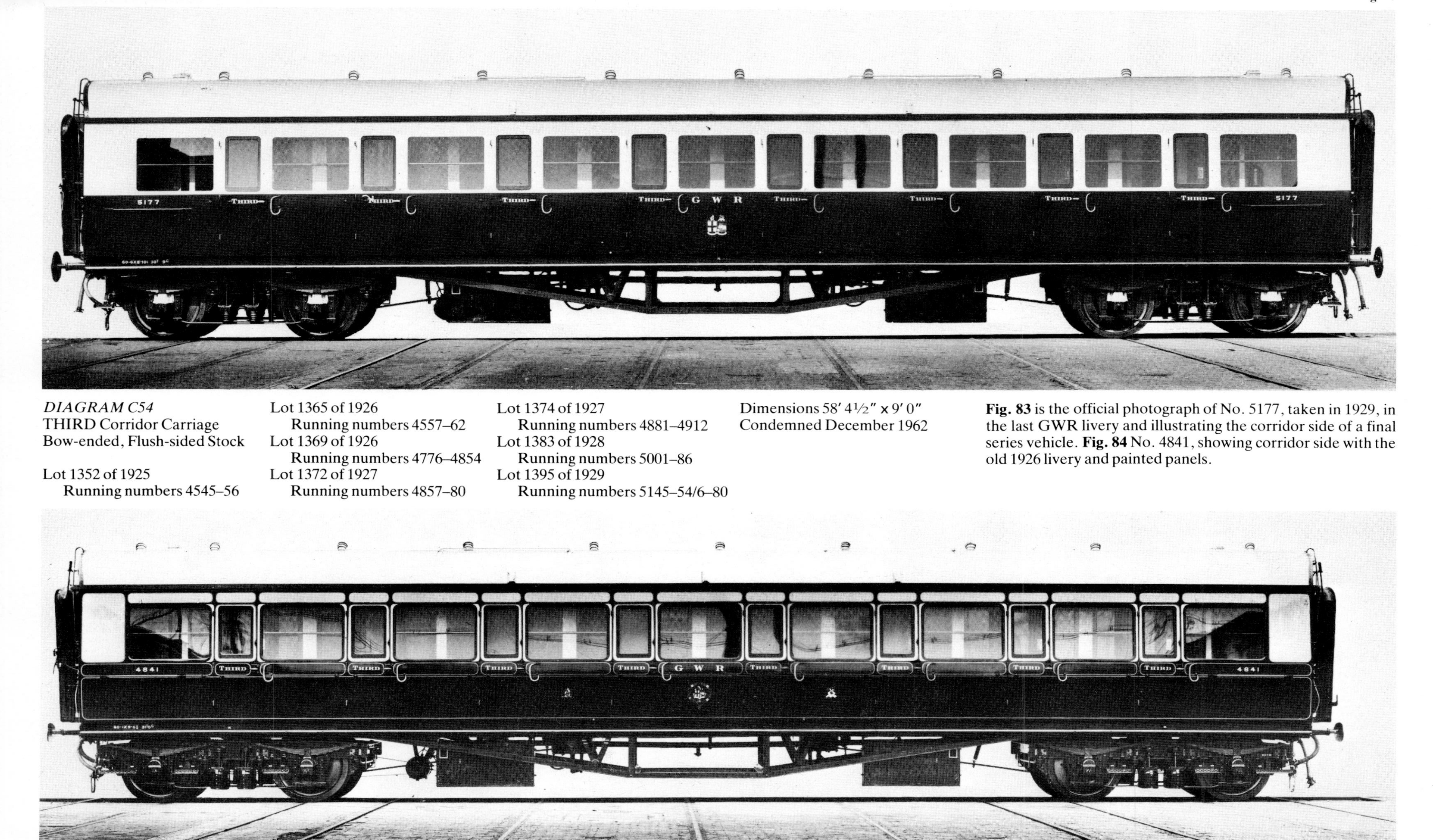

DIAGRAM C54
THIRD Corridor Carriage
Bow-ended, Flush-sided Stock

Lot 1352 of 1925
Running numbers 4545–56
Lot 1365 of 1926
Running numbers 4557–62
Lot 1369 of 1926
Running numbers 4776–4854
Lot 1372 of 1927
Running numbers 4857–80
Lot 1374 of 1927
Running numbers 4881–4912
Lot 1383 of 1928
Running numbers 5001–86
Lot 1395 of 1929
Running numbers 5145–54/6–80

Dimensions 58′ 4½″ x 9′ 0″
Condemned December 1962

Fig. 83 is the official photograph of No. 5177, taken in 1929, in the last GWR livery and illustrating the corridor side of a final series vehicle. **Fig. 84** No. 4841, showing corridor side with the old 1926 livery and painted panels.

Fig. 84

Fig. 85

DIAGRAM C54
Fig. 85 shows No. 5013 in 1928, illustrating the new livery and the panelled roof. The corridor side is nearest the camera.

Fig. 86 No. 4556 is seen in the first BR livery at Old Oak Common in 1955. Roof boards read 'Channel Islands Boat Express' in yellow letters on maroon background.

Fig. 86

Fig. 87

DIAGRAM C58
THIRD Corridor Carriage
Bow-ended, Flush-sided Stock

Lot 1411 of 1929
Running numbers 5181–5230
Lot 1395
Running numbers 5156–80
Dimensions 58′ 4½″ x 8′ 10¾″
Condemned December 1962
This series had larger lavatories tha
C55

Fig. 87 No. 5212, showing the corridc side at Old Oak Common in 1952. Th opposite side of the same vehicle ca be seen in **Fig. 88**.

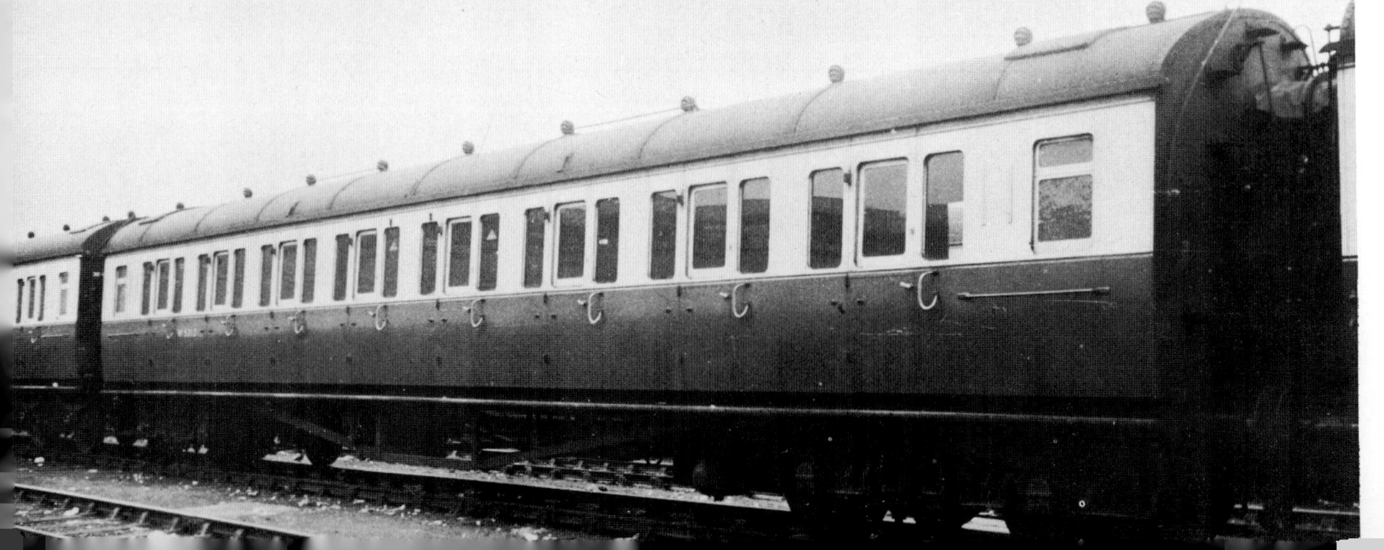

Fig. 88

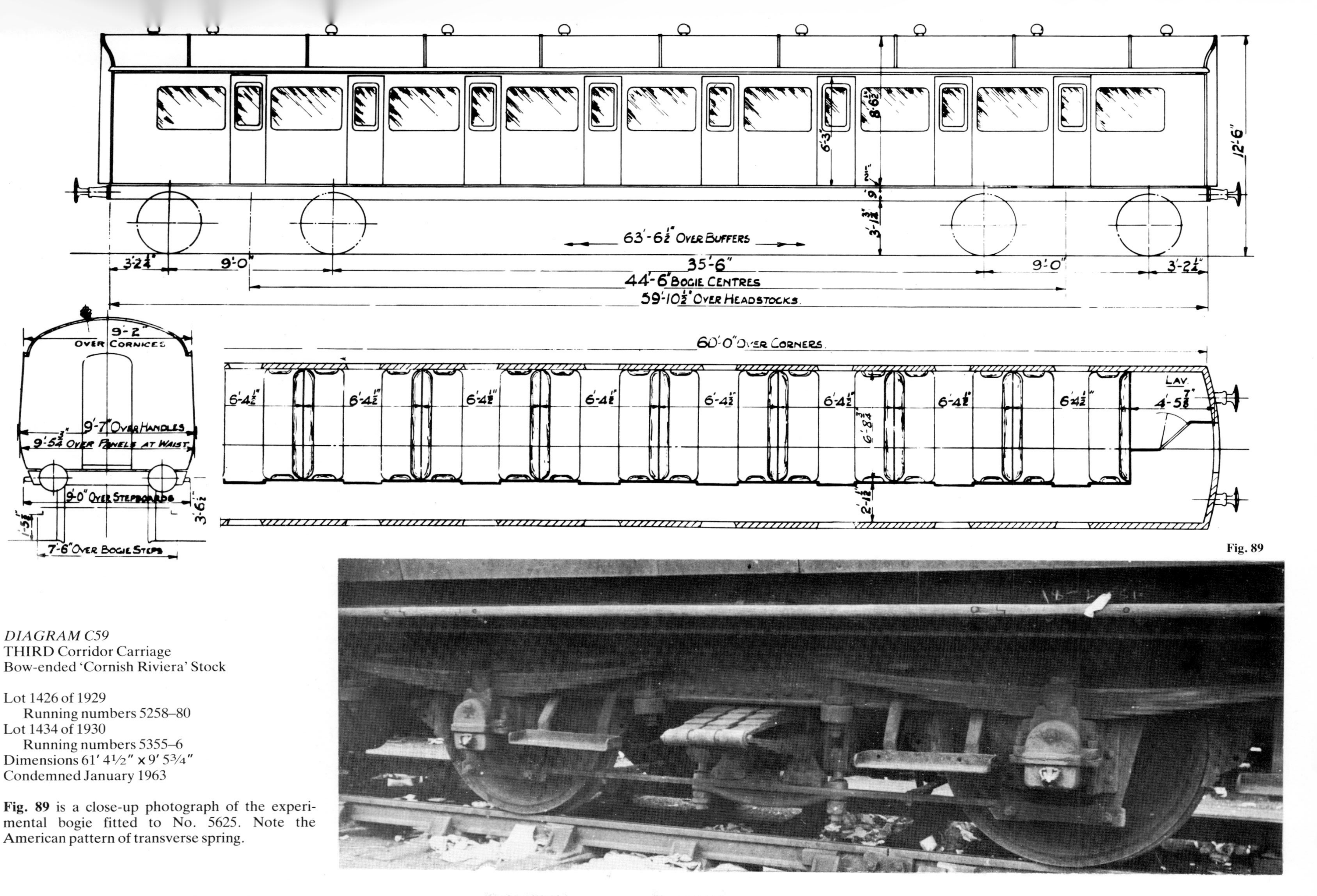

Fig. 89

DIAGRAM C59
THIRD Corridor Carriage
Bow-ended 'Cornish Riviera' Stock

Lot 1426 of 1929
Running numbers 5258–80
Lot 1434 of 1930
Running numbers 5355–6
Dimensions 61′ 4½″ x 9′ 5¾″
Condemned January 1963

Fig. 89 is a close-up photograph of the experimental bogie fitted to No. 5625. Note the American pattern of transverse spring.

Fig. 90

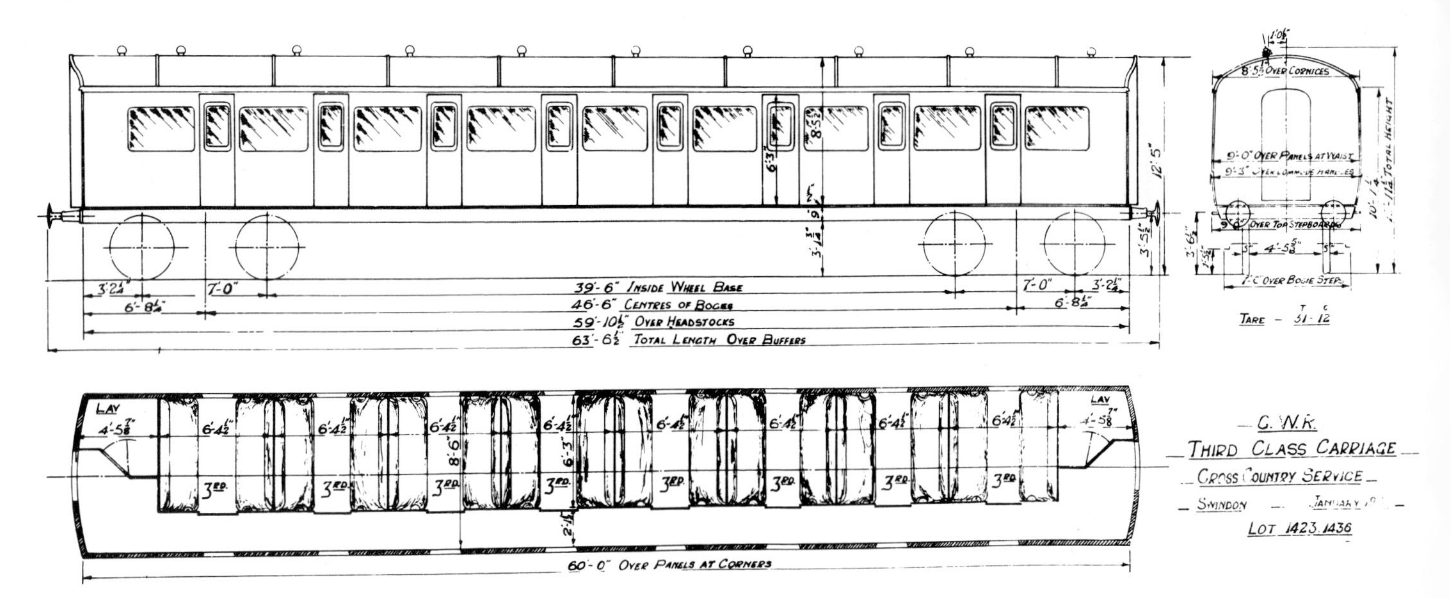

DIAGRAM C60
THIRD Corridor Carriage
Bow-ended Stock

Lot 1423
Running numbers 5243–57
Lot 1436 of 1930
Running numbers 5315–54
Lot 1466 of 1931
Running numbers 5689–5708
Dimensions: 61′ 4½″ x 9′ 0″
Condemned December 1963

Fig. 90 No. 5331, photographed at Old Oak Common in 1951, displays the corridor side of the series, while **Fig. 91** illustrates the compartment side of No. 5353, also at Old Oak, but in 1952. Both are seen in the first BR livery of strawberry and cream.

Fig. 91

Fig. 92

DIAGRAM C62
THIRD Corridor Carriage
Bow-ended Stock

Fig. 93

Lot 1447 of 1930
Running numbers 5357–60
Lot 1453 of 1931
Running numbers 5369–72
Lot 1475 of 1932
Running numbers 5381–84
Lot 1477 of 1932
Running numbers 5393–5446
Dimensions: 61′ 4½″ x 9′ 3″
Centre of bogies: 46′ 6″
Condemned March 1963

Fig. 92 No. 5409, compartment side, at Old Oak Common in 1953. **Fig. 93** is the corridor side of No. 5424, also at Old Oak Common, this time in 1952. In **Fig. 94** No. 5428 is shown as rebuilt in 1951 after the original body was destroyed by fire at Stratten Park.

Fig. 94

Fig. 95

DIAGRAM C62
The top two photographs on this page show the *Diagram C62* series in the 1936 condition (**Fig. 95**), and No. 5428 as rebuilt after being completely burnt out (**Fig. 96**). The latter is an official Swindon photograph dated 1951, and gives good detail of the fittings at the side of the vehicle.

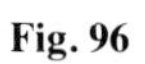
Fig. 96

DIAGRAM C63
THIRD Non-Corridor Carriage
9-compartment Bow-ended Stock

Lot 1465 of 1932
Running numbers 5673–88
Dimensions: 61′ 2″ x 9′ 0″

Fig. 97 No. 5676 standing at Cardiff Queen Street in 1952, painted in the BR strawberry and cream livery.

Fig. 97

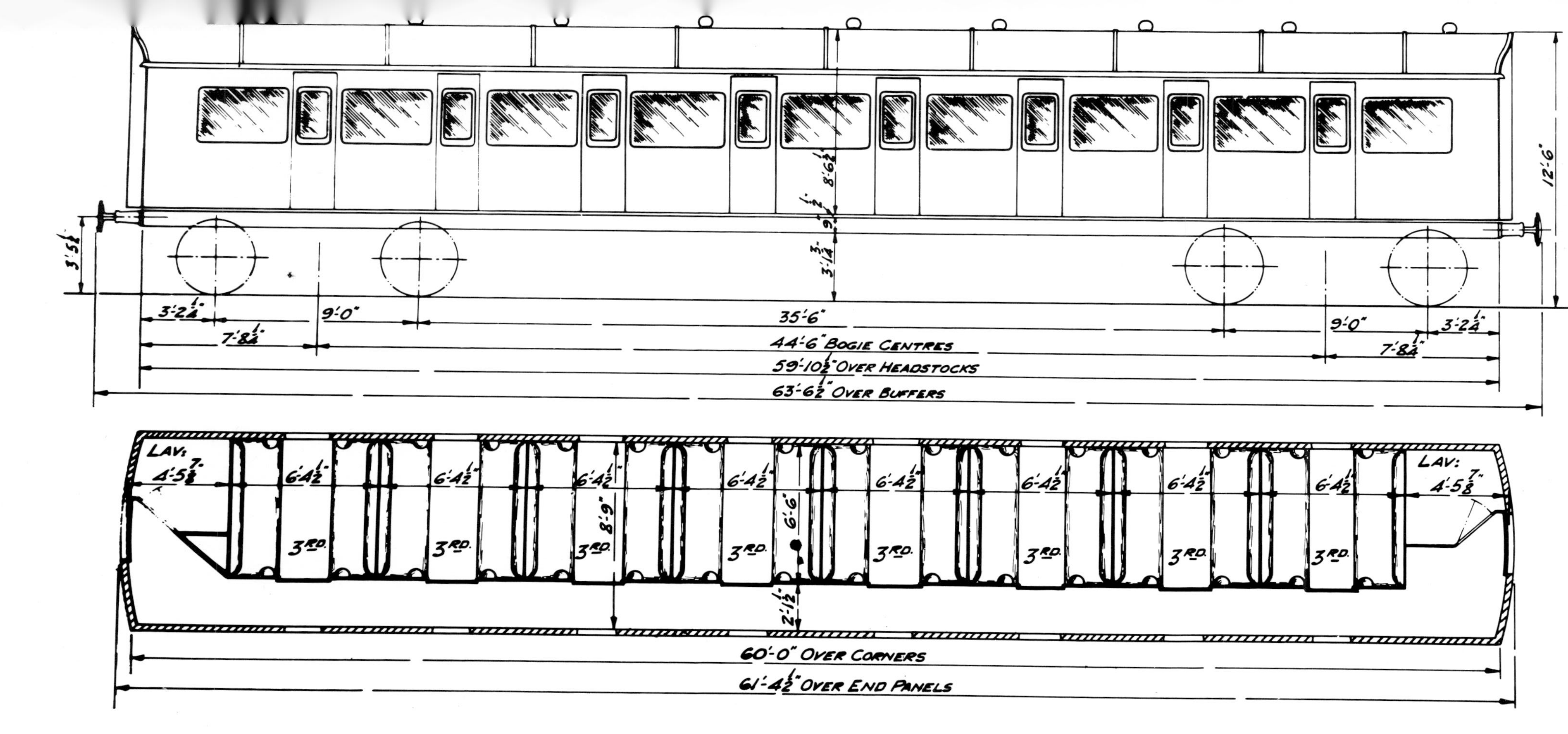

Fig. 98 is the official photograph of the *C64* series as built in 1933. It shows No. 5709 in GWR chocolate and cream livery with white roof and double lining at the waist.

Fig. 98

DIAGRAM C64
THIRD Corridor Carriage
Bow-ended Stock

Lot 1489 of 1933
Running numbers 5709–43
Dimensions: 61′ 4½″ x 9′ 3″
Centre of bogies: 44′ 6″
Condemned October 1963

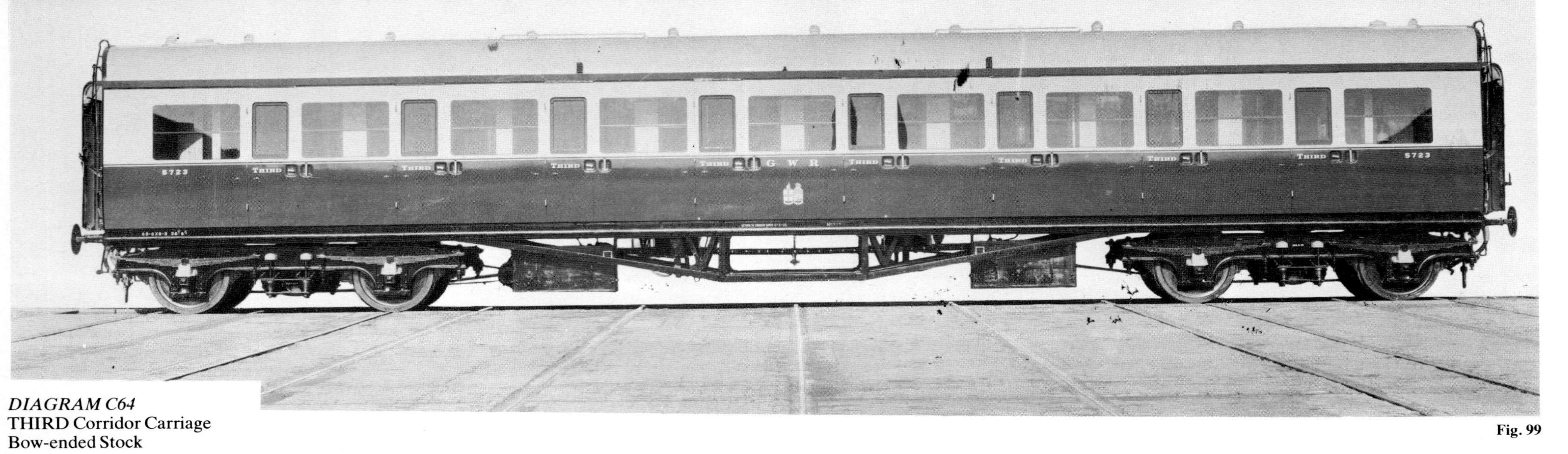

Fig. 99

DIAGRAM C64
THIRD Corridor Carriage
Bow-ended Stock

Fig. 99 Official photograph of No. 5723, showing variation of waist lining. **Fig. 101** Compartment side of No. 5729 pictured at Old Oak Common in 1952, and at the same site and date is seen the corridor side of this vehicle (**Fig. 102**). Both 5723 and 5729 are in BR livery.

DIAGRAM C65
THIRD Corridor Carriage
Flat-ended Stock

Lot 1489 of 1933
Running numbers 5744–78
Dimensions: 60′ 0″ x 9′ 3″

Condemned September 1963

Fig. 103 Another corridor-side view, this time of No. 5771 at Old Oak Common in 1953. **Fig. 104** illustrates the compartment side of No. 5748, seen at Old Oak in 1953.

Fig. 100 This official Swindon photograph illustrates No. 5745 as built and carrying GWR livery with single waist lining.

Fig. 100

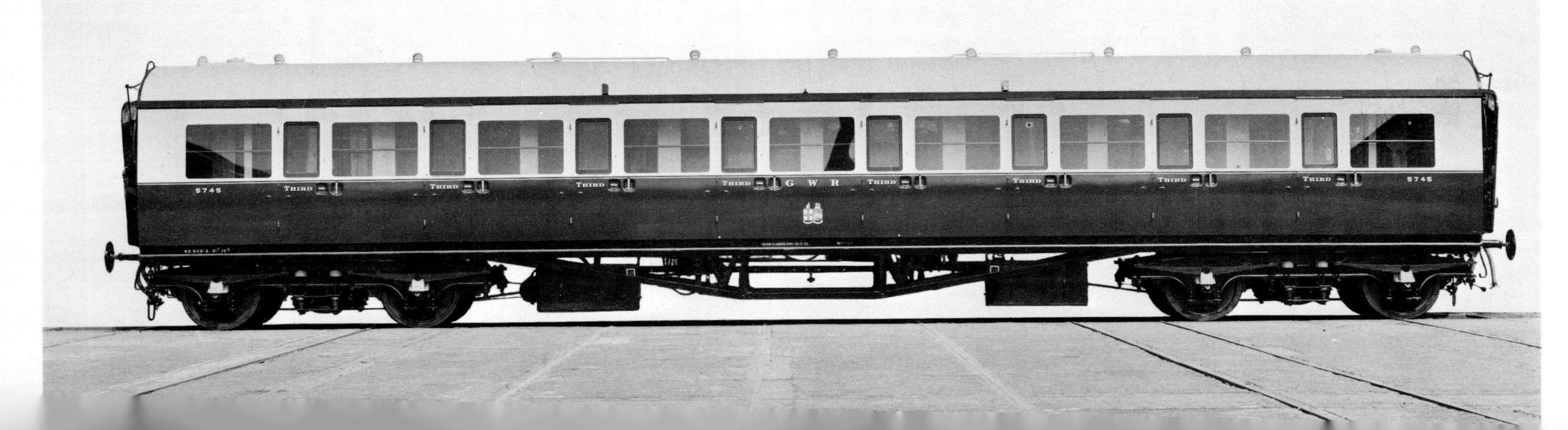

Fig. 101

Fig. 102

△ Fig. 103

Fig. 104

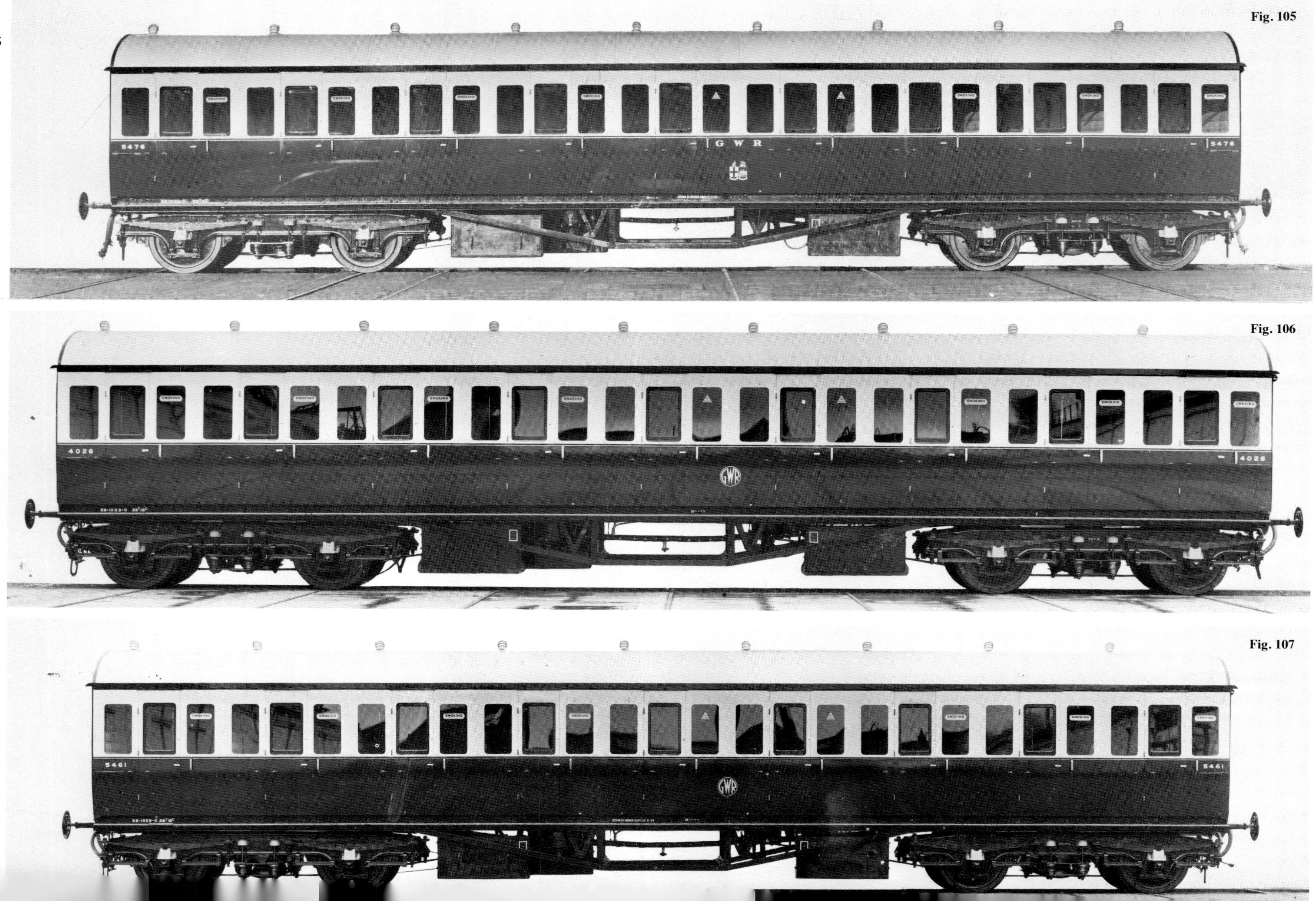

Fig. 105

Fig. 106

Fig. 107

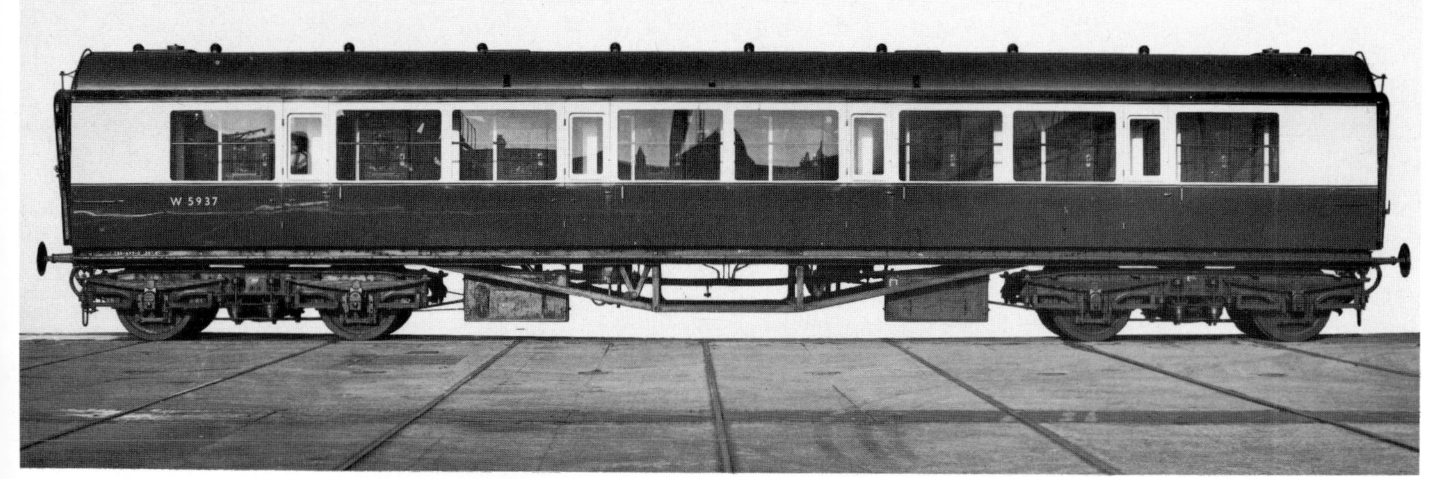

Fig. 108

DIAGRAM C66
THIRD Non-Corridor Carriage
Flush-sided Flat-ended Stock

Lot 1492 of 1934
  Running numbers 5471–90
Lot 1506 of 1934
  Running numbers 5461–70
Lot 1524 of 1936
  Running numbers 4244–91
Lot 1551 of 1935
  Running numbers 4026–65
Dimensions: 55′ 3½″ x 9′ 0″
Condemned December 1963

Fig. 109

Fig. 105 shows No. 5476 as built in 1934. **Fig. 106** depicts No. 4026 in similar conditions two years later. **Fig. 107** No. 5461 displays the GWR 'roundel' livery in late 1934.

Three pictures of the *Diagram C67* series in British Railways livery. **Fig. 108** shows No. 5937 at Swindon factory in 1951, illustrating the corridor side. **Fig. 109** The compartment side of No. 5821 at Swindon yard in 1953. **Fig. 110** depicts the opposite side of the same vehicle.

DIAGRAM C67
THIRD Corridor Carriage
Flush-sided Flat-ended Stock

Lot 1509 of 1935
  Running numbers 5808–67
Lot 1513 of 1934
  Running numbers 5888–5927
Lot 1527 of 1935
  Running numbers 5928–82
Dimensions: 57′ 0″ x 9′ 0″

Fig. 110

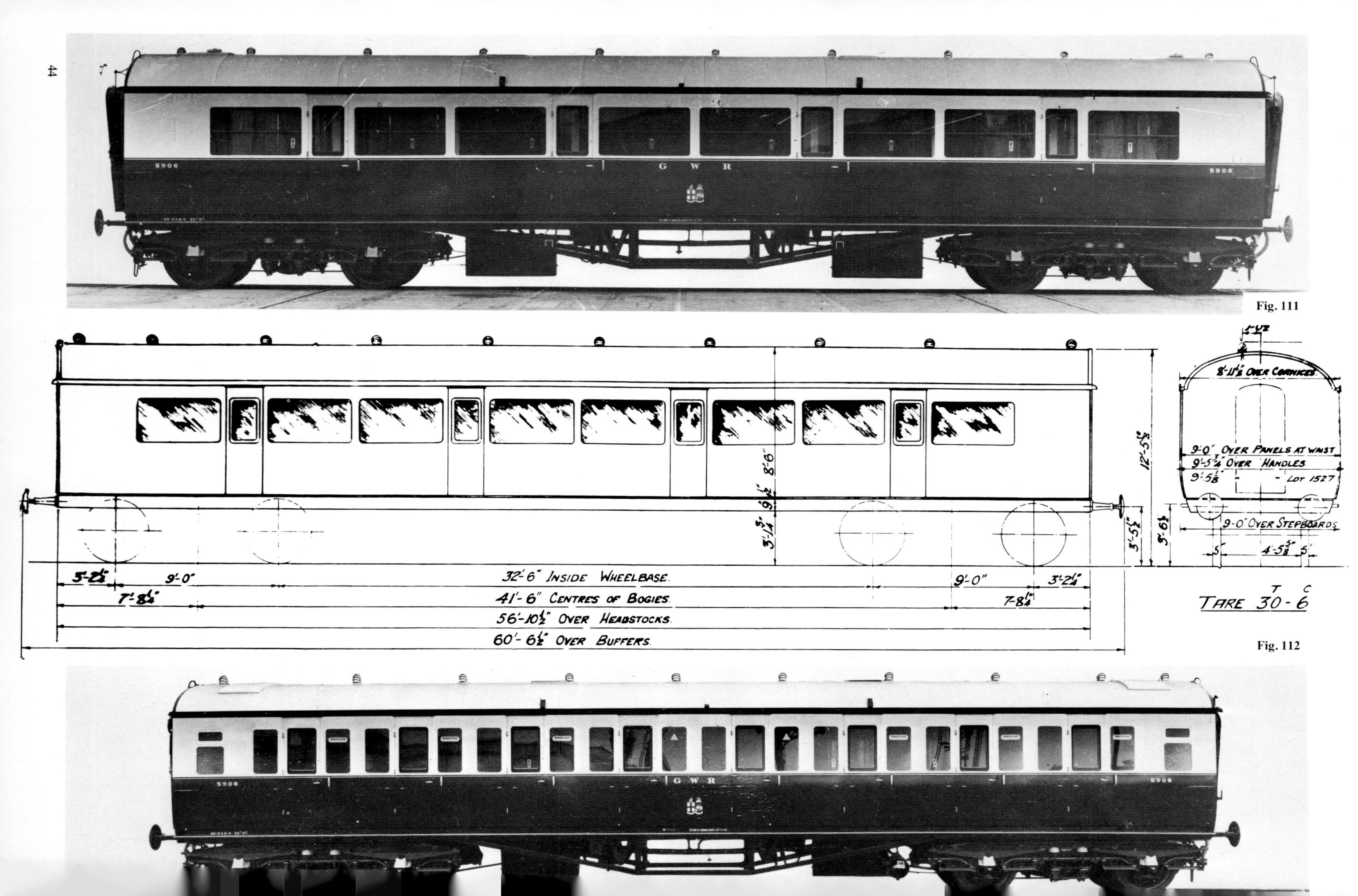

Fig. 111

Fig. 112

Fig. 113

◁ *DIAGRAM C67*
THIRD Corridor Carriage

Fig. 111 (opposite page) is the official photograph of No. 5906 in ex-works condition, showing the corridor side; and the compartment side of the same vehicle is seen in **Fig. 112**. Note the cantrail strip, which was painted in a milk chocolate colour, and the white roof.

△ *DIAGRAM C67*
THIRD Corridor Carriage

Fig. 113 End view of No. 5825, showing details of the end step and hand rails, corridor gangway and suspension, and buffing and drawgear,etc. Note the coach weight numerals on the left-hand side of the black painted end.

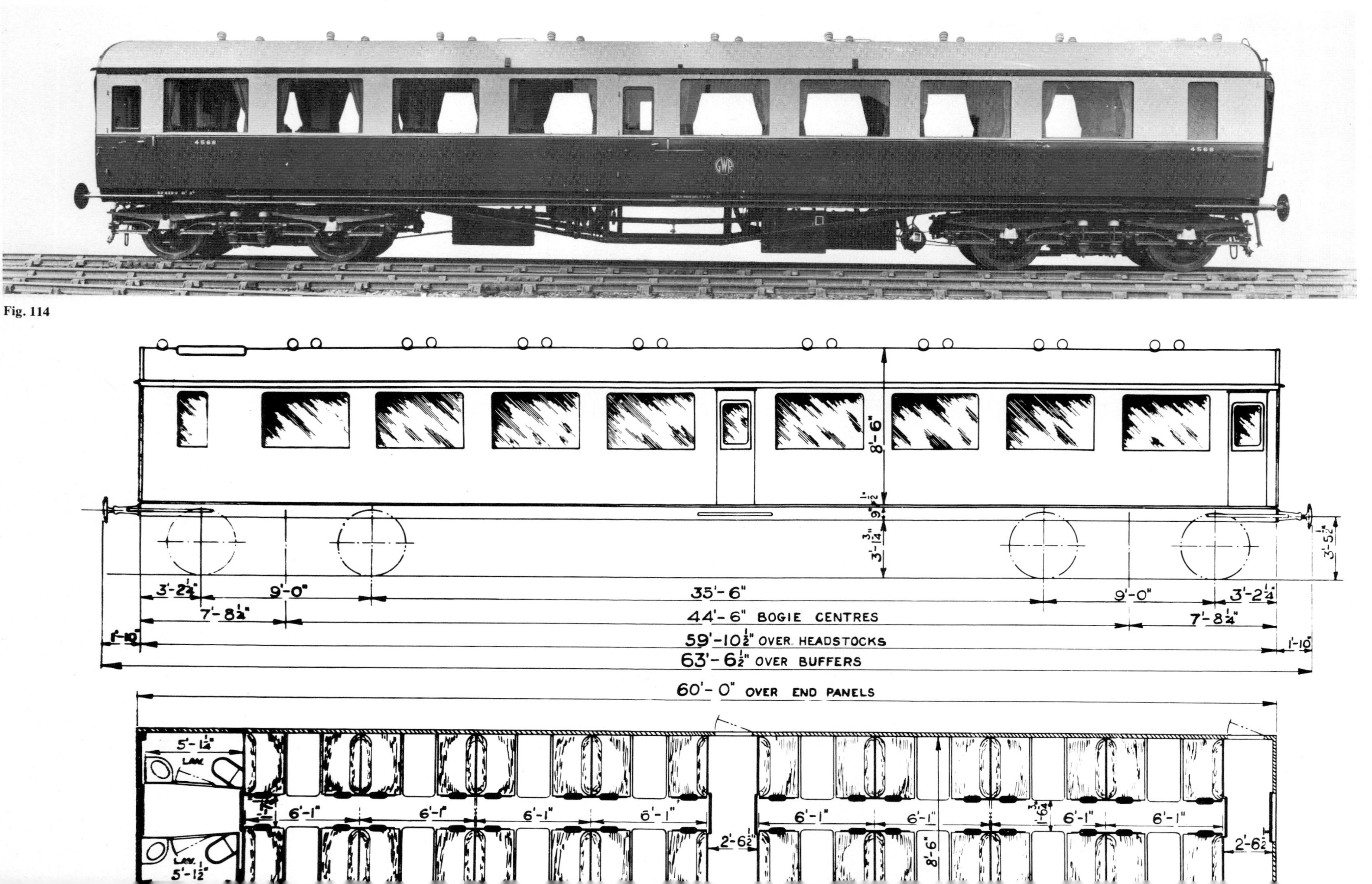

4568
GWR
8'-6"
9½"
3'-1¾"
3'-5½"
3'-2¼"
9'-0"
35'-6"
7'-8¼"
44'-6" BOGIE CENTRES
1'-10"
59'-10½" OVER HEADSTOCKS
63'-6½" OVER BUFFERS
60'-0" OVER END PANELS
5'-1¼"
LAV
5'-1½"
6'-1"
2'-6½"
1'-6¾"

Fig. 114

Fig. 115

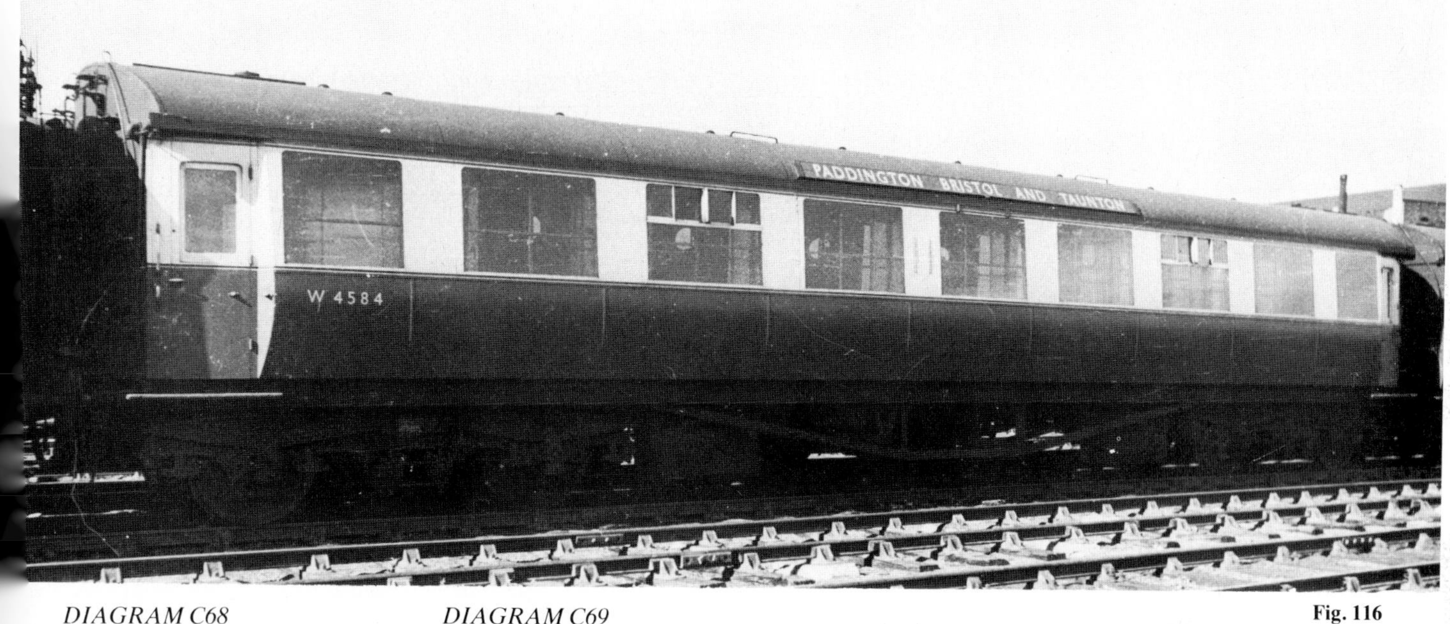

Fig. 116

DIAGRAM C68
THIRD Centre Corridor Saloon
Excursion Stock

Lot 1530 of 1935
Running numbers 4563–70
Dimensions: 60′ 0″ x 9′ 0″
Condemned January 1965

DIAGRAM C69
THIRD Corridor Carriage
'Centenary' Stock

Lot 1537 of 1935
Running numbers 4581–86
Dimensions: 61′ 4½″ x 9′ 7″
Condemned September 1963

Fig. 116 shows the corridor side of No. 4584 at Old Oak Common in 1952, carrying roof boards branded 'Paddington, Bristol and Taunton'. **Fig. 117** No. 4582 at Old Oak Common in 1953, with the compartment side towards the camera.

◁ **Fig. 114 (opposite page)** The official Swindon photograph of No. 4568, ex-works in 1935.
Fig. 115 shows No. 4565 in 1951 at Old Oak Common.

Fig. 117

Fig. 118

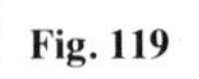

Fig. 119

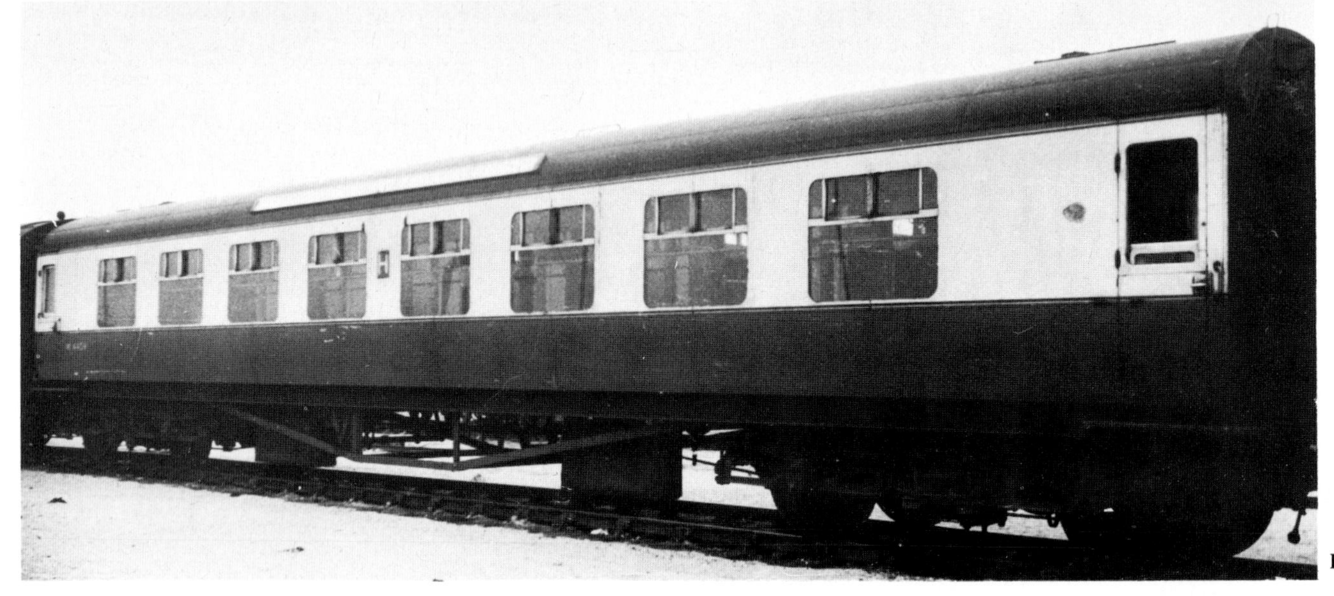

Fig. 120

Fig. 12

DIAGRAM C70
THIRD Corridor Carriage
Flush-sided Stock

Lot 1554 of 1936
Running numbers 4304–31

Lot 1559 of 1936
Running numbers 4444–83
Dimensions: 6′ 11¼″ x 9′ 0″
Condemned 1964
Provided with end doors only.

Fig. 118 No. 4312 is seen in this Swindon official picture of 1936. Note the painted numbers on cream panels. **Fig. 119** No. 4459 at Old Oak Common in 1951, showing the compartment side and roof boards reading 'Paddington, Cardiff and Fishguard Harbour'. **Fig. 120** shows the corridor side of this vehicle at the same location. **Fig. 121** depicts No. 4164 at Aberystwyth in the first BR livery in 1955.

DIAGRAM C71
THIRD Centre Corridor Saloon
Excursion Stock

Lot 1558 of 1936
Running numbers 4158–67
Dimensions: 60′ 0″ x 9′ 0″
Condemned November 1964
The only difference between this series and *C68* was a 2″ wider centre gangway. *C71* also had one large window per seating bay.

Fig. 122 shows the series as built in 1936; No. 4161 is seen with the 'roundel' livery.

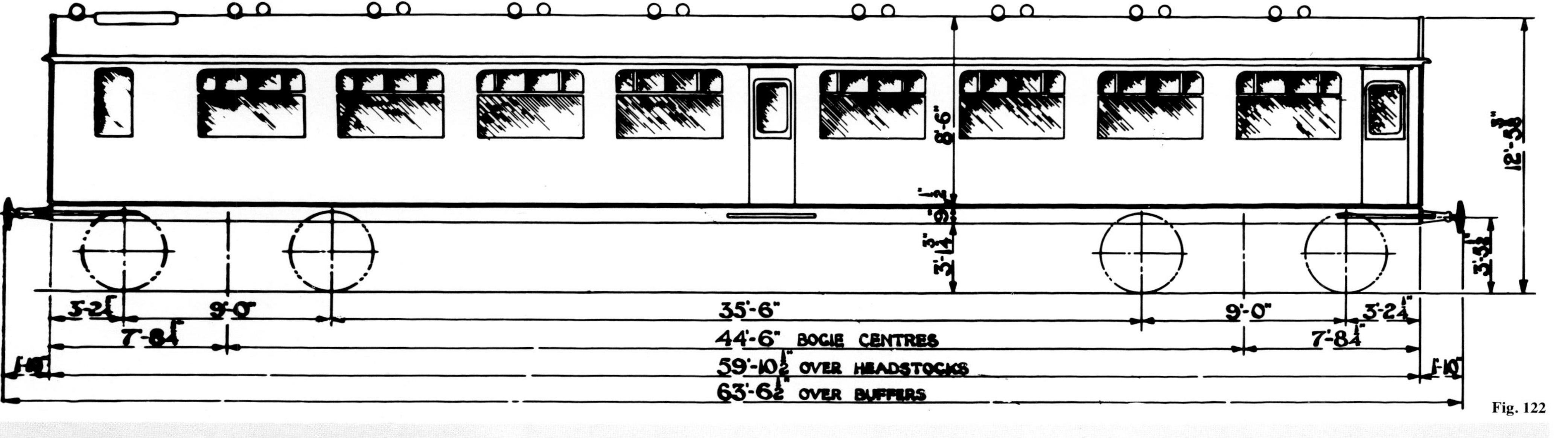

Fig. 122

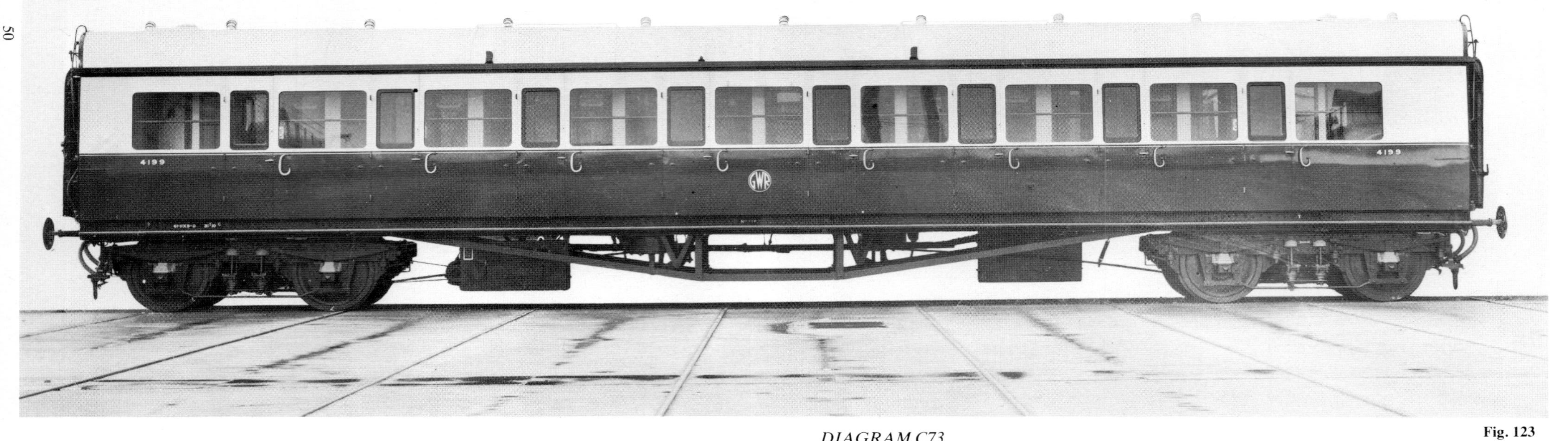

Fig. 123

DIAGRAM C72
THIRD Corridor Carriage
Ex-Articulated Stock

Lots 1361 and 1362
  Rebuilt running numbers 4190–4201
Dimensions: 59′ 9″ x 9′ 0″
Condemned December 1962
Originally built to *Diagrams C51* and *C52*.

Fig. 123 is the official picture of the *C72* series as rebuilt in 1936, showing the corridor side.

DIAGRAM C73
THIRD Corridor Carriage

Lot 1573 of 1937
  Running numbers 1442–1516
Dimensions: 60′ 11¼″ x 9′ 0″

Fig. 124 The corridor side of one of the series, No. 1456, as turned out of factory in 1937. Note the new type of deep windows.

Fig. 124

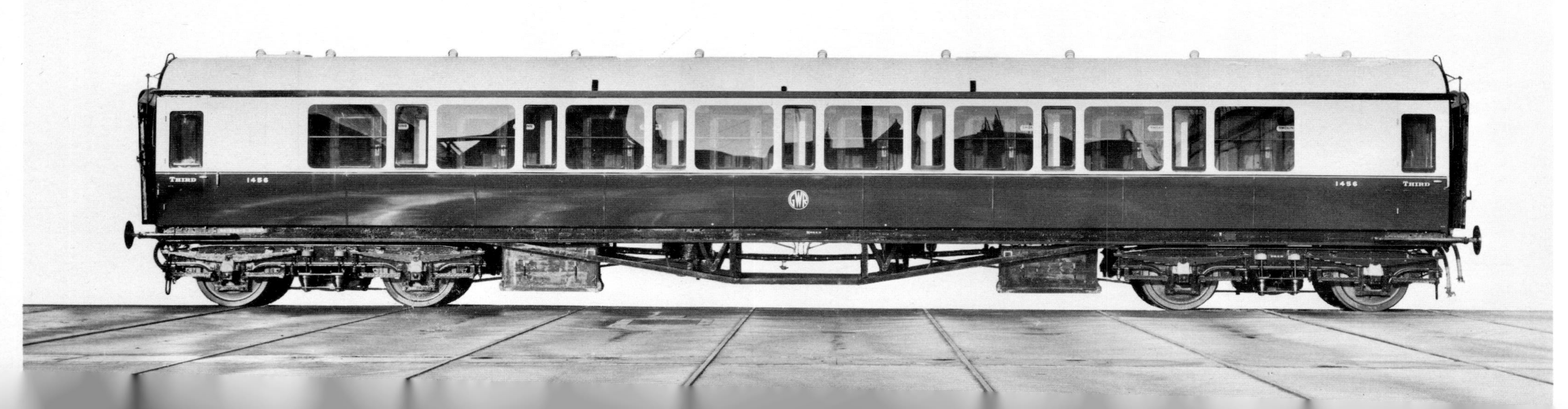

DIAGRAM C74
THIRD Centre Corridor
Excursion Stock

Lot 1575 of 1937
Running numbers 1271–97
Dimensions: 60′ 0″ x 9′ 0″
All these vehicles had single-sided seats at each end, facing the vehicle's ends. In 1949 these were turned, facing inwards. Only two doors were provided in each side.

No. 1285 is seen in **Fig. 125** at Old Oak Common in 1951.

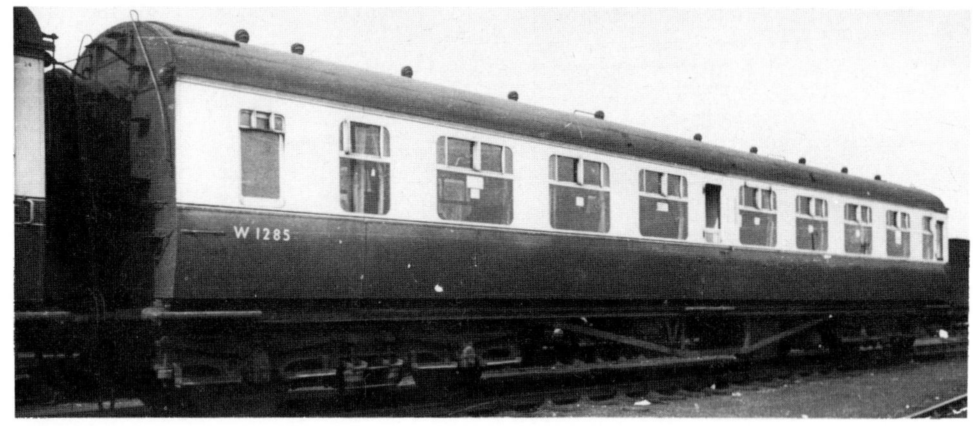

Fig. 125

DIAGRAM C76
THIRD Centre Corridor
Excursion Stock

Lot 1591 of 1938
Running numbers 1530–39
Lot 1625 of 1939
Running numbers 626–37
Lot 1643 of 1940
Running numbers 644–49
Dimensions: 60′ 11¼″ x 8′ 11″
C76 differed from *C74* in being slightly longer, the extra length being used in the lavatories and vestibules.

Fig. 126 shows No. 648 at Old Oak Common in 1951.

Fig. 126

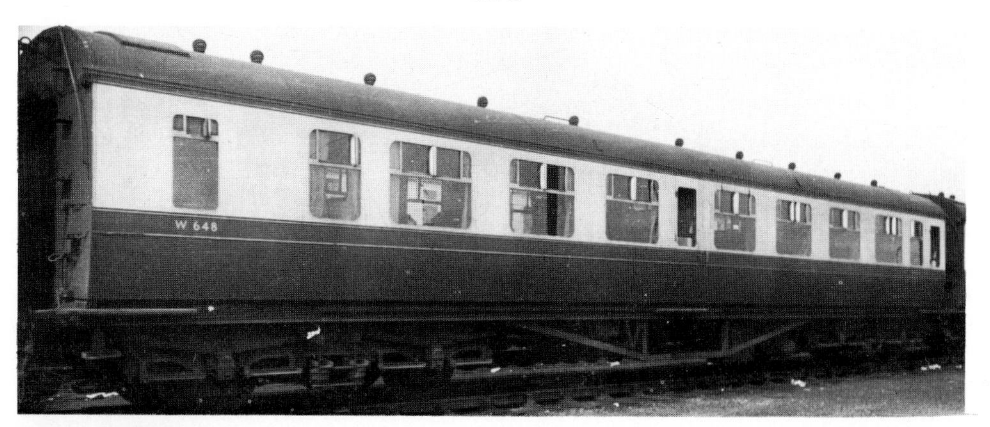

DIAGRAM C77
THIRD Side Corridor Carriage

Lot 1593 of 1938
Running numbers 1080–9, 93–8, 1100–16/18–28/30–4/36–55
Lot 1623 of 1940
Running numbers 501–95
Dimensions: 60′ 11¼″ x 8′ 11″

One of these vehicles, No. 1096, was altered to work between diesel cars Nos. 37 and 38 to form a three-coach train.

Fig. 127

Fig. 127, taken at Old Oak Common in 1951, illustrates the corridor side of No. 1139. **Fig. 128** Compartment side of No. 553 at Old Oak Common in 1955; the roof boards read 'Channel Islands Boat Express' in yellow letters on strawberry coloured background.

Fig. 128

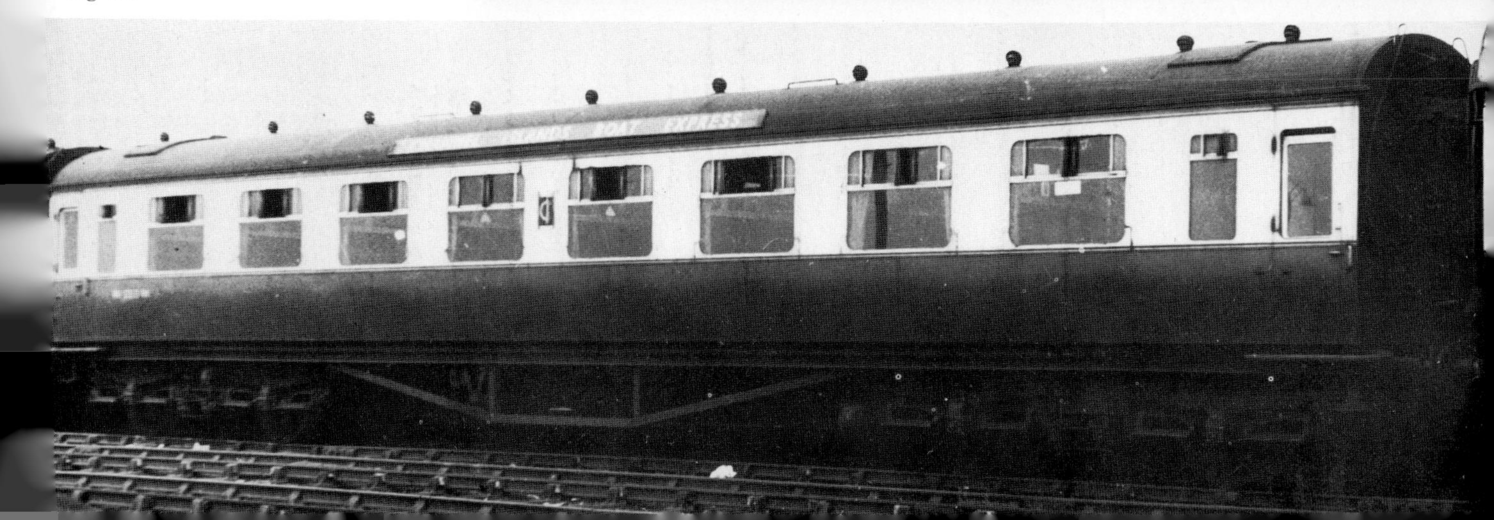

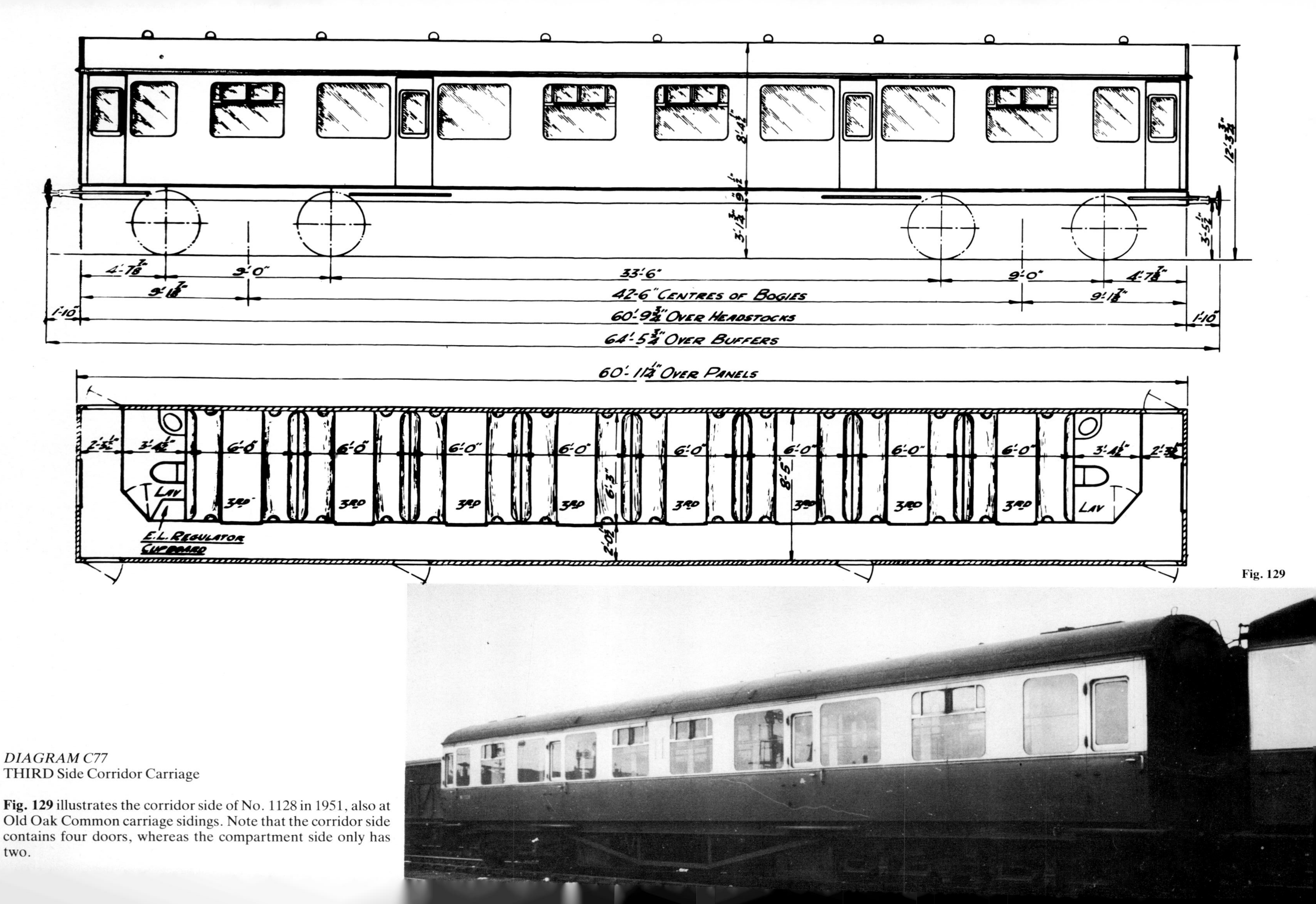

Fig. 129

DIAGRAM C77
THIRD Side Corridor Carriage

Fig. 129 illustrates the corridor side of No. 1128 in 1951, also at Old Oak Common carriage sidings. Note that the corridor side contains four doors, whereas the compartment side only has two.

Fig. 130

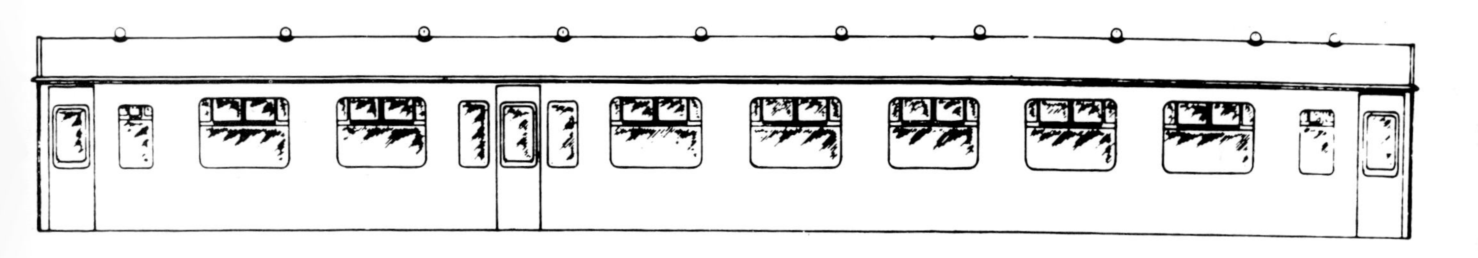

DIAGRAM C81
THIRD Corridor Carriage

Lot 1641 of 1941
Running numbers 751–80
Dimensions: 60′ 11¼″ x 8′ 11″
An unusual feature of this stock was that it was provided with four doors on the corridor side but only one door at each end on the compartment side, *plus* a single door fitted to the compartment third from left (viewed from the compartment side).

Fig. 130 shows this feature to advantage, on No. 761 at Old Oak Common in 1953. **Fig. 131** illustrates the corridor side of No. 768, also at Old Oak Common, but in 1952.

Fig. 131

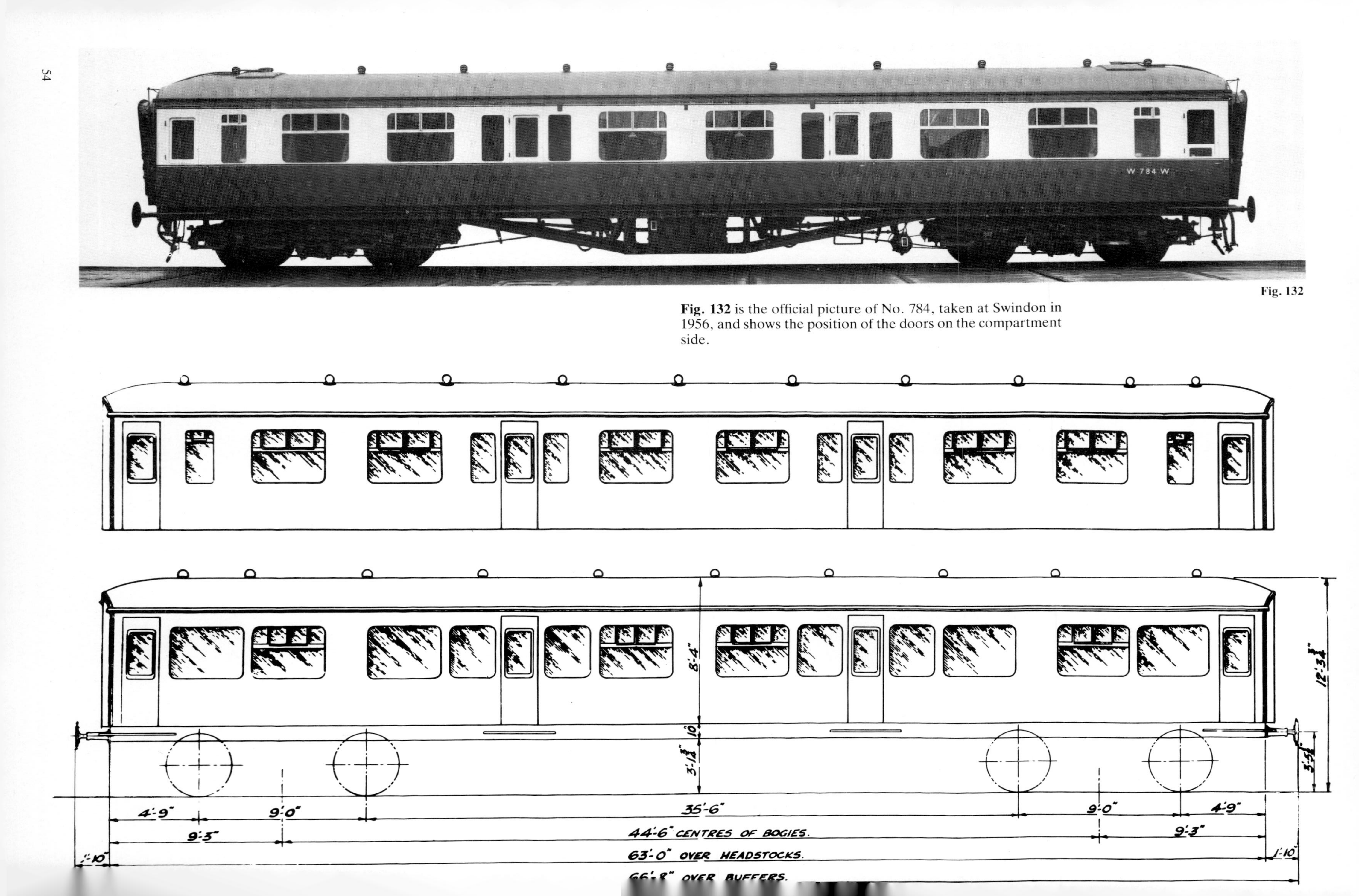

Fig. 132 is the official picture of No. 784, taken at Swindon in 1956, and shows the position of the doors on the compartment side.

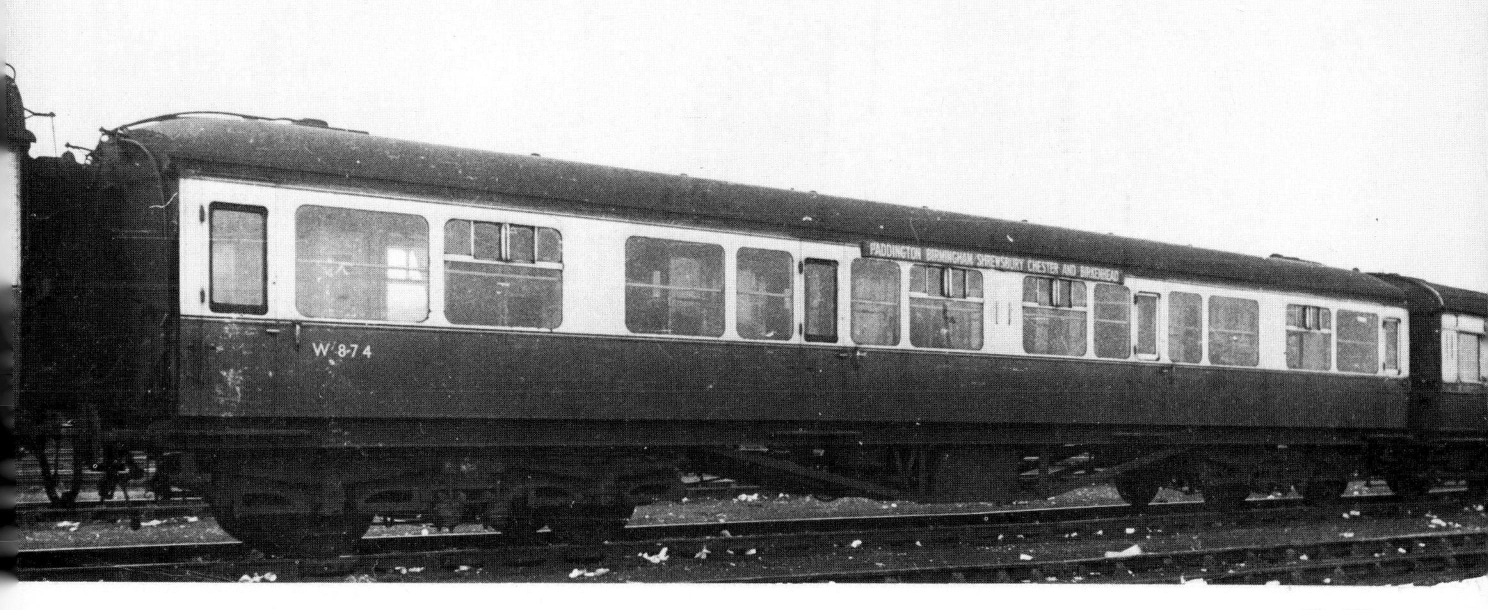

Fig. 133

DIAGRAM C82
THIRD Carriage Corridor
'Hawksworth' Stock

Lot 1691 of 1948
Running numbers 781–832
Lot 1714 of 1948 (built by Gloucester C & W Co.)
Running numbers 855–924
Dimensions: 64′ 0″ x 8′ 11″
This dome-roofed, round-ended stock had four doors each side, only two compartments being so provided.

Fig. 133 shows No. 874 at Old Oak Common in 1952 with the corridor side nearest the camera. Destination boards are now at cantrail level, and read 'Paddington, Birmingham, Shrewsbury, Chester and Birkenhead'.

DIAGRAM C84
THIRD Corridor Carriage
'Hawksworth' Stock

Lot 1706 of 1948
Running numbers 1717–37
Lot 1720 of 1949 (built by Gloucester C & W Co.)
Running numbers 2107–36
Lot 1735 of 1950
Running numbers 2264–92
Dimensions: 64′ 0″ x 8′ 11″ (identical to *C82*)

Fig. 134 Official three-quarter view of No. 784 of the *C82* series, showing the compartment side.

Fig. 134

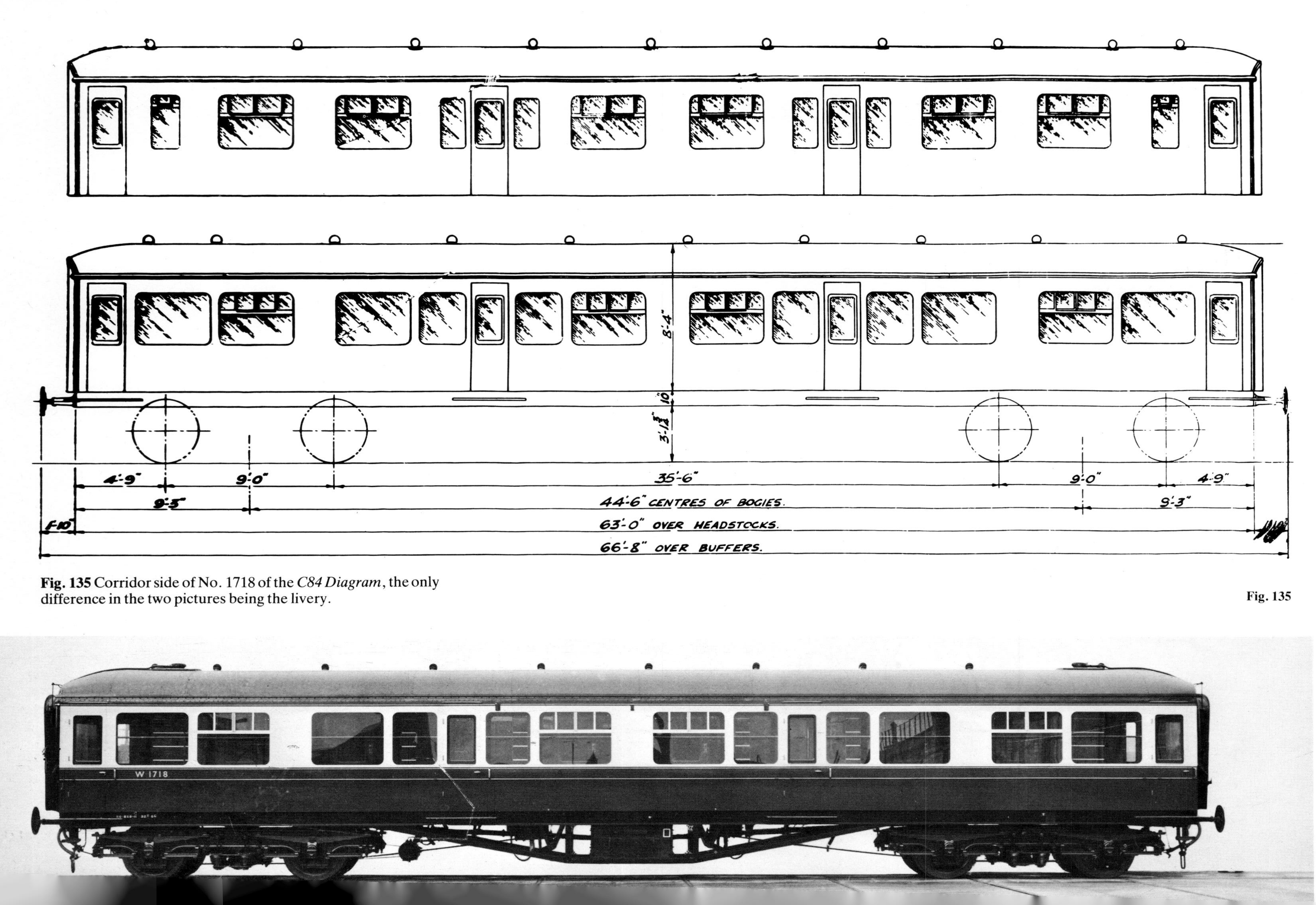

Fig. 135 Corridor side of No. 1718 of the *C84 Diagram*, the only difference in the two pictures being the livery.

Fig. 135

△ **Fig. 136**

▽ **Fig. 137**

Fig. 136 illustrates the compartment and lavatory side of the *C84* series in this picture of No. 2123 at Old Oak Common in 1952.

DIAGRAM C84
THIRD Corridor Carriage
'Hawksworth' Stock

Fig. 137 No. 2276 of Lot 1735 at Old Oak Common in 1952 with the corridor side towards the camera.

DIAGRAM C85
Experimental

Lot 1685 of 1950
One vehicle only: No. 2239
This vehicle was constructed in light alloy, reducing the weight from 31t 14cwt to 27t 12cwt, a saving of four tons. All other details were identical to *C84* and *C82 Diagrams.*

Fig. 138 illustrates the corridor side of this one-off vehicle at Swindon in 1950. Note the white painted roof and unpainted aluminium chassis.

Fig. 138

DIAGRAM C83
THIRD Non-Corridor Carriage
10-compartment Stock

Fig. 139

Lot 1693 of 1948
Running numbers 374–413
Lot 1712 of 1949
Running numbers 2002–16
Lot 1739 of 1950
Running numbers 2017–26
Lot 1726 of 1950
Running numbers 1840–59
Lot 1745 of 1951
Running numbers 2601–90, 2700–20
Lot 1748 of 1951
Running numbers 2797–2832
Dimensions: 63′ 0¾″ x 8′ 11″
Seated 100 passengers.

Fig. 140

Fig. 139 Official broadside view of No. 383 in GWR colours and lettering, photographed at Swindon in August 1947. **Fig. 140** shows No. 408 at Old Oak Common in 1951, still in GWR livery with crest.

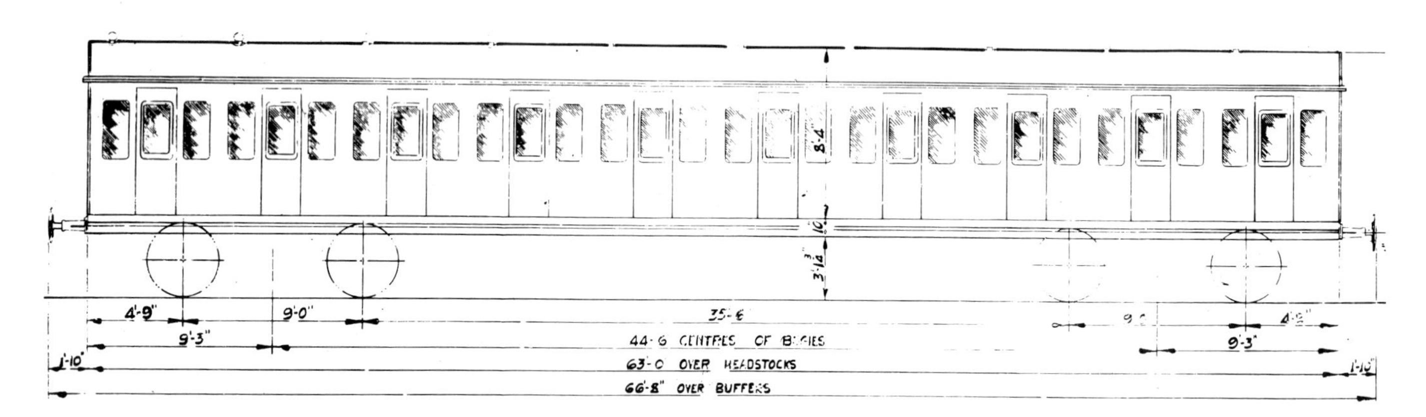

DIAGRAM C83
THIRD Non-Corridor Carriage

10-compartment Stock
Lot 1748 of 1951

Fig. 141 An official Swindon broadside view of No. 2800 in British Railways maroon livery.

Fig. 141

Fig. 142 No. 2800 is also the subject of this three-quarter view which shows clearly the end-detail of the series. Although the roof appears white in this picture, the painting at this time was grey.

SECOND Corridor Carriage
BR Standard Stock
BR Lot 30059, built by Cravens Ltd.

Fig. 143 shows a three-quarter view of No. W24701 in strawberry and cream livery.

BR Lot 30068 of 1952, built at Swindon.
Fig. 144 A broadside photograph of No. W24540 in British Railways livery, as above.

Fig. 143

Fig. 144

DIAGRAM BR 93
SECOND Corridor Carriage
BR Main Line Stock
BR Lot 30079 of 1953, Type J

Fig. 145 Official Swindon picture of No. W3789, built at York, showing gangway detail and buck-eye couplings.

Fig. 164

DIAGRAMS D30 and *D31*
BRAKE THIRD Corridor Carriage
Clerestory Stock

Lot 931 of 1900
Running numbers 2059/60/4/82/3, built to *D31*
Running numbers 2813/5 (right-hand vans), 2084–6, built to *D30*
Lot 955 of 1900
Running numbers 3424–32, built to *D30*
Condemned August 1949

BRAKE THIRD Corridor Carriage
Clerestory Stock

Lot 953 of 1900
Running numbers 3415/7/9/21/2
Dimensions: 56′ 0¾″ x 8′ 6¾″
Condemned September 1952
Built to *D31*. Identical to Lots 931 and 955, but all provided with left-hand vans.

Fig. 164 is one of a pair of official photographs showing the corridor side of No. 2085, as built in 1900, and in **Fig. 165**, the compartment side.

Fig. 165

DIAGRAM BR 93
SECOND Corridor Carriage
BR Main Line Stock
BR Lot 30079 of 1953, Type J

Fig. 145 Official Swindon picture of No. W3789, built at York, showing gangway detail and buck-eye couplings.

THIRD Non-Corridor Carriage
BR Standard Suburban Stock
BR Lot 30037 of 1954, built at Swindon. Type 3

Fig. 146-A three-quarter view of maroon-liveried No. W46033 at Swindon in 1954. **Fig. 147** A broadside photograph of the same vehicle, also taken at Swindon.

Fig. 147

DIAGRAM BR 147
THIRD Open Gangwayed Carriage
BR Standard Stock
BR Lot 30149 of 1955, Type J

DIAGRAM BR 147
THIRD Gangwayed Carriage
BR Main Line Stock
BR Lot 30027 of 1954, Type C

Fig. 148 Official photograph of No. W24750, showing the compartment side.

Fig. 148

Fig. 149 No. S4002, showing the lavatory side.

Fig. 149

Fig. 150

Fig. 151

SECOND Open Gangwayed Carriage
BR Standard Stock
BR Lot 30230 of 1957, built by Metro-Cammell

Figs. 150 and **151** show No. W25165, in both broadside and three-quarter views at Swindon in 1957.

Fig. 152

Fig. 153

THIRD Passenger Carriage
Narrow Gauge Bogie Stock
Vale of Rheidol Railway, ex-Cambrian Railways stock.

Fig. 152 shows coach No. 2 at Aberystwyth station in 1923. **Fig. 153**, also taken at Aberystwyth, illustrates carriage No. 7 of the Cambrian Railways just after the Grouping.

THIRD Open Toast-rack Carriage
Narrow Gauge Stock
Vale of Rheidol Railway, ex-Cambrian Railways stock.

Fig. 154 depicts open bogie car No. 12 at Aberystwyth in 1923.

Fig. 154

Fig. 155

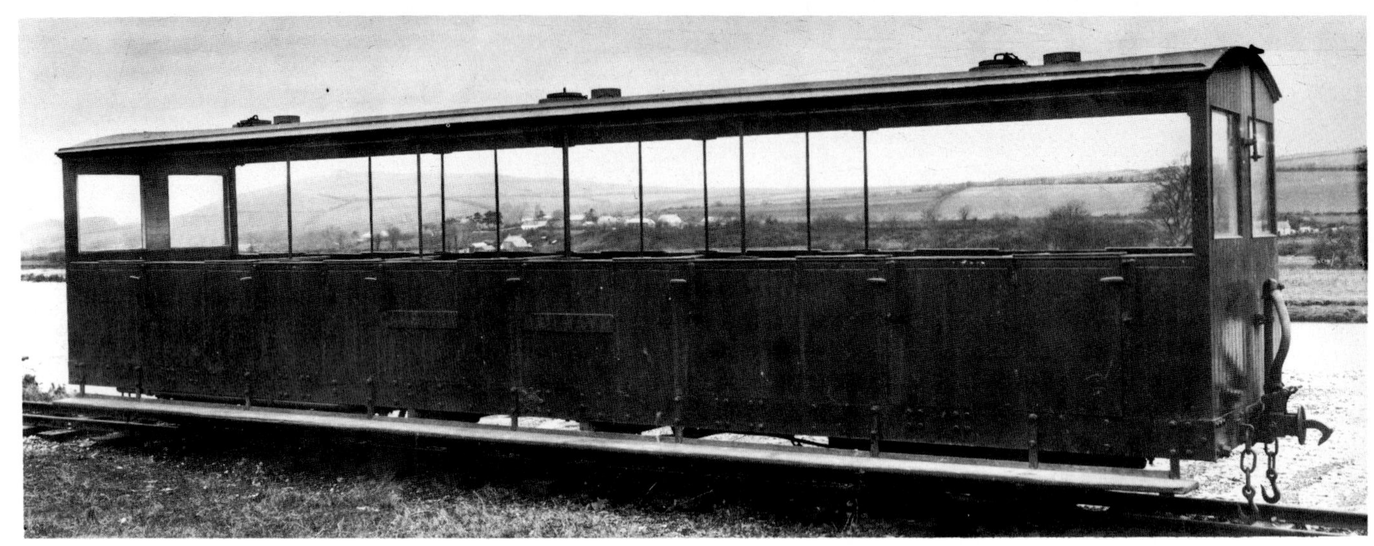

Fig. 156

DIAGRAM C48
THIRD Open Carriage
Narrow Gauge Bogie Stock

Lot 1333 of 1923
Running numbers 4997–5000
Lot 1618 of 1939
Running numbers 4149–51
Dimensions: 32′ 0⅝″ x 6′ 4″
Gauge 1′ 8½″
Vale of Rheidol Railway, ex-Cambrian Railways stock.

Fig. 155 illustrates two open four-wheel cars of the Cambrian Railways, Nos. 16 and 17, at Aberystwyth.

Fig. 156 shows carriage No. 11, an open vehicle with panelled sides. **Fig. 157** No. 4998 of Lot 1333, built at Swindon by the GWR for the Vale of Rheidol service.

Fig. 157

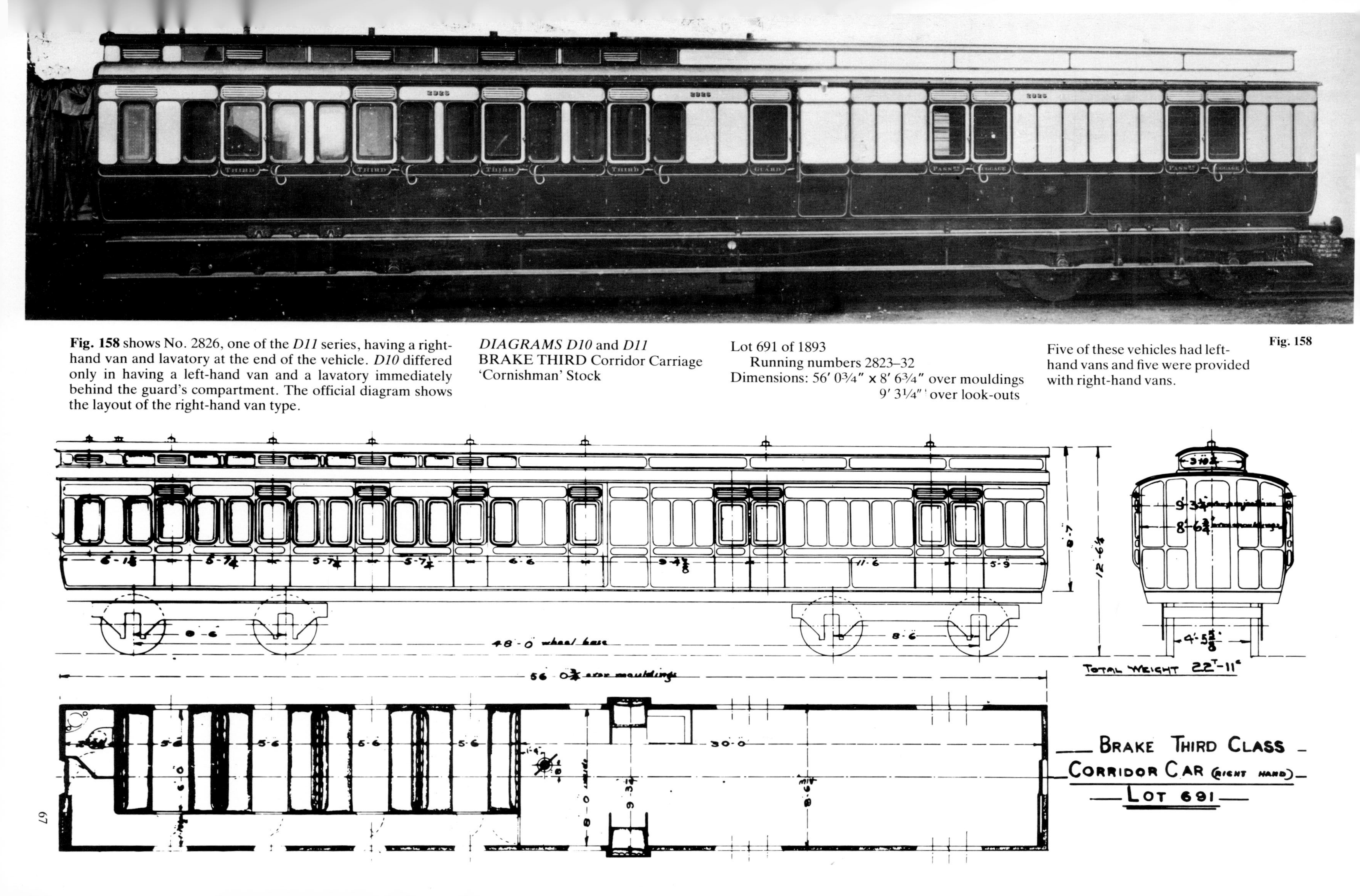

Fig. 158

Fig. 158 shows No. 2826, one of the *D11* series, having a right-hand van and lavatory at the end of the vehicle. *D10* differed only in having a left-hand van and a lavatory immediately behind the guard's compartment. The official diagram shows the layout of the right-hand van type.

DIAGRAMS D10 and *D11*
BRAKE THIRD Corridor Carriage
'Cornishman' Stock

Lot 691 of 1893
Running numbers 2823–32
Dimensions: 56′ 0¾″ × 8′ 6¾″ over mouldings
9′ 3¼″ over look-outs

Five of these vehicles had left-hand vans and five were provided with right-hand vans.

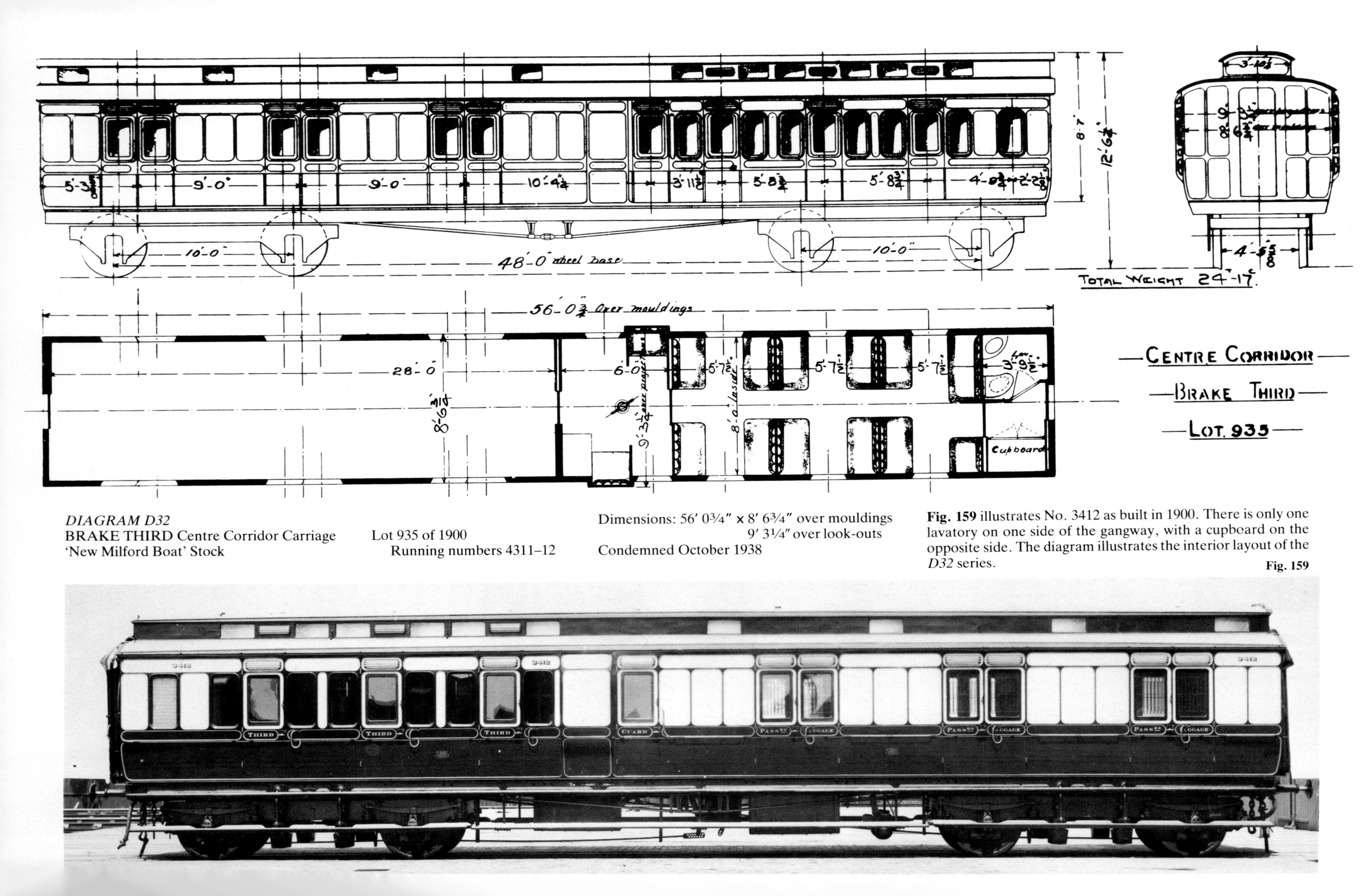

DIAGRAM D32
BRAKE THIRD Centre Corridor Carriage
'New Milford Boat' Stock

Lot 935 of 1900
Running numbers 4311–12

Dimensions: 56′ 0¾″ x 8′ 6¾″ over mouldings
9′ 3¼″ over look-outs
Condemned October 1938

Fig. 159 illustrates No. 3412 as built in 1900. There is only one lavatory on one side of the gangway, with a cupboard on the opposite side. The diagram illustrates the interior layout of the *D32* series.

Fig. 159

DIAGRAM D8
BRAKE THIRD Non-Corridor Carriage
Clerestory Stock

Lot 613 of 1892
  Running numbers 2241–50
Lot 673 of 1893
  Running numbers 2801–04
Lot 769 of 1895
  One replacement vehicle for No. 2245 of Lot 613
Dimensions: 48′ 6¾″ x 8′ 0¾″
Last vehicle condemned December 1948

Fig. 160 depicts No. 2803, complete with look-outs.

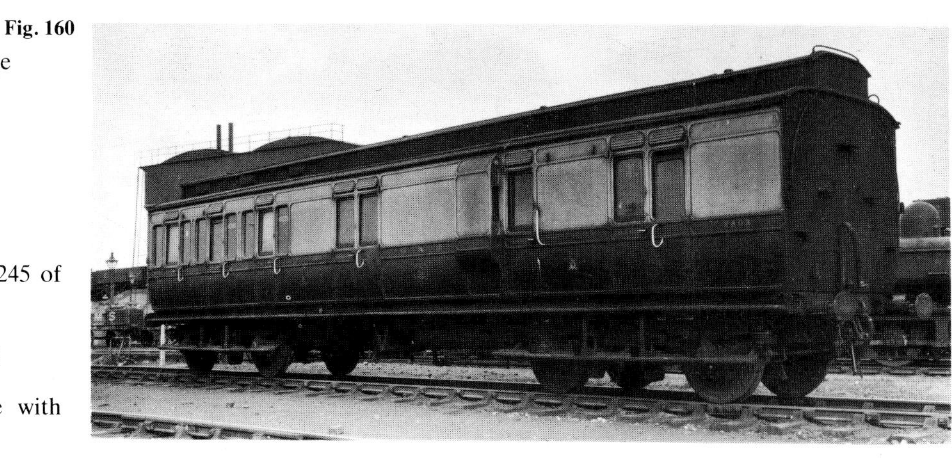
Fig. 160

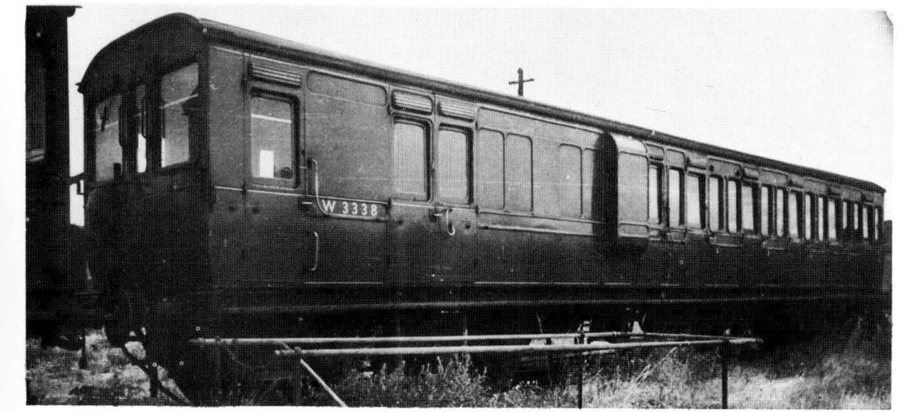

Fig. 161

DIAGRAM D27
BRAKE THIRD Non-Corridor Carriage
3-arc Low-roof Stock

Lot 872 of 1898
  Running numbers 3331–40
Dimensions: 51′ 0¾″ x 8′ 0¾″
Modified to Clifton Downs autocar profile, and condemned in August 1949.

Fig. 161 shows the driving end of No. 3338 in BR days.

DIAGRAM D29
BRAKE THIRD Corridor Carriage
3-compartment Clerestory Stock
Condemned December 1950

Lots 917, 923, 998, 1009, 1019, 1036, and 1050 of 1899 to 1904
  Running numbers 3351–60, 3301–10, 3445–48, 3449–54, 2332–36, 2337–41
Dimensions: 56′ 0¾″ x 8′ 6¾″

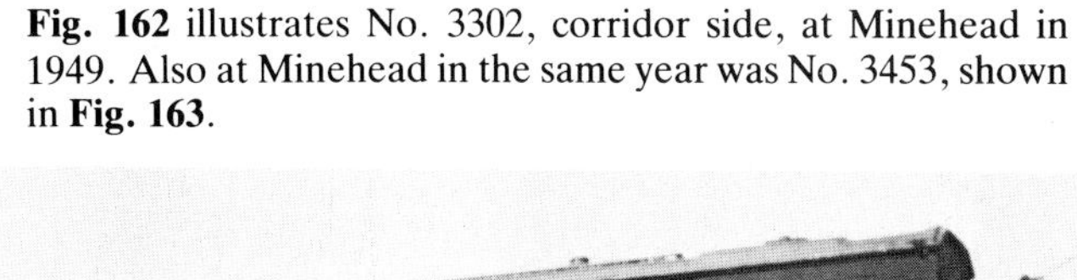
Fig. 162 illustrates No. 3302, corridor side, at Minehead in 1949. Also at Minehead in the same year was No. 3453, shown in **Fig. 163**.

△ **Fig. 162**

Fig. 163

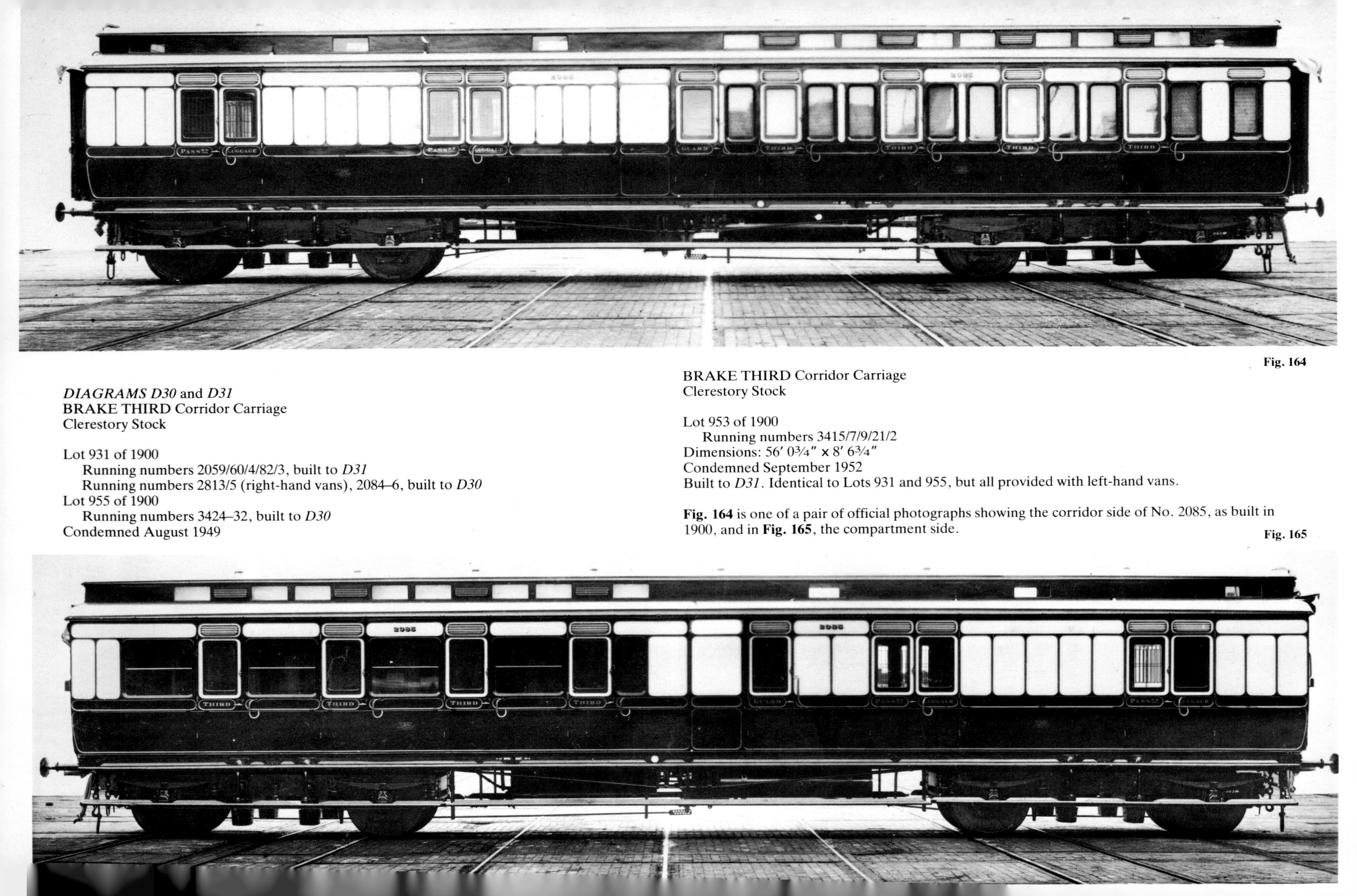

Fig. 164

DIAGRAMS D30 and *D31*
BRAKE THIRD Corridor Carriage
Clerestory Stock

Lot 931 of 1900
  Running numbers 2059/60/4/82/3, built to *D31*
  Running numbers 2813/5 (right-hand vans), 2084–6, built to *D30*
Lot 955 of 1900
  Running numbers 3424–32, built to *D30*
Condemned August 1949

BRAKE THIRD Corridor Carriage
Clerestory Stock

Lot 953 of 1900
  Running numbers 3415/7/9/21/2
Dimensions: 56′ 0¾″ x 8′ 6¾″
Condemned September 1952
Built to *D31*. Identical to Lots 931 and 955, but all provided with left-hand vans.

Fig. 164 is one of a pair of official photographs showing the corridor side of No. 2085, as built in 1900, and in **Fig. 165**, the compartment side.

Fig. 165

Fig. 166

Fig. 167

DIAGRAM D42
BRAKE THIRD Corridor Carriage
Lots 1066 and 1085
Running numbers 3467–78
Dimensions: 70′ 0″ x 9′ 6″
Condemned January 1954

Fig. 166 No. 3476 started life as a 'Dreadnought' (see small inset, **Fig. 167**) and after being burnt out in 1926 was rebuilt to the 1922 'South Wales' design, as illustrated here.

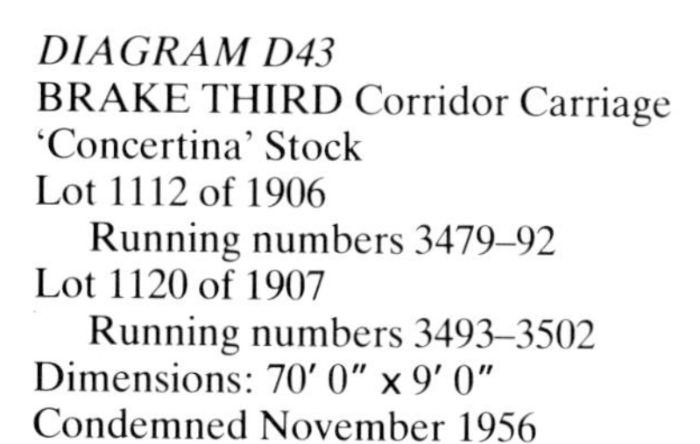

DIAGRAM D43
BRAKE THIRD Corridor Carriage
'Concertina' Stock
Lot 1112 of 1906
Running numbers 3479–92
Lot 1120 of 1907
Running numbers 3493–3502
Dimensions: 70′ 0″ x 9′ 0″
Condemned November 1956

Fig. 168 No. 3482 at Old Oak Common in 1949 with compartment side nearest camera. The roof boards read 'Paddington, Birmingham, Shrewsbury, Chester and Birkenhead'.

DIAGRAM D44
BRAKE THIRD Corridor Carriage
3-Compartment 'Toplight' Stock
Lot 1135 of 1908
Running numbers 3503–17
Dimensions: 57′ 0″ x 9′ 0″
All sold toWD and converted to continental ambulance train stock in First World War. Several examples were brought back but were not rebuilt to original *D44* design.

Fig. 169 shows No. 3506 returned to GWR stock and converted to *Diagram D56*. The vehicle is seen at Tyseley in 1950, with the corridor side nearest the camera.

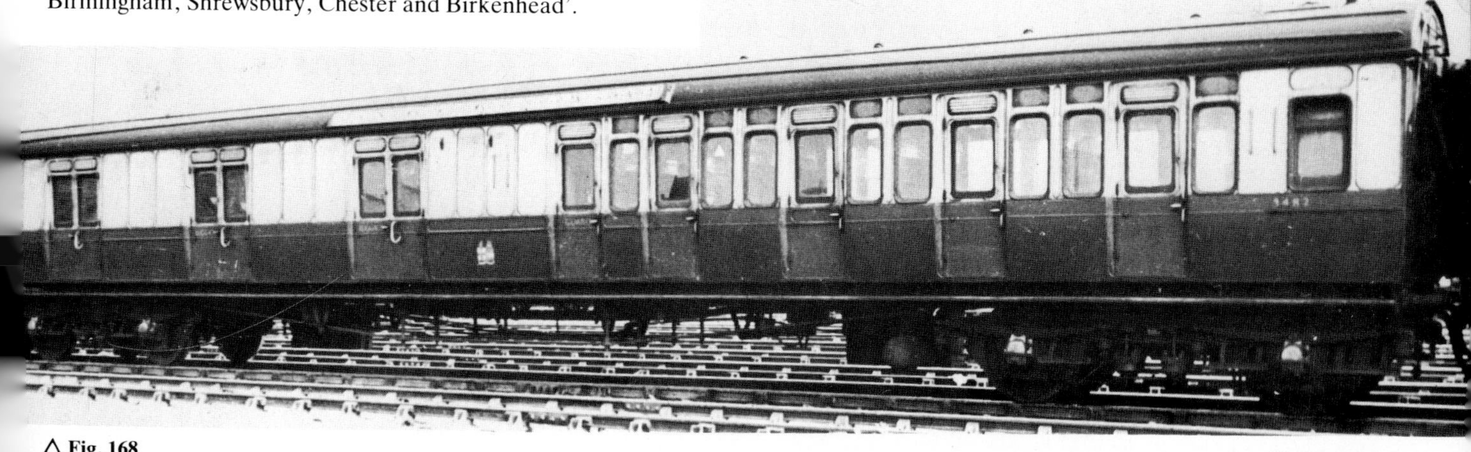

△ **Fig. 168**

▽ **Fig. 169**

Fig. 170

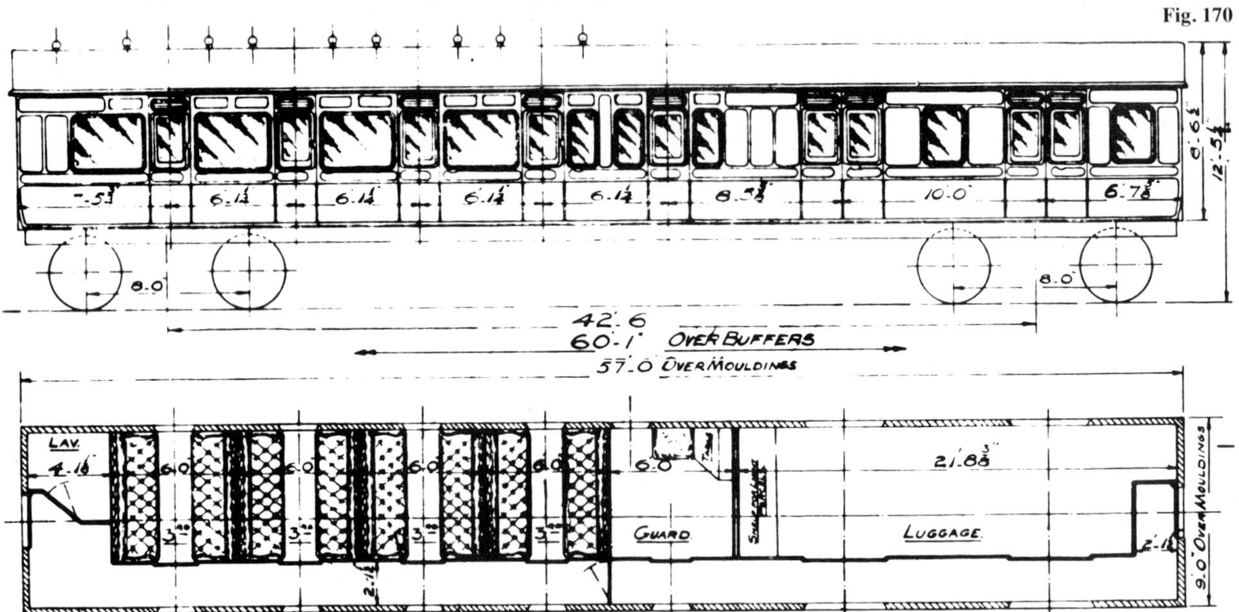

DIAGRAM D45
BRAKE THIRD Corridor Carriage
4-Compartment 'Toplight' Stock

Lot 1146
Running numbers 3518–33
Lot 1152 of 1908
Running numbers 3534–5
Lot 1156 of 1909
Running numbers 3536–45
Dimensions: 57′ 0″ x 9′ 0″
Condemned March 1962

All this series were sold to WD. Several were later repurchased but none were rebuilt to *Diagram D45*.

Fig. 170 No. 3543 at Old Oak Common in 1950 with toplights still in place, and with compartment side nearest camera.
Fig. 171 No. 3537 at Old Oak in 1951 with the toplights and panels plated over. The small drawings show the interior arrangements and the corridor side elevation as built.

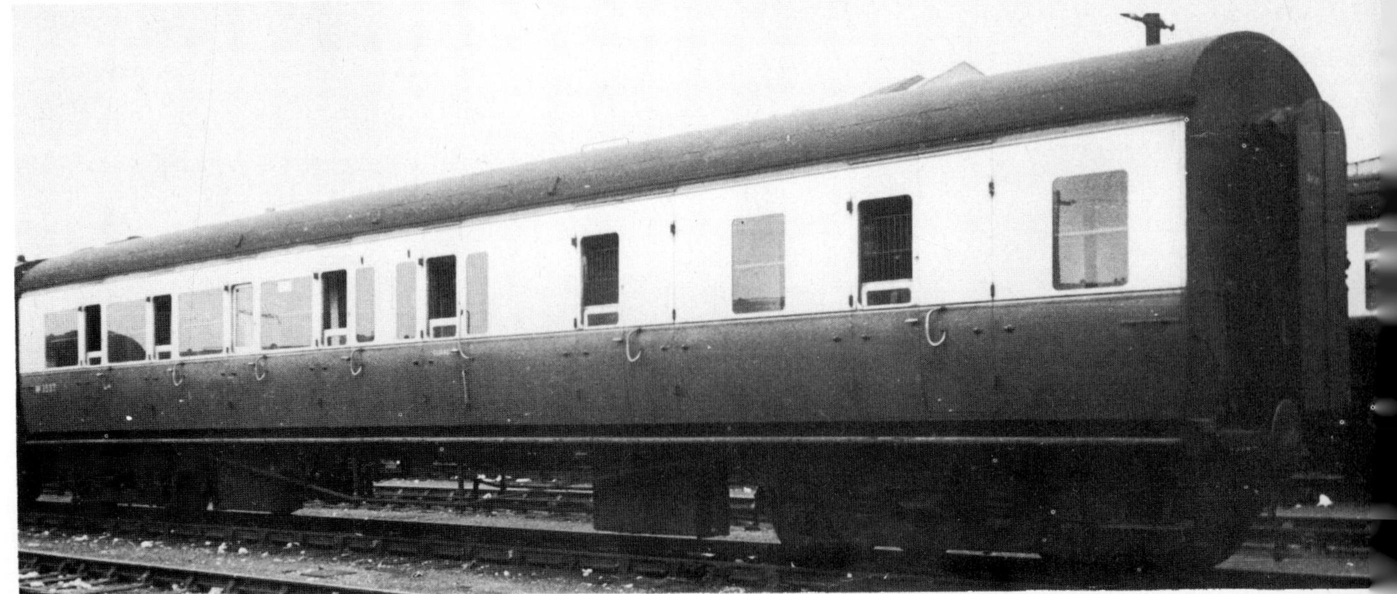

Fig. 171

Fig. 172

DIAGRAM D46
BRAKE THIRD Corridor Carriage
4-Compartment 'Toplight' Stock, Bars I
Lot 1168 of 1910
Running numbers 2342–45
Lot 1174 of 1911
Running numbers 2356–65
Dimensions: 56′ 0″ x 9′ 0″
Condemned March 1962
This series was almost identical to *D45* but was one foot shorter, taken out of the lavatory and luggage compartments.

Fig. 172 No. 2362, compartment side, seen at Old Oak Common in 1952. **Fig. 173** No. 2343 in BR livery, also at Old Oak Common in 1952. **Fig. 174** depicts the corridor side of No. 2362, again at Old Oak in 1952.

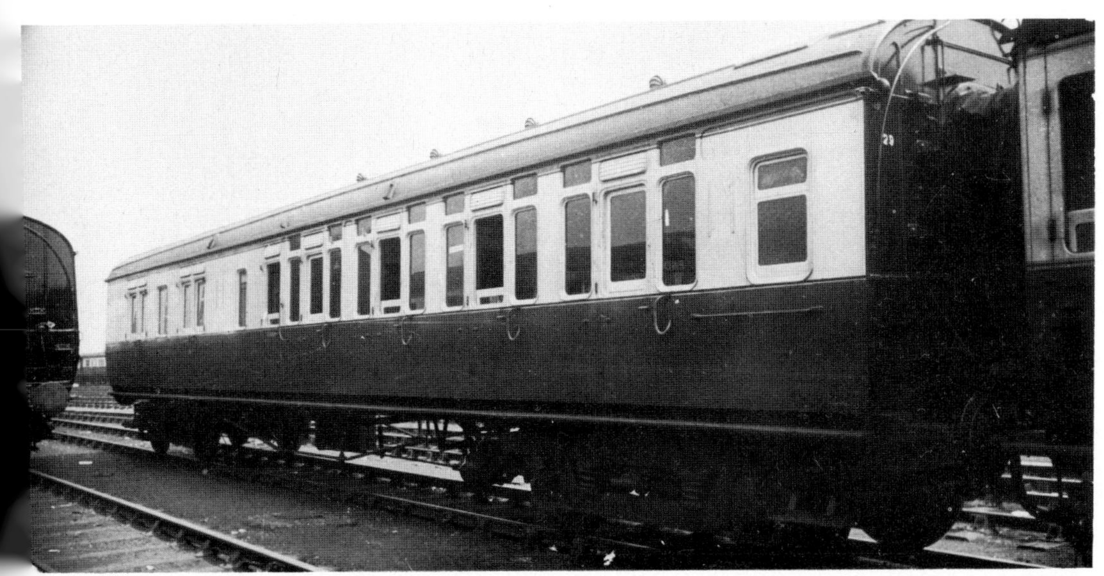

Fig. 173

Fig. 174

Fig. 175

Fig. 176

DIAGRAM D47
BRAKE THIRD Corridor Carriage
'Toplight' Stock, Bars I
Lots 1173, 1180 and 1195 of 1911–12
Running numbers 2346–55 Bars I RH
Running numbers 2367–81, 3551–59 Bars II
Lot 1314 of 1922 (sold to WD as ambulance sets)
Running numbers 3509/11–13 Bars II
Running numbers 3551–56 Bars II RH
Running numbers 3557–59 Bars II LH
Dimensions: 57′ 0″ x 9′ 0″
Condemned March 1962
This series differs from *D45* in having a shorter lavatory and a longer luggage compartment.

Fig. 175 shows the compartment side of No. 2377 at Old Oak in 1952. The roof boards read 'Paddington, Bristol and Taunton'.

DIAGRAM D48
BRAKE THIRD Corridor Carriage
3-Compartment 'Toplight' Stock
Lot 1181 of 1910
One vehicle only: No. 2366
Dimensions: 70′ 0″ x 9′ 0″
Condemned April 1955

Fig. 176 shows the compartment side of this vehicle at Swindon in 1952. Built with 9′ American bogies, but later fitted with 12-wheel bogies.

Fig. 177

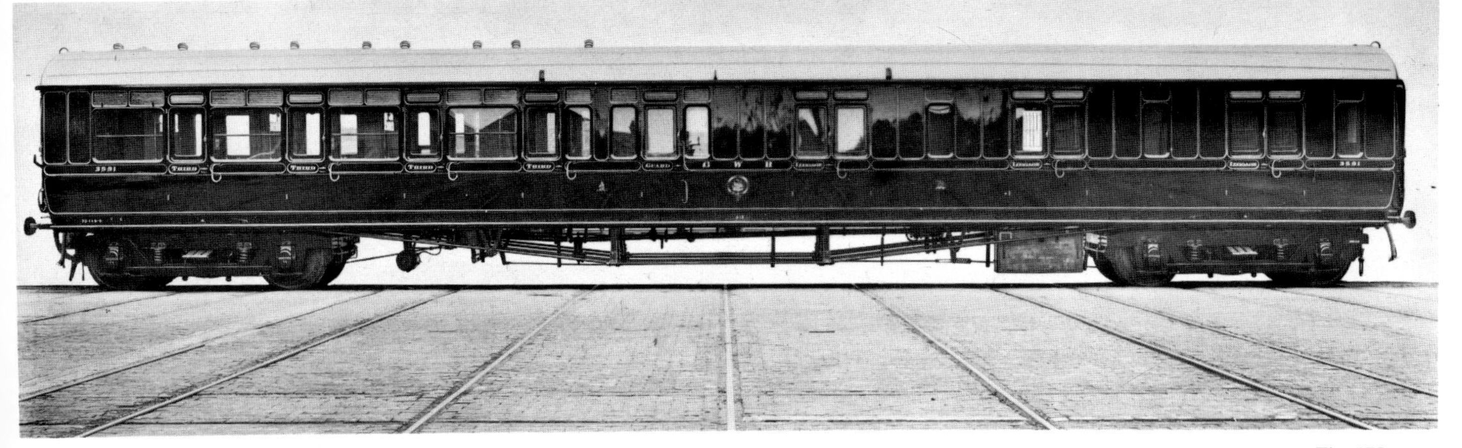

Fig. 178

DIAGRAM D49
BRAKE THIRD Non-Corridor Carriage
6-Compartment 'Toplight' Stock
Lot 1188 of 1911
◁ Running numbers 2388–95
Dimensions: 57′ 0″ x 9′ 0″
Condemned April 1955

Fig. 177 depicts No. 2392 at Reading Station in 1947, painted in the last GWR livery.

Fig. 179

DIAGRAM D51
BRAKE THIRD Corridor Carriage
'Toplight' Stock, Bars II
Lot 1207 of 1912
Running numbers 3575–84
Lot 1215 of 1913
Running numbers 3585–92
Dimensions: 70′ 0″ x 9′ 0″
Condemned October 1959

Fig. 178 is the official Swindon picture of No. 3591, as built in 1913, showing the corridor side and painted in the GWR maroon livery. **Fig. 179** shows No. 3575 at Old Oak Common in 1952 with the compartment side nearest the camera. **Fig. 180** illustrates No. 3576, also at Old Oak Common in 1952, but in BR strawberry and cream livery and with steel panelled sides.

Fig. 180

Fig. 181

DIAGRAM D51
BRAKE THIRD

Fig. 181 Corridor side of No. 3589, still with panelling in place but with toplights plated over. This right-hand van vehicle is seen at Old Oak Common in 1951. **Fig. 182** Also photographed at Old Oak Common in 1951 is the van end of No. 3587 with toplights still in position. **Fig. 183** shows a left-hand van pattern vehicle, No. 3583, at Old Oak in 1950 with its toplights plated over and the corridor side nearest the camera.

DIAGRAM D52
BRAKE THIRD Corridor Carriage
3-Compartment 'Toplight' Stock, Bars II
As originally constructed the series comprised the following:
Lot 1195 of 1912
Running numbers 3560–69
Lot 1203 of 1912
Running numbers 3570–74, of which 3573/4 were sold to WD
Various vehicles were re-purchased from WD and rebuilt to *Diagram D52* as follows:
Lot 1296 of 1921 (originally *D52* and built as ambulance stock)
Running number 3573 (left-hand van)
Lot 1314 of 1922 (originally *D52* and built as ambulance stock)
Running number 3510 (left-hand van)
Dimensions: 57′ 0″ x 9′ 0″
Condemned April 1962

Fig. 184 shows No. 3566 at Swindon Station in 1947, and fitted with 8′ American bogies.

Fig. 182

Fig. 183

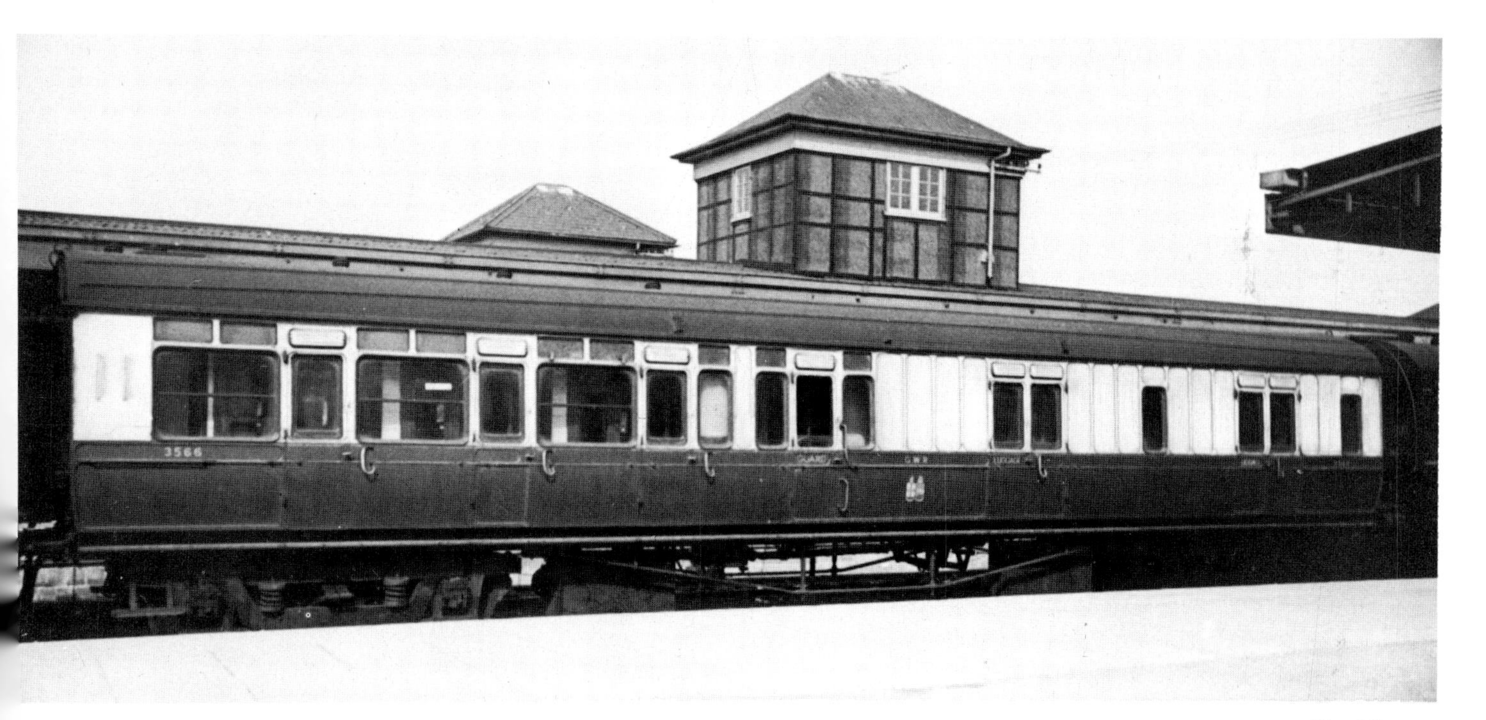

Fig. 184

DIAGRAM D53
BRAKE THIRD Non-Corridor Carriage
'Toplight' Stock, Multibar
Lot 1229 of 1913
Running numbers 3735–46
Dimensions: 56′ 11¼″ x 8′ 11¼″
Condemned June 1956

Fig. 185 is the official photograph of No. 3735 as built in 1913 with the GWR maroon livery. **Fig. 186** shows the opposite side of No. 3741 at Tyseley in 1950. Although the diagram of *D53* indicates the luggage doors as being opposite each other on the body, this does not tally with these two photographs.

DIAGRAM D55
BRAKE THIRD Non-Corridor Carriage
Birmingham Division 'Toplight' Stock, Multibar
Lot 1227 of 1913
Running numbers 1070–77
Dimensions: 69′ 11¼″ x 8′ 11¼″
Condemned December 1956

Fig. 185

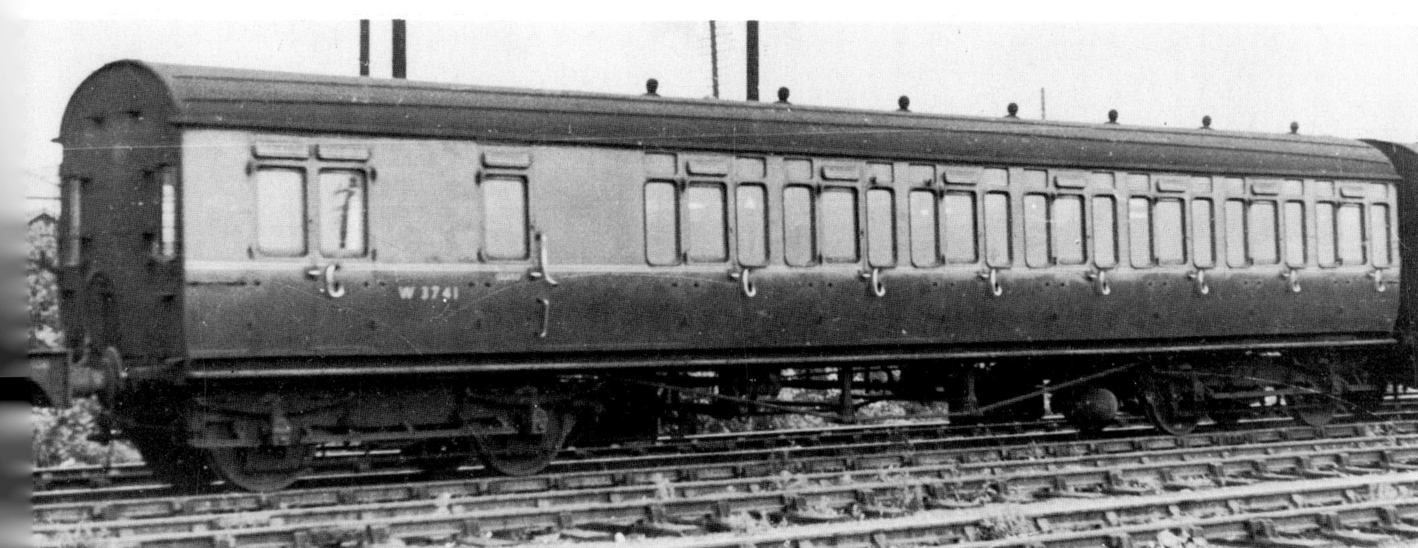

Fig. 186

DIAGRAM D56
BRAKE THIRD Corridor Carriage
3-Compartment 'Toplight' Stock, Multibar
Lot 1235
Running numbers 3593–95, Multibar, RH
Running numbers 3596–98, Multibar, LH
Lot 1247
Running numbers 3763–70, of which 3770 was sold to WD
Running numbers 3771–72, angle trusses, RH
Running numbers 3773–77, angle trusses, RH, sold to WD*
Lot 1257
Running numbers 3778–86, angle trusses, RH, sold to WD*
Lot 1270
Running numbers 3787–92, angle trusses, RH
Lot 1279
Running numbers 3805–10, angle trusses, RH, sold to WD*
Lot 1291 (originally *D56* and built as ambulance stock)
Running number 3503, re-purchased from WD
Lot 1293 (originally *D56* and built as ambulance stock)
Running numbers 3505–06, re-purchased from WD
Lot 1315 (*Diagram D56A*, rebuilt from *C28* ambulance stock)
Running number 3515
Lot 1339 (*Diagram D56A*, rebuilt from *D58* ambulance stock)
Running number 4243
Dimensions: 56′ 11¼″ x 8′ 11¼″
Condemned December 1963
*Of the coaches sold to the WD and re-purchased, all resumed their original numbers except Nos. 3773/80/83, 3810.

Fig. 187

Fig. 187 shows No. 1071 in 1920, painted maroon with white roof and branded 'Birmingham Division 5'. Note the 9′ American bogies fitted to this vehicle.

Fig. 188

Fig. 188 illustrates the series as first built in 1914 with maroon livery and white roof.

Fig. 189

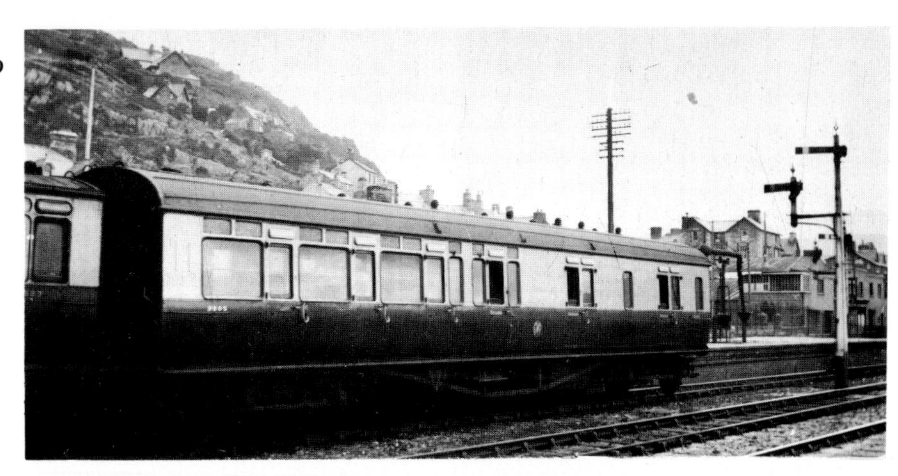

DIAGRAM D56
BRAKE THIRD Corridor Carriage
'Toplight' Stock, Multibar

Fig. 190

This page shows well the subtle difference between left-hand and right-hand van vehicles. At the top, **Fig. 189** illustrates the corridor side of No. 3805 (right-hand van) at Barmouth in 1938, while **Fig. 190** depicts No. 3598 at Paddington in 1950, showing the left-hand van pattern, this example being fitted with American pattern 8′ bogies. **Fig. 191** No. 3596 was photographed at Old Oak Common in 1950 and displays roof boards reading 'Paddington, Newport, Cardiff, Swansea and Neyland'. This carriage is of the left-hand type, and an example of the complementary right-hand series, No. 3791, can be seen in **Fig. 192**. Both vehicles are shown with their compartment sides nearest the camera.

Fig. 191

Fig. 192

Fig. 193

Fig. 194

DIAGRAM D57
BRAKE THIRD Corridor Carriage
'Toplight' Stock, Multibar
Lot 1237 of 1914
Running numbers 3759–62
Dimensions: 69′ 11¼″ x 8′ 11¼″
Condemned May 1958

Fig. 193 illustrates No. 3760 as built at Swindon in 1914 with the maroon livery. This is a left-hand van example. **Fig. 194** shows No. 3761 of the right-hand van pattern at Reading in 1947, and in **Fig. 195** No. 3759 is seen at Old Oak Common in 1953 with the compartment side facing the camera. The roof boards read 'Paddington, Gloucester and Cheltenham Spa'.

Fig. 195

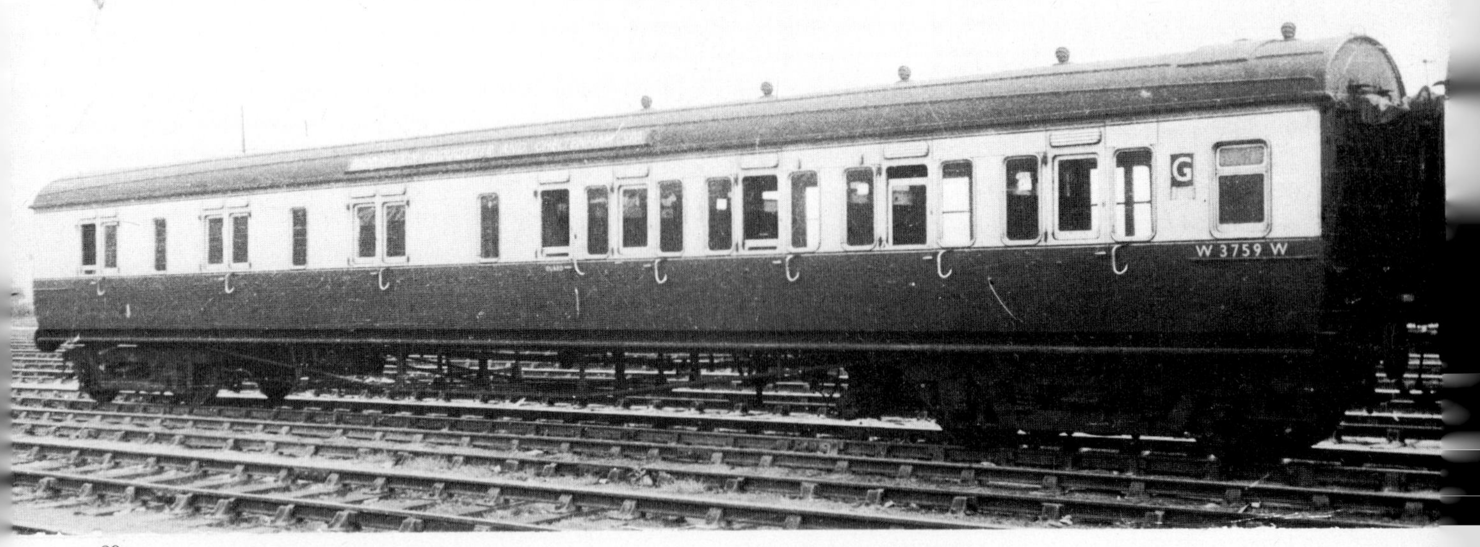

Fig. 196

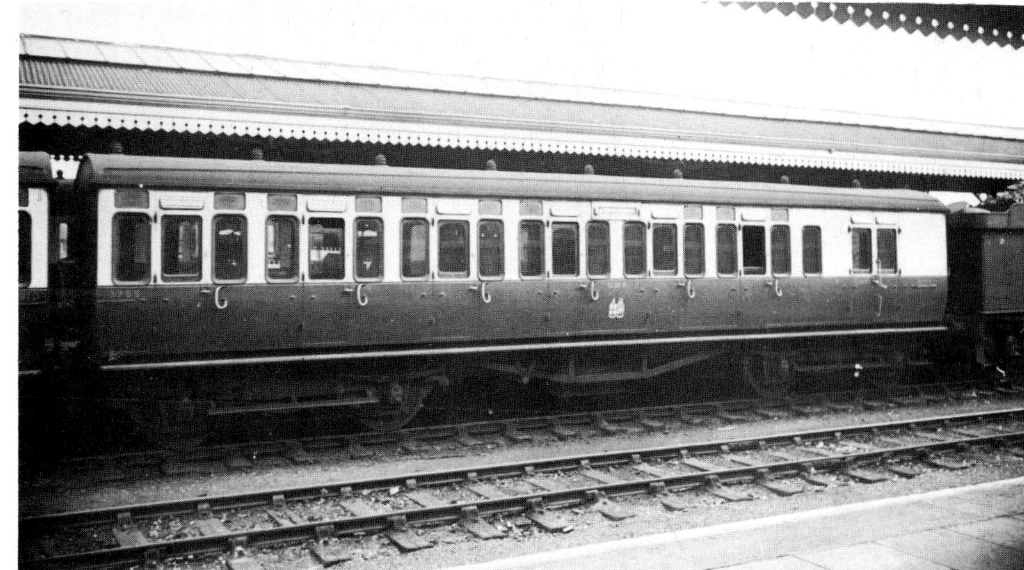

DIAGRAM D62
BRAKE THIRD Non-Corridor Carriage
6-Compartment, Low-roof Main Line & City Stock
Lot 1263 of 1919
    Running numbers 3747–48
Lot 1275 of 1921
    Running numbers 3749–58
Dimensions: 48′ 0″ x 8′ 5¼″
Condemned January 1965
These vehicles had normal buffing gear at the van end and short buffers at the compartment ends.

Fig. 196 shows No. 3755 at Reading in 1946.

DIAGRAM D67
BRAKE THIRD Non-Corridor Carriage
High-roof 'Toplight' Stock, Multibar
Lot 1283 of 1922
    Running numbers 3811–18
    Renumbered in 1953: 3411–18
Lot 1304 of 1922
    Running numbers 3819–26
    Renumbered in 1953: 3819–23 to 3419–23
Dimensions: 56′ 11¼″ x 8′ 11¼″
Condemned February 1966

Fig. 197

Fig. 197 No. 3826 was carrying GWR chocolate and cream livery when photographed at Reading in 1946, whereas No. 3821 (**Fig. 198**) displayed the GWR crimson lake livery of the period at Swindon in original condition in 1922.

Fig. 198

Fig. 199

DIAGRAM D69
BRAKE THIRD Corridor Carriage
4-Compartment 'Toplight' Stock, Multibar
Lot 1278 of 1921
Running numbers 3793–3804
Renumbered in 1953: 3393–3404
Dimensions: 69′ 11¼″ x 8′ 11¼″
Condemned February 1962

Fig. 199 is the official photograph of the series as built in 1922. No. 3794 is seen in the maroon livery of 1922. Clerestory stock of Lots 70 to 79 was refurbished in 1922 to build up stock lists.

Fig. 200

DIAGRAM D80
BRAKE THIRD Corridor Carriage
'Toplight' Stock, Bars I
Lot 1314 (originally *D44*)
Running numbers 3507–08
Lot 1338 (originally *D44*)
Running numbers 4225–32/41
Dimensions: 57′ 0″ x 9′ 0″
Condemned May 1962

These were ex-ambulance vehicles taken back into stock in 1922 and refurbished.

Fig. 200 illustrates No. 4228 at Old Oak Common in 1951 showing the corridor side of a left-hand van vehicle. **Fig. 201** shows No. 4227 at Tyseley in 1950, the compartment side of this right-hand van example being nearest the camera. Note that one vehicle displays single waistline and its companion has double lining but no cantrail lines.

Fig. 201

Fig. 202

DIAGRAM D82
BRAKE THIRD Corridor Carriage
'South Wales' Stock with one bow end and one flat end
Lot 1309 of 1923
Running numbers 3518–19
Lot 1321 of 1924
Running numbers 4613/5/7/9

Dimensions: 70′ x 9′ 0″
Condemned January 1959
Originally fitted with automatic couplings at the bowed ends.
This was the last series of 70′ stock to be built by the GWR.

Fig. 203

Fig. 202 No. 4613 at Old Oak Common in 1952 with the compartment side facing the camera. **Fig. 203** The van end and corridor side of No. 4613; the same side, but opposite end, of this vehicle is seen (**Fig. 204**) in Old Oak Common stock shed, also in 1952. The two pictures show, respectively, the flat end and the bowed end of this series.

Fig. 204

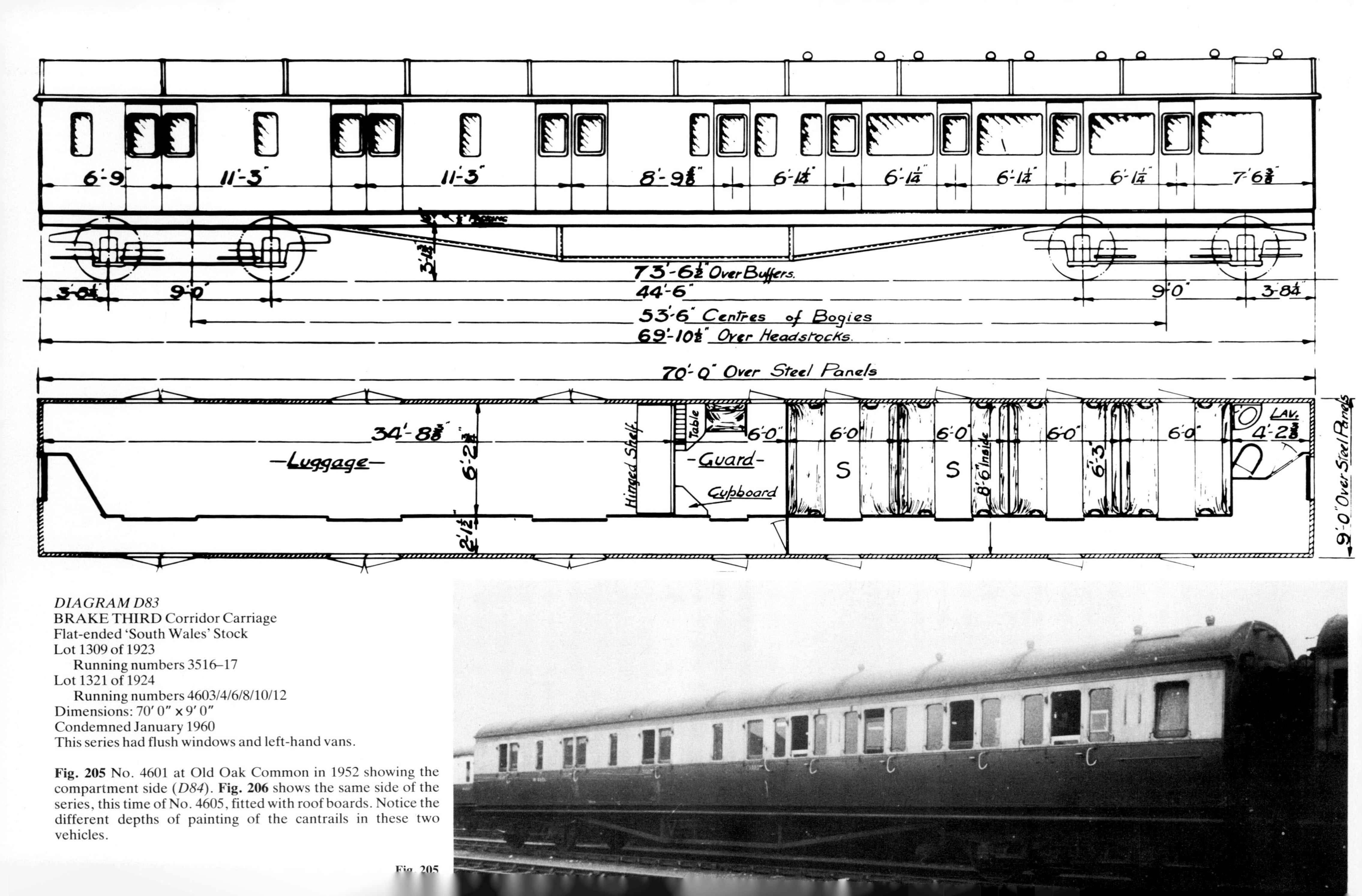

DIAGRAM D83
BRAKE THIRD Corridor Carriage
Flat-ended 'South Wales' Stock
Lot 1309 of 1923
Running numbers 3516–17
Lot 1321 of 1924
Running numbers 4603/4/6/8/10/12
Dimensions: 70′ 0″ x 9′ 0″
Condemned January 1960
This series had flush windows and left-hand vans.

Fig. 205 No. 4601 at Old Oak Common in 1952 showing the compartment side (*D84*). **Fig. 206** shows the same side of the series, this time of No. 4605, fitted with roof boards. Notice the different depths of painting of the cantrails in these two vehicles.

Fig. 205

Fig. 206

Fig. 207

DIAGRAM D84
BRAKE THIRD Corridor Carriage
'South Wales' Stock
Lot 1321 of 1923
    Running numbers 4601/2/5/7/9/11
Dimensions as for *D83*
Condemned May 1962
Identical to *D83* but with right-hand vans.

Fig. 207 shows No. 4601 as built in 1923 and with corridor side nearest camera. Note the pseudo panel painting.

DIAGRAM D85
BRAKE THIRD Non-Corridor Carriage
Steel-panelled Stock
Lot 1318 of 1924
    Running numbers 4399–4408
Lot 1329 of 1924
    Running numbers 4434–43
Dimensions: 57′ 0″ x 9′ 0″
Condemned August 1960

Fig. 208 shows No. 4408 as built in 1924 and, as with *D84* above, painted with the panels, which are in fact only plain steel sheeting!

Fig. 208

Fig. 209

DIAGRAM D86
BRAKE THIRD Non-Corridor Carriage
6-Compartment Bow-ended Suburban Stock
Lot 1335 of 1925
Running numbers 4652–77
Dimensions: 58′ 2″ x 9′ 0″
Condemned July 1960

Fig. 209 shows No. 4661 at Windsor in 1951 painted in BR maroon livery.

Fig. 210

DIAGRAM D87
BRAKE THIRD Corridor Carriage
Ex-Ambulance Stock, Bars I
Lot 1326 of 1924
Running numbers 4621/9/32/3/41–47, originally *C31*
Lot 1332 of 1924
Running numbers 4630/34–38, originally *C32*
Running numbers 4631/9/40, originally *C28*
Dimensions: 57′ 0″ x 9′ 0″
Condemned November 1961

This series identical to *D88* below, but had right-hand vans. Certain running numbers have been placed in both series where it is not known whether they were left- or right-hand vehicles.

Fig. 210 illustrates No. 4631 at Minehead in 1949 with corridor side and van end nearest camera. **Fig. 211** shows the opposite side of the same vehicle.

Fig. 211

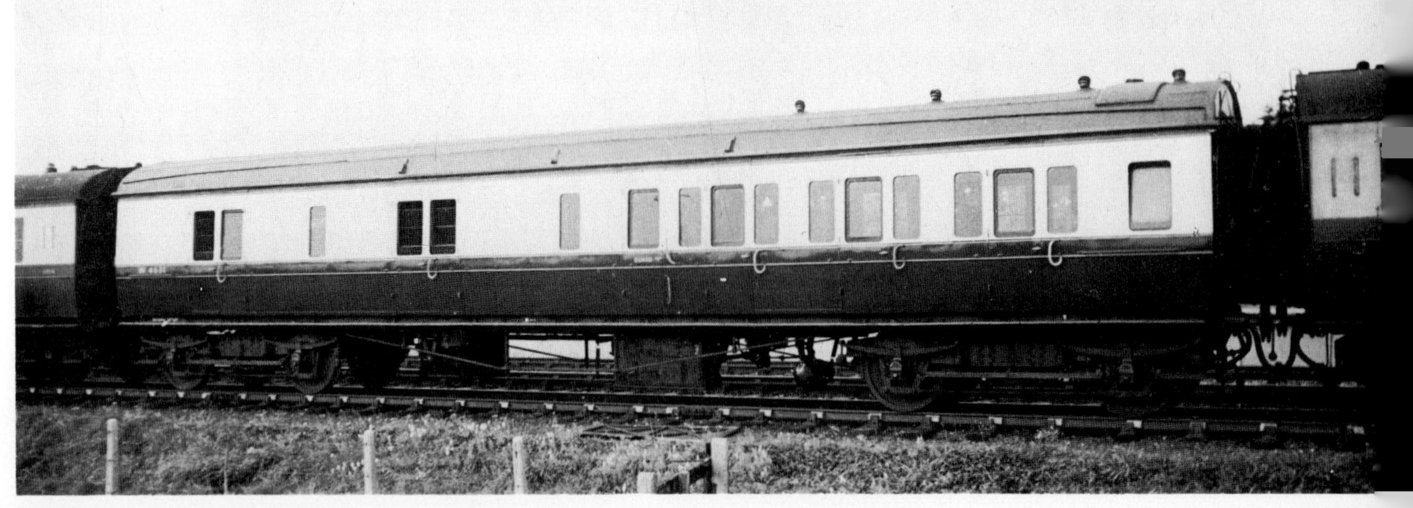

DIAGRAM D88
BRAKE THIRD Corridor Carriage
Ex-Ambulance Stock
Lot 1326
    Running numbers 4622/4/6/8/30/2/4/6/8/40
Lot 1332
    Running numbers 4642/4/6
Dimensions: as *D87*
Condemned January 1961
These vehicles handed back to GWR and refitted in 1924. Series identical to *D87* but constructed with right-hand vans.

Fig. 212 depicts the corridor side of No. 4638 in 1947.

Fig. 212

Fig. 213

DIAGRAM D90
BRAKE THIRD Corridor Carriage
'South Wales' Stock with one bow end and one flat end
Lot 1321
    Running numbers 4614/6/8/20
Dimensions: 70′ 8¼″ x 9′ 0″
Condemned May 1958

This series was almost identical to *D83*, but had bow ends at the compartment end and flat ends to the van section. They were originally fitted with buckeye couplers at the compartment ends.

Fig. 213 No. 4618 at Old Oak Common in 1955 showing the corridor side with left-hand van. **Fig. 214** shows the compartment side of No. 4620 inside the stock shed at Old Oak in 1954.

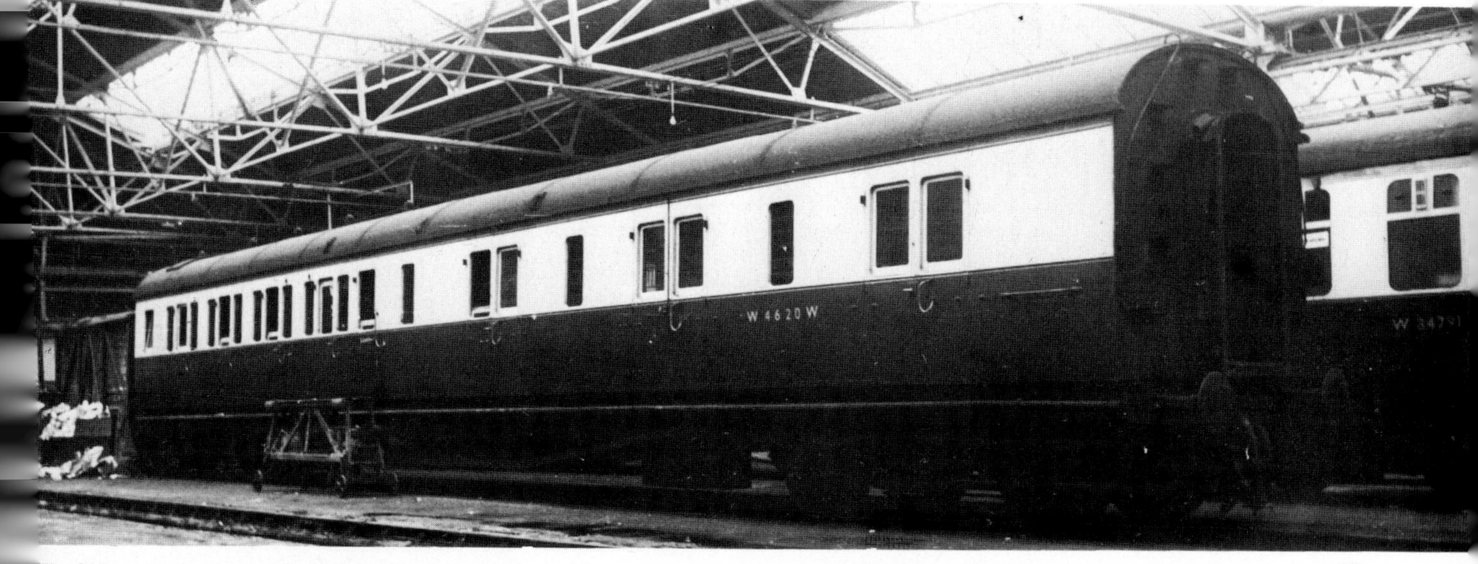

Fig. 214

Fig. 215

DIAGRAM D91
BRAKE THIRD Non-Corridor Carriage
6-Compartment Suburban Stock
Lot 1335 of 1925 (second half)
Running numbers 4658–4705
Dimensions: 58′ 2″ x 9′ 0″
Condemned November 1962
This series only differed from *D86* in having a straight back and seat in the end compartment, whereas in the *D86* pattern these were curved to fit the bow ends of the vehicles.

Fig. 216

Fig. 217

Fig. 215 is the official photograph of No. 4704 as built in 1925 with painted-on panels and white roof. **Fig. 216** is a detail picture of the '1914' type bogie usually fitted to these vehicles. **Fig. 217** depicts one of the series, No. 4694, showing the van end at Windsor in 1951.

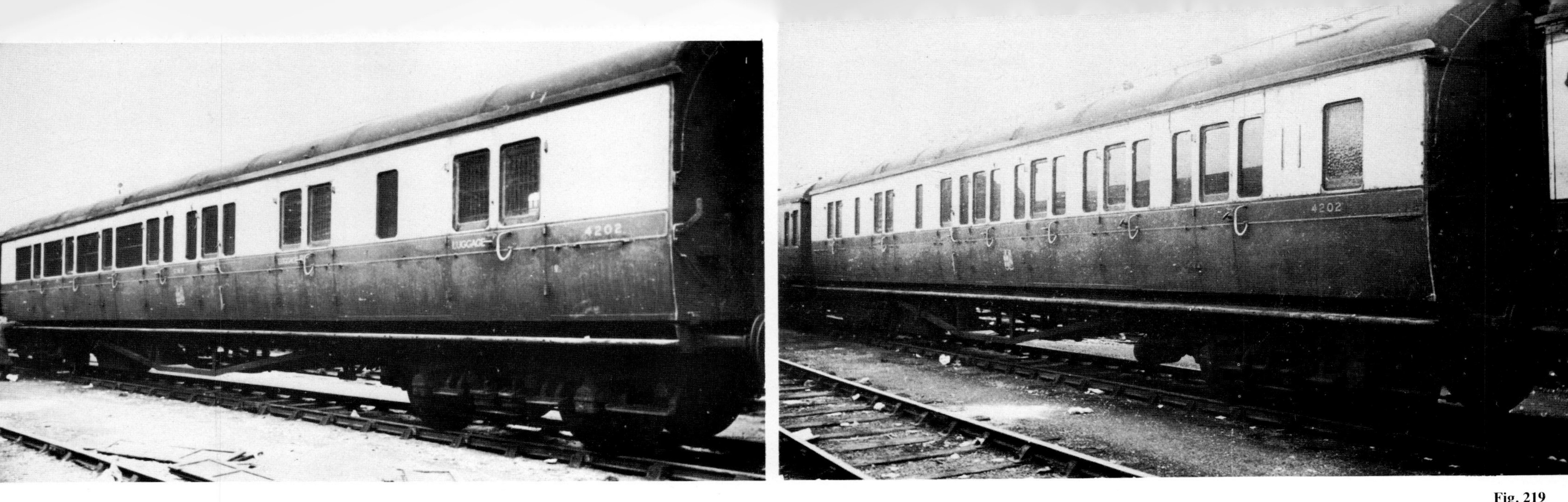

Fig. 219

Fig. 220

DIAGRAM D92
BRAKE THIRD Corridor Carriage
Ex-Articulated Stock of 1925
Lot 1360, sets rebuilt in 1936–7 as separate vehicles.
Renumbered 4202–07
Dimensions: 58′ 0¾″ x 9′ 0″
Condemned December 1962
Altered to the above dimensions by the addition of one extra 3rd class compartment. Diagram re-allotted *D112*.

Fig. 218 shows No. 4202 at Old Oak Common in 1951, corridor side and van end nearest camera. **Fig. 219** illustrates the opposite side of the same vehicle, and **Fig. 220**, taken at Tiverton Junction in 1951, depicts the van end and compartment side, also of No. 4202.

Fig. 221

DIAGRAM D93
BRAKE THIRD Non-Corridor Carriage
Articulated Main Line & City Suburban Stock
Lot 1342 of 1925
Running numbers 9801/6/7/12/3/8
Dimensions: 48′ 0″ x 8′ 6″
Condemned July 1960

Fig. 221 shows No. 9812 at Banbury in 1953 in BR maroon livery.

Fig. 222

DIAGRAM D94
BRAKE THIRD Corridor Carriage
3-Compartment Bow-ended Stock
Lot 1354 of 1925
Running numbers 4763–9, with right- and left-hand vans
Lot 1353 of 1925
Running numbers 4751–62, with right- and left-hand vans
Dimensions: 58′ 4½″ x 9′ 0″
Condemned April 1962
Provided with flush windows.

Fig. 222 Corridor side of No. 4753 at Exeter in 1946, seen here in the 1945 GWR livery.

DIAGRAM D95
BRAKE THIRD Corridor Carriage
4-Compartment Bow-ended Stock
Lot 1375 of 1927
Running numbers 4913–44, with right- and left-hand vans
Lot 1384 of 1928
Running numbers 5087–5132, with right- and left-hand vans
Dimensions: 58′ 4½″ x 9′ 0″
Condemned 1963
Provided with flush windows.

Fig. 223 shows No. 4932 as built at Swindon in 1927 with painted panels, and depicting the corridor side of this left-hand van pattern carriage.

Fig. 223

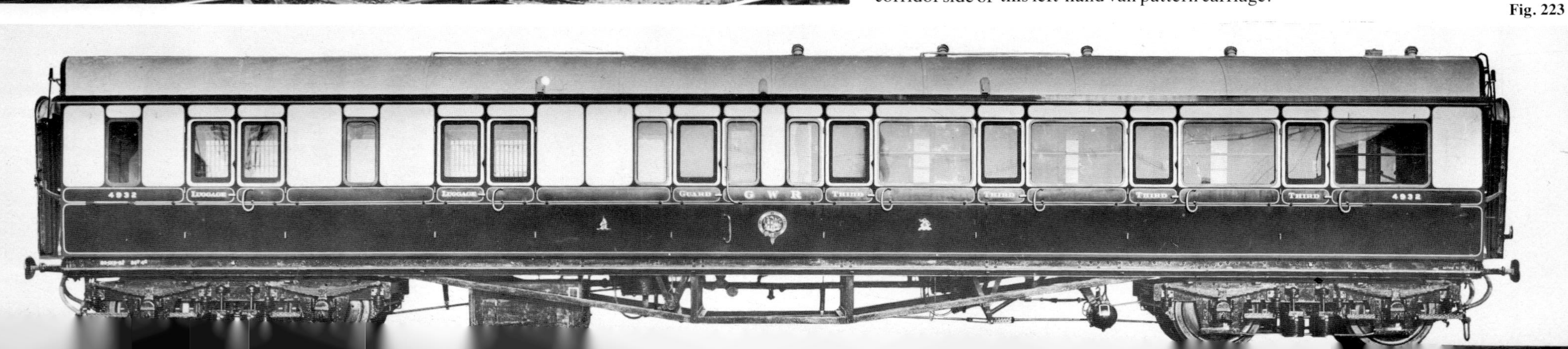

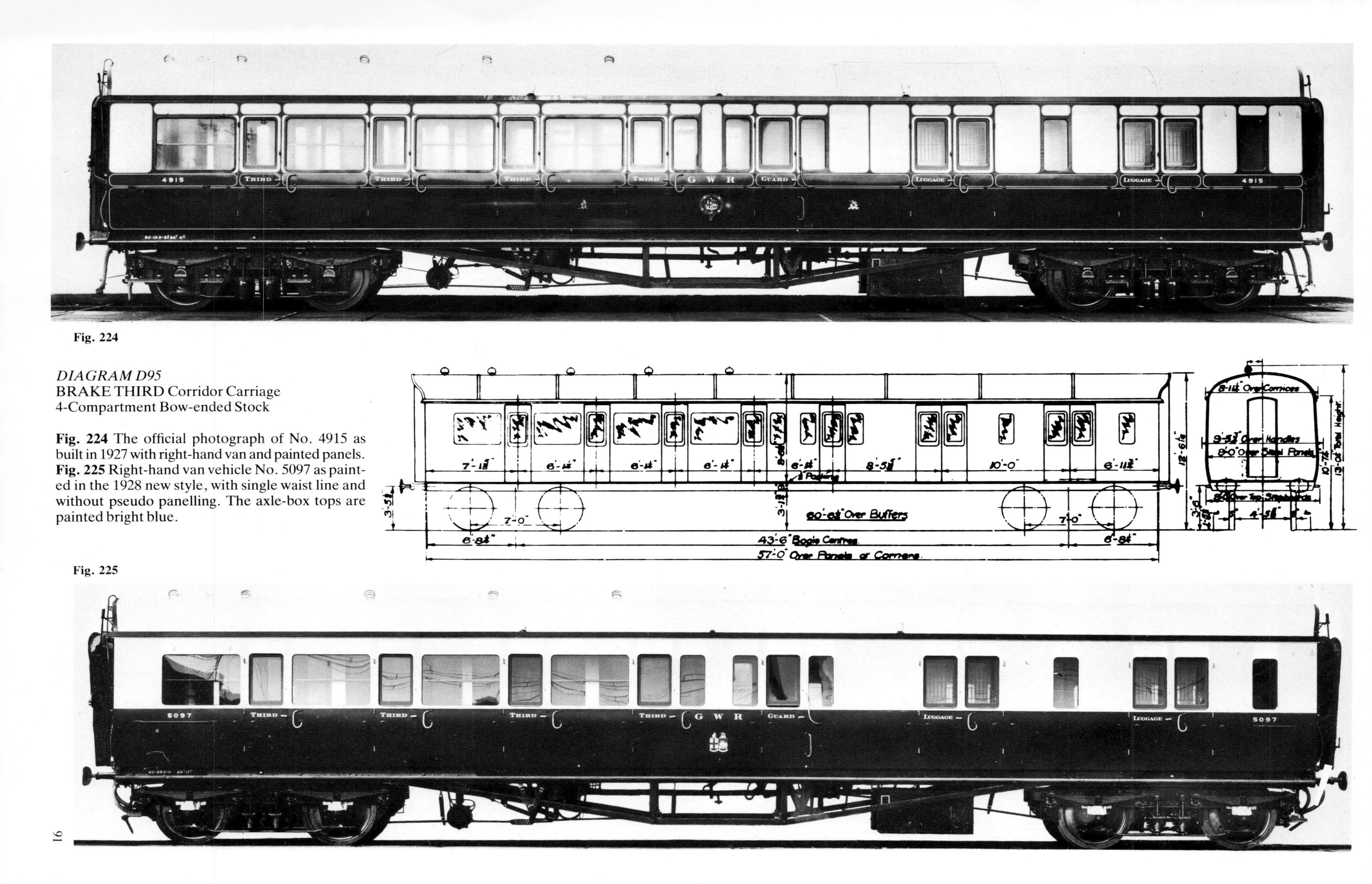

Fig. 224

DIAGRAM D95
BRAKE THIRD Corridor Carriage
4-Compartment Bow-ended Stock

Fig. 224 The official photograph of No. 4915 as built in 1927 with right-hand van and painted panels. **Fig. 225** Right-hand van vehicle No. 5097 as painted in the 1928 new style, with single waist line and without pseudo panelling. The axle-box tops are painted bright blue.

Fig. 225

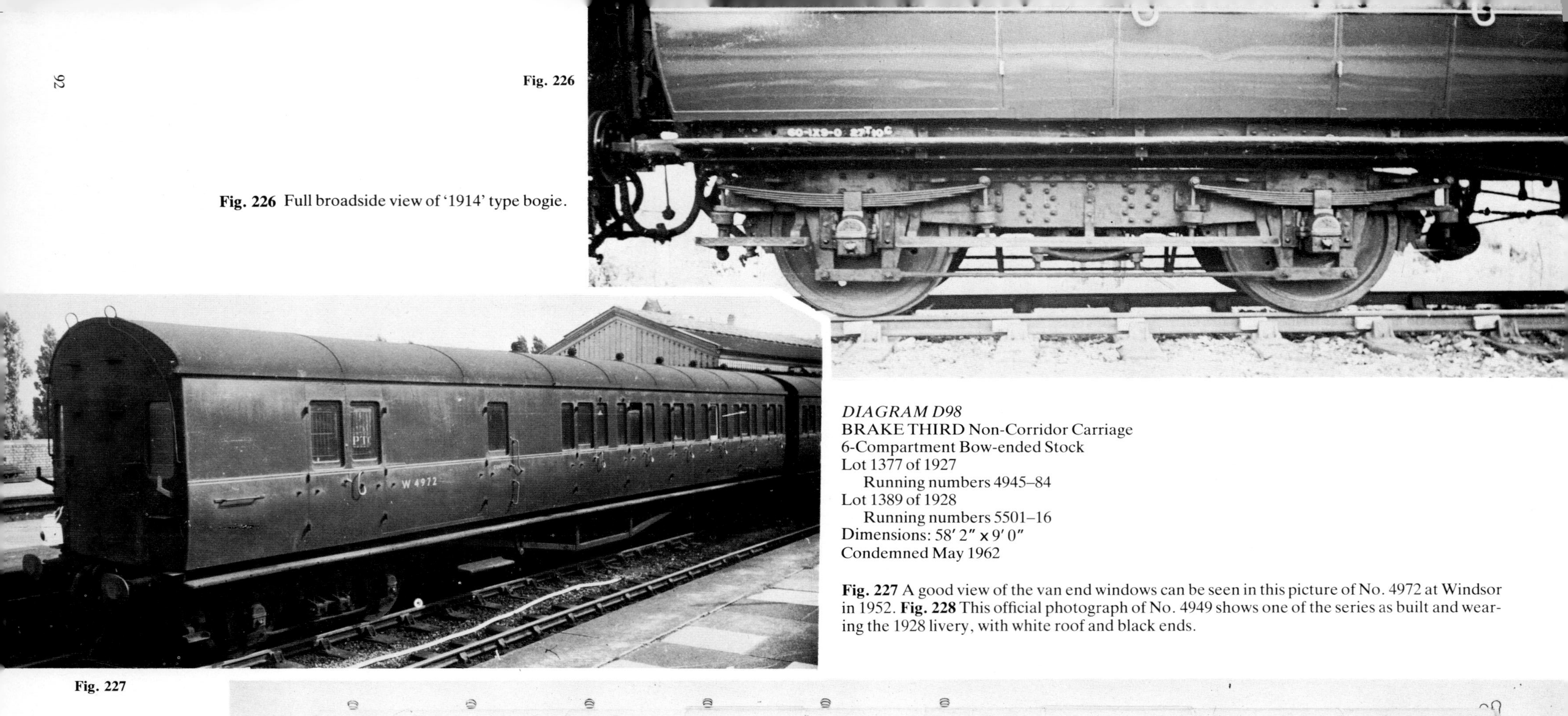

Fig. 226

Fig. 226 Full broadside view of '1914' type bogie.

DIAGRAM D98
BRAKE THIRD Non-Corridor Carriage
6-Compartment Bow-ended Stock
Lot 1377 of 1927
  Running numbers 4945–84
Lot 1389 of 1928
  Running numbers 5501–16
Dimensions: 58′ 2″ x 9′ 0″
Condemned May 1962

Fig. 227 A good view of the van end windows can be seen in this picture of No. 4972 at Windsor in 1952. **Fig. 228** This official photograph of No. 4949 shows one of the series as built and wearing the 1928 livery, with white roof and black ends.

Fig. 227

Fig. 228

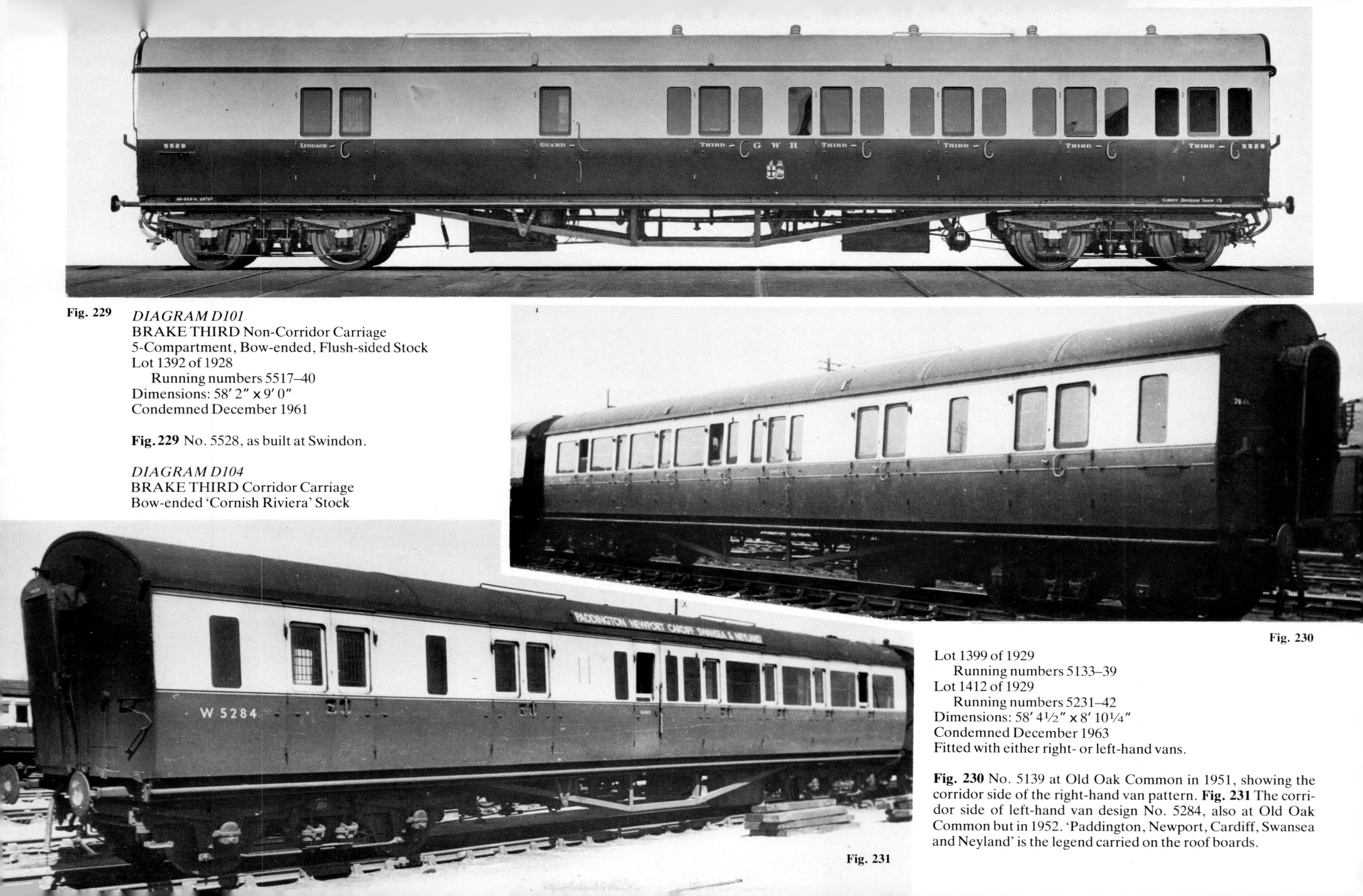

Fig. 229

DIAGRAM D101
BRAKE THIRD Non-Corridor Carriage
5-Compartment, Bow-ended, Flush-sided Stock
Lot 1392 of 1928
Running numbers 5517–40
Dimensions: 58′ 2″ x 9′ 0″
Condemned December 1961

Fig. 229 No. 5528, as built at Swindon.

DIAGRAM D104
BRAKE THIRD Corridor Carriage
Bow-ended 'Cornish Riviera' Stock

Fig. 230

Lot 1399 of 1929
Running numbers 5133–39
Lot 1412 of 1929
Running numbers 5231–42
Dimensions: 58′ 4½″ x 8′ 10¼″
Condemned December 1963
Fitted with either right- or left-hand vans.

Fig. 231

Fig. 230 No. 5139 at Old Oak Common in 1951, showing the corridor side of the right-hand van pattern. **Fig. 231** The corridor side of left-hand van design No. 5284, also at Old Oak Common but in 1952. 'Paddington, Newport, Cardiff, Swansea and Neyland' is the legend carried on the roof boards.

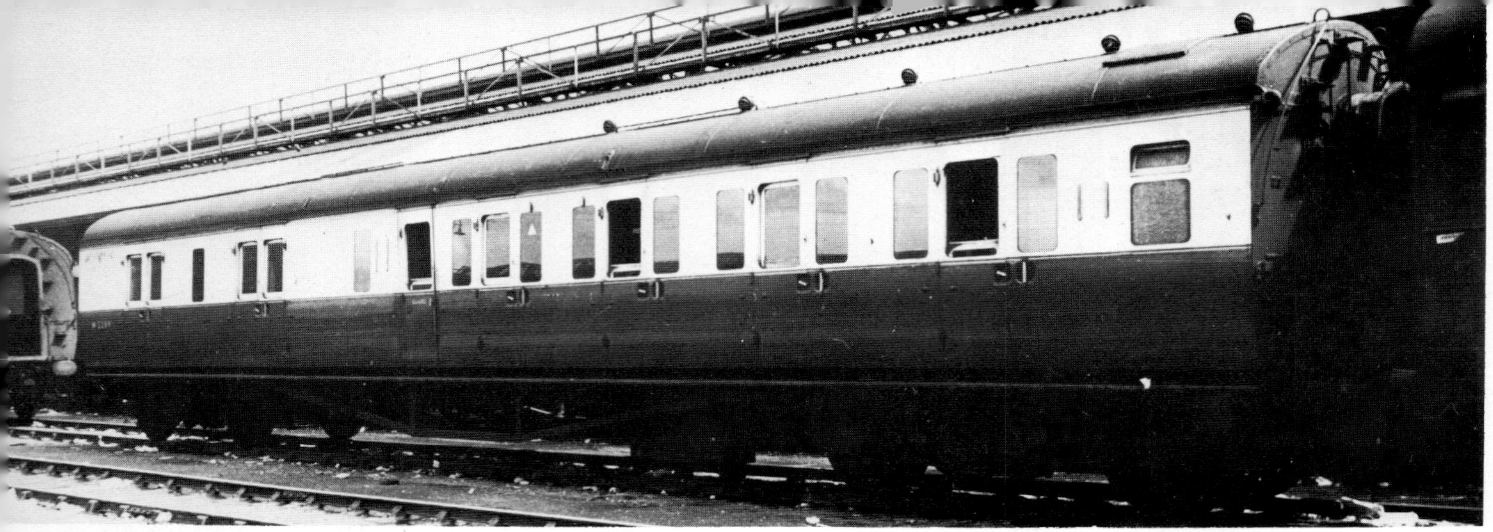

Fig. 232

DIAGRAM D105
BRAKE THIRD Corridor Carriage
4-Compartment, Bow-ended, 'Cornish Riviera' Stock
Lot 1427 of 1929
Running numbers 5281–92
Dimensions: 61′ 4½″ x 9′ 5¾″
Condemned December 1961
This series had a flat door to the guard's compartment.

Fig. 232 shows No. 5289 outside Old Oak Common stock shed in 1952, with the compartment side nearest the camera.

DIAGRAM D106
BRAKE THIRD Corridor Carriage
2-Compartment, Bow-ended 'Cornish Riviera' Stock
Lot 1428 of 1929
Running numbers 5293–98
Dimensions: 61′ 4½″ x 9′ 5¾″
Condemned January 1962

Fig. 233 No. 5296 was photographed in 1956 at Old Oak Common with the compartment side nearest the camera. The single flat door to the guard's compartment can be seen in this picture. **Fig. 234**, taken at Truro in 1950, shows the corridor side of No. 5296 when the vehicle was painted in the double waist lining style.

Fig. 233

Fig. 234

Fig. 235

DIAGRAM D106

Fig. 235 is the official photograph of No. 5293 as built at the factory in 1929. It is seen here carrying 'Cornish Riviera' roof boards, painted daffodil cream with milk chocolate lettering.

Fig. 236

DIAGRAM D107
BRAKE THIRD Corridor Carriage
Cross-Country Service Bow-ended Stock
Lot 1437 of 1930
Running numbers 5303–14
Dimensions: 61′ 4½″ x 9′ 0″
Condemned June 1962
Fitted with 7′ plate bogies.

Fig. 236 No. 5306 at Swindon in 1952 with the compartment side towards the camera. **Fig. 237** shows the corridor side of No. 5306, also at Swindon in 1952. The van end of the vehicle is illustrated.

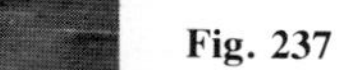

Fig. 237

Fig. 238

Fig. 238 An official photograph of the series taken in 1946. No. 5619 is seen in the final GWR livery with the deep cantrail painted brown and with lead-grey roof.

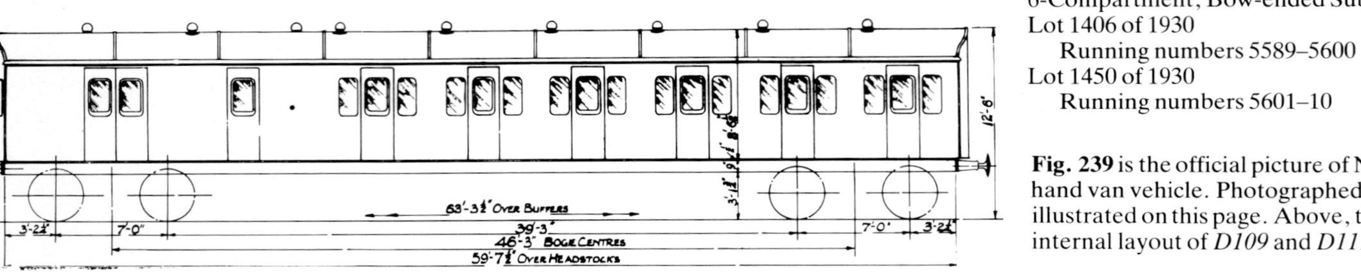

DIAGRAM D109
BRAKE THIRD Non-Corridor Carriage
6-Compartment, Bow-ended Suburban Stock
Lot 1406 of 1930
Running numbers 5589–5600
Lot 1450 of 1930
Running numbers 5601–10
Lot 1457 of 1931
Running numbers 5611–30
Dimensions: 61′ 2″ x 9′ 3″
Condemned December 1962
End windows in van

Fig. 239 is the official picture of No. 5368 as built in 1930, and showing the corridor side of this left-hand van vehicle. Photographed at Swindon. It is of interest to compare the two styles of painting illustrated on this page. Above, the 1946 style and, below, the 1930 pattern. The drawings show the internal layout of *D109* and *D111*.

Fig. 239

DIAGRAM D111
BRAKE THIRD
Corridor Carriage
Details on following page

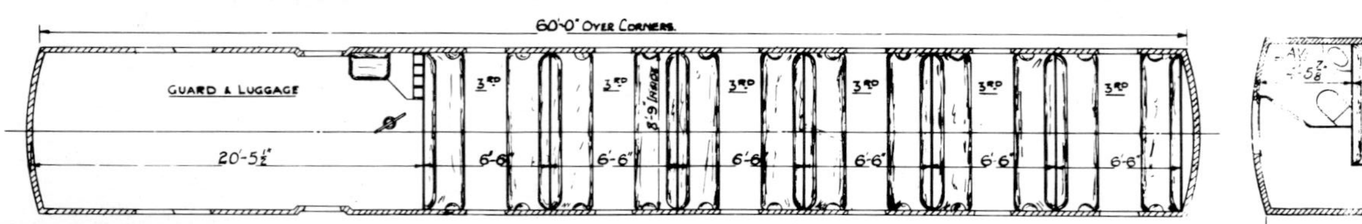

Fig. 240

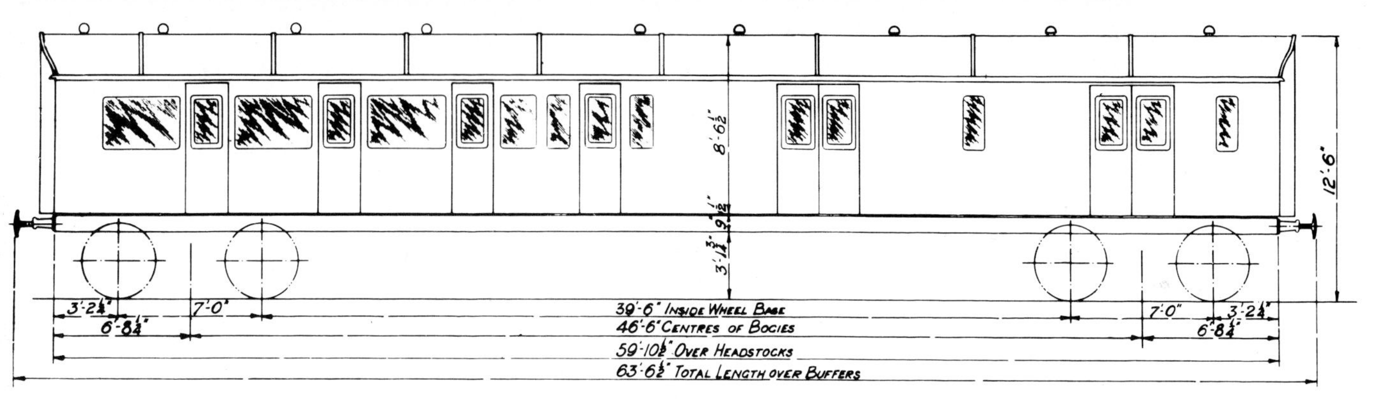

DIAGRAM D111
BRAKE THIRD Corridor Carriage
3-Compartment, Bow-ended General Service Stock
Lot 1448 of 1930
    Running numbers 5361–68
Lot 1454 of 1931
    Running numbers 5373–80
Dimensions: 61′ 4½″ x 9′ 3″
Condemned December 1962

Fig. 240 illustrates No. 5367 and shows the corridor side of this right-hand van vehicle at Old Oak Common in 1951, painted in the first BR colours. **Fig. 241** shows the compartment side of No. 5362, a left-hand van design, also at Old Oak Common during 1951. These carriages had ventilators in the van roof as well as over the compartments. 7′ plate bogies are fitted to both examples illustrated on this page.

Fig. 241

Fig. 242

DIAGRAM D115
BRAKE THIRD Corridor Carriage
4-Compartment Bow-ended General Service Stock
Lot 1476 of 1932
Running numbers 5385–92
Lot 1478 of 1932
Running numbers 5447–60
Dimensions: 61′ 4½″ x 9′ 3″
Condemned December 1962
There was an extra window on the compartment side of the van end of this series.

Fig. 242 shows the compartment side of No. 5387, pictured at Goodrington in 1952. This was a right-hand van vehicle. **Fig. 243** No. 5448, photographed at Old Oak Common in 1951, provides an example of the left-hand van pattern. The roof boards read 'Paddington, Gloucester and Cheltenham Spa'.

DIAGRAM D116 (on next page)
BRAKE THIRD Corridor Carriage
4-Compartment, Flat-ended General Service Stock
Lot 1490 of 1933
Running numbers 5779–97
Dimensions: 57′ 0″ x 9′ 0″
Condemned February 1964
Fitted with 9′ plate bogies.

Fig. 244 An official photograph of No. 5794, as built in 1933, showing the compartment side. **Fig. 245** shows the corridor side of No. 5780. A feature of note in both pictures is that the GWR coat of arms is not centrally positioned. **Fig. 246** illustrates No. 5788 in early BR condition at Old Oak Common in 1952, with a view of the compartment side. The opposite side of the same carriage is displayed in **Fig. 247**. ▷

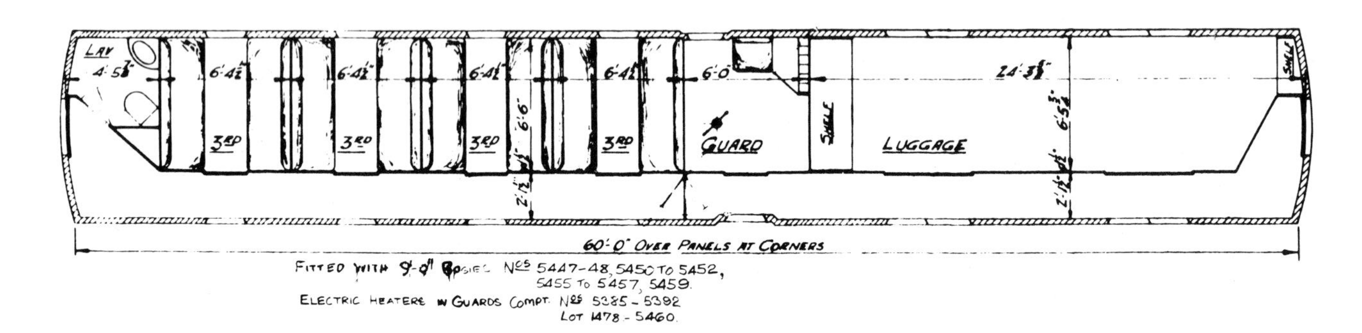

Fig. 243

Fig. 245

Fig. 246

Fig. 247

Fig. 248

Fig. 249

Fig. 250

Fig. 251

◁ **Fig. 248** Official photograph of No. 4006 as built in 1936, carrying the 'roundel' livery of that period.

DIAGRAM D117
BRAKE THIRD Non-Corridor Carriage
5-Compartment Flat-ended Suburban Stock
Lot 1493 of 1934
Running numbers 5491–5500
Lot 1507 of 1934
Painted numbers 5868–77
Lot 1525 of 1935
Painted numbers 4342–67, except Nos. 4350 and 4364
Lot 1552 of 1936
Painted numbers 4001–20
Dimensions: 57′ 0″ x 9′ 0″
Condemned December 1963

◁ **Fig. 249** The Swindon picture of No. 5886, with the compartment side facing the camera. **Fig. 250** shows the corridor side of No. 5878, as built in 1934.

DIAGRAM D118
BRAKE THIRD Corridor Carriage
4-Compartment General Service Stock
Lot 1510 of 1934
Running numbers 5798–5807
Lot 1514 of 1934
Running numbers 5878–87
Lot 1528 of 1935
Running numbers 5983–95
Dimensions: 57′ 0″ x 9′ 0″
Condemned December 1963

DIAGRAM D118
Fig. 251 shows the compartment side of No. 5878 at Old Oak Common in 1953, displaying the BR strawberry and cream livery.
Fig. 252 A photograph taken at the same location in 1952 illustrates the corridor side of No. 5803.

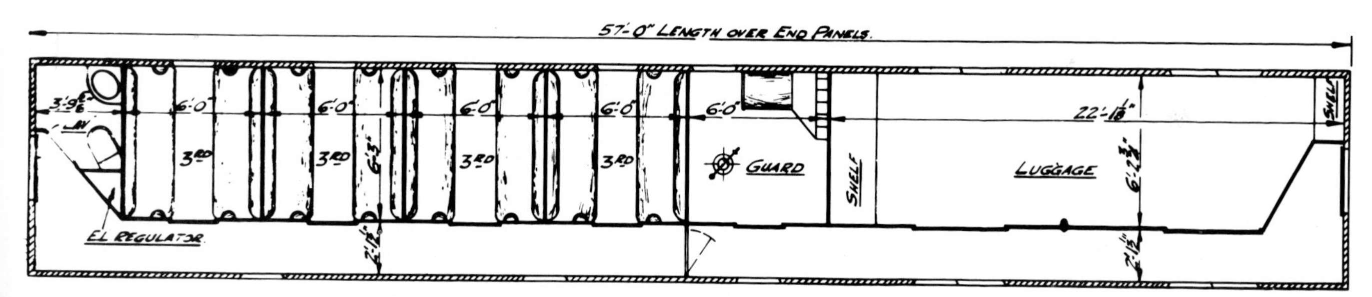

Fig. 252

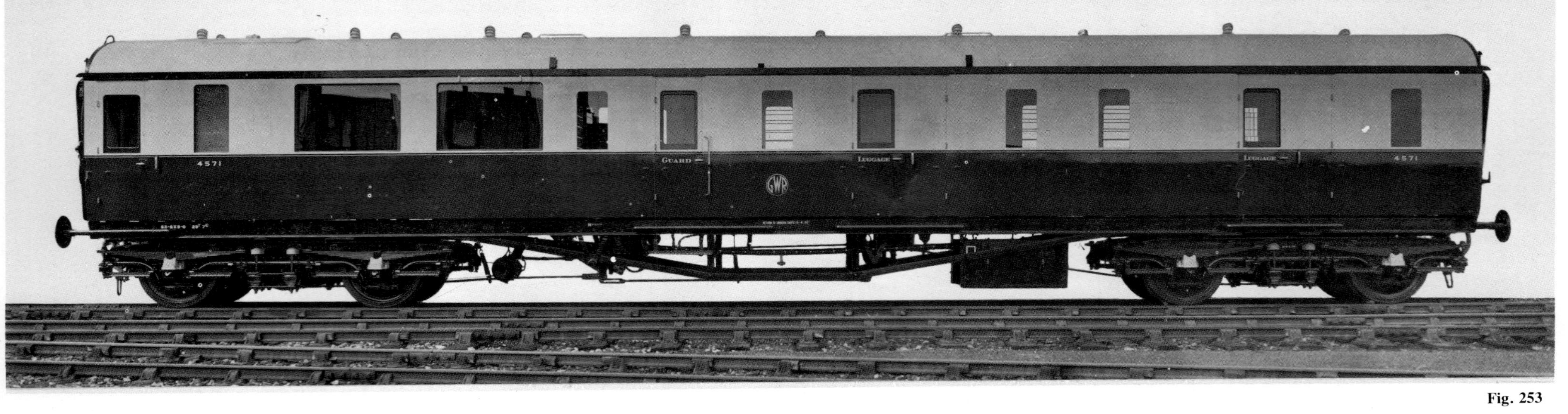

Fig. 253

60'-0" Over End Panels
Lav
Lav
2'-6½"
5'-4¼"
6'-1"
6'-1"
8'-6"
E.L. Regulator
Guard
6'-0"
Shelf
8'-5½"
Luggage
33'-0½"
Shelf

DIAGRAM D119
BRAKE THIRD Centre Corridor Carriage
16-Seat Saloon Excursion Stock
Lot 1531 of 1935
Running numbers 4571–74
Dimensions: 60' 0" x 9' 0"
Condemned December 1964

Fig. 253 shows No. 4571 at Swindon, as built in 1935.

Fig. 254

DIAGRAM D120
BRAKE THIRD Corridor Carriage
'Centenary' Stock
Lot 1536 of 1935
Painted numbers 4575–80
Dimensions: 61' 4½" x 9' 7"
Condemned September 1963
4 vehicles constructed with right-hand vans and 2 with left-hand vans.

Fig. 254 shows No. 4577 at Newton Abbot in 1952, with the compartment side nearest the camera. For details of other 'Centenary' stock, see *A Pictorial Record of Great Western Coaches, Part Two,* published by Oxford Publishing Co.

Fig. 255

DIAGRAM D121
BRAKE THIRD Corridor Carriage
4-Compartment, Low-waisted Large-window Stock
Lot 1555 of 1936
Running numbers 4066–69/73–4102/04–25
Dimensions: 60′ 11¼″ x 9′ 0″
Condemned December 1963

Fig. 256

Fig. 255 is the official photograph of the series as built in 1936, and shows the corridor side of No. 4073. Notice the gold-lettered transfer running number on the cream panels. **Fig. 256** shows the corridor side of No. 4084 at Kingsbridge in 1950, wearing the first BR livery with double waist lines. **Fig. 257** illustrates the compartment side of No. 4120 at Paddington in 1950. The roof boards read 'Paddington, Birmingham and Wolverhampton'.

Fig. 257

Fig. 258

DIAGRAM D122
BRAKE THIRD Corridor Carriage
Ex-articulated Stock
Lot 1360 of 1936
Running numbers 4202–07
Dimensions of rebuild: 58′ 0¾″ x 9′ 0″
Condemned December 1962
Originally *Diagram D92* of 1925.

Fig. 258 shows the corridor side of No. 4206 after being rebuilt at Swindon in 1936.

DIAGRAM D123
BRAKE THIRD Centre Corridor Carriage
32-seat Excursion Stock
Lot 1576 of 1937
Running numbers 1298–1301
Dimensions: 60′ 0″ x 9′ 0″
Condemned January 1966

Fig. 259 illustrates the saloon end of No. 1300 at Kingswear in 1952.

DIAGRAM D124
BRAKE THIRD Corridor Carriage
4-Compartment General Purpose Stock
Lot 1574 of 1937
Running numbers 1583–1603/5–26
Dimensions: 60′ 11¼″ × 9′ 0″

Fig. 260 The official record photograph taken at Swindon in 1937 of No. 1593 as built, with the corridor side nearest the camera.

Fig. 261

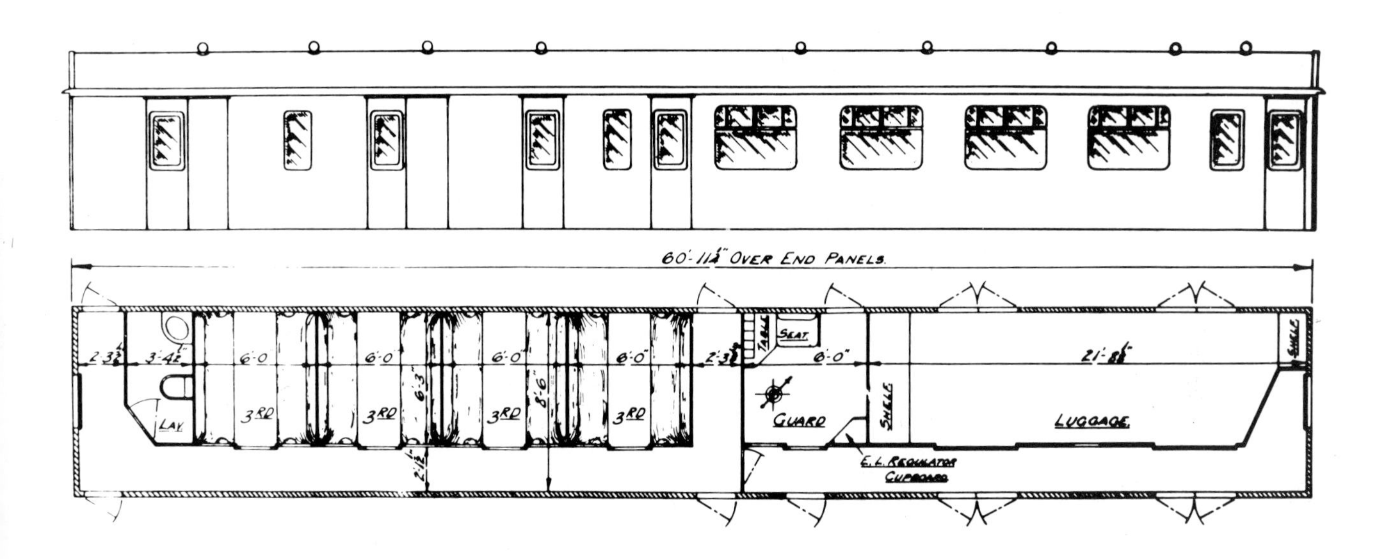

Fig. 262

DIAGRAM D124

Fig. 261 shows No. 1602 in Old Oak Common carriage sidings in 1952, with the compartment side in view. **Fig. 262** depicts No. 1594 at Old Oak Common in 1951, with the corridor side and deep windows in prominence. Note how these windows extend from cantrail to waist and, unlike the *D121* series, the small windows and droplights are now much deeper.

Fig. 263

Fig. 264

DIAGRAM D127
BRAKE THIRD Corridor Carriage
Large-window 'Sunshine' Stock
Lot 1594 of 1938
Running numbers 1627–47/9-54
Lot 1595 of 1938
Running numbers 1655–7, specially fitted for coupling to Pullman gangways
Lot 1624 of 1939
Running numbers 601–25
Lot 1642 of 1941
Running numbers 652–75
Dimensions: 60′ 11¼″ x 8′ 11″
This series was slightly reduced in size to travel over the LMS and LNER restricted routes and carried a yellow disc on the end of each vehicle.

Fig. 263 A Swindon picture of No. 1630, as built in 1938, showing the corridor side. The compartment side of No. 618 is seen in **Fig. 264** and was photographed at Old Oak Common in 1951. **Fig. 265** The van end and corridor side of No. 1628, also at Old Oak in 1951.

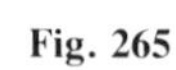
Fig. 265

Fig. 266

Fig. 266 is the official photograph of No. 651 and was taken at Swindon in 1940. This carriage was one of only two vehicles made to this design.

Fig. 267

DIAGRAM D130
BRAKE THIRD Centre Corridor Carriage
40-seat Open Saloon Stock
Lot 1644 of 1940
Running numbers 650–1
Dimensions: 60′ 11$\frac{1}{4}$″ x 8′ 11″
Condemned February 1965

DIAGRAM D132
BRAKE THIRD Non-Corridor Carriage
60-seat Stock
Lot 1694 of 1948
Running numbers 414–38
Lot 1713 of 1950
Running numbers 2087–2106
Lot 1746 of 1952
Running numbers 2721–65/76–90
Lot 1764 of 1953
Running numbers 4126–31/3/4/6/7/9/40–2/52
Dimensions: 63′ 0$\frac{3}{4}$″ x 8′ 11″
Condemned December 1963

Fig. 267 The Swindon photograph of No. 416 of 1948 in the first BR livery. **Fig. 268** Another official view of the same series; this vehicle is No. 2090, and is depicted as turned out of the factory in 1949 and painted in BR maroon with yellow lining.

Fig. 268

Fig. 269

DIAGRAM D132
BRAKE THIRD Non-Corridor Stock
Built by Gloucester Carriage & Wagon Co. to the Western *D132* design.

Fig. 269 No. 2721, part of Lot 1746, seen from the van end at Swindon in 1952. The official broadside view of the same vehicle (**Fig. 270**) clearly shows the plain BR maroon livery with black underframe ends and grey roof.

Fig. 270

Fig. 271

Fig. 272

Fig. 273

DIAGRAM D133
BRAKE THIRD Corridor Carriage
'Hawksworth' Stock
Lot 1707 of 1949
Running numbers 1772–86
Lot 1732 of 1950
Running numbers 2137–85/87–2223/5–8
Lot 1744 of 1951
Running numbers 2240–59
Dimensions: 64′ 0″ x 8′ 11″

Fig. 271 No. 2251 is seen at Swindon factory in 1950, painted in the BR strawberry and cream livery. The compartment side is nearest the camera. **Fig. 272** shows No. 2184 at Old Oak Common in 1951, also with the compartment side towards the viewer. The roof boards, painted with yellow letters on a maroon background, read 'Paddington and Bristol'. **Fig. 273** illustrates No. 2188 at Paddington in 1952, and this shows the corridor side, including a single window with ventilators.

Fig. 274

DIAGRAM BR 182
BRAKE THIRD Corridor Carriage
BR Standard Gangwayed Stock
Lot 30200 of 1955
Built by Gloucester Carriage & Wagon Co.

Fig. 274 is the official Swindon photograph of No. W34810, with the corridor side facing the camera.

DIAGRAM BR 183
BRAKE THIRD Open Carriage
BR Standard Gangwayed Stock
BR Lot 30170 of 1956
Built at Doncaster

Fig. 275 shows No. W9257 at Swindon in 1956.

Fig. 275

DIAGRAM BR 182

Fig. 276 The final picture of the brake thirds (or seconds) to be recorded in this work. This official photograph is a three-quarter view of No. W34810, previously seen in broadside on page 110. Details of the bogies, coupling and buffing gear are particularly clear in this photograph.

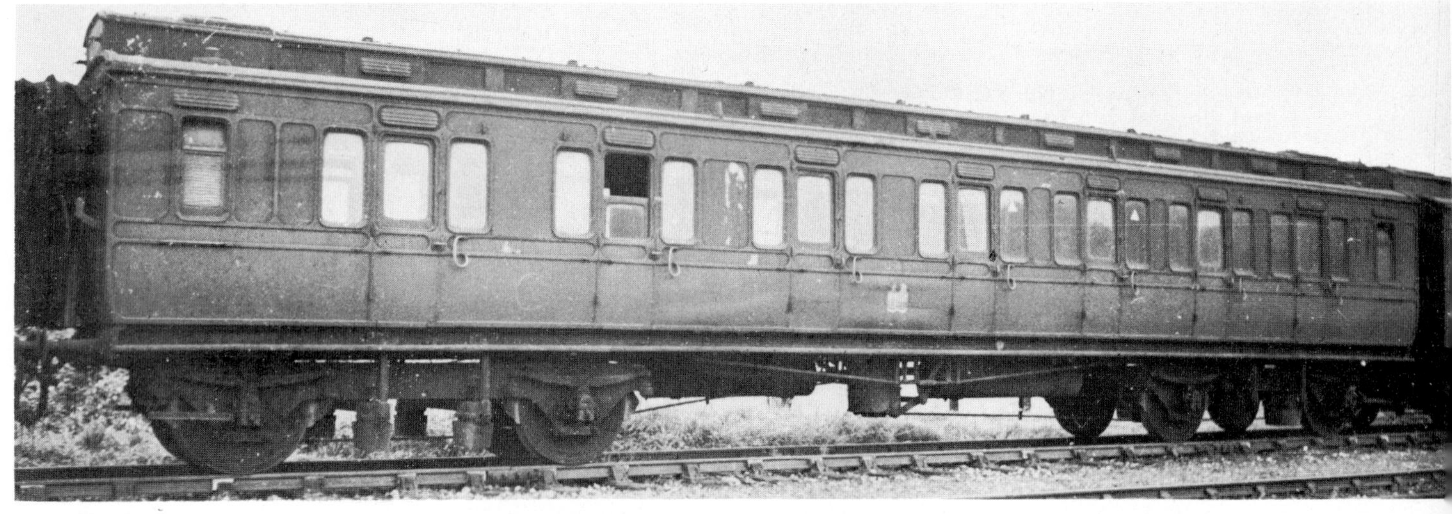

Fig. 277

Fig. 279

DIAGRAMS E65 and E66
COMPOSITE Corridor Carriage
Clerestory Roof Stock
Lot 910 of 1899
Running numbers 7421–35
Lot 918 of 1899
Running numbers 7436–45
Dimensions: 55′ 0¾″ x 8′ 6¾″
All condemned by July 1948
Passenger accommodation comprised three 1sts, four 3rds, 2 lavatories. This series was provided with Dean 10′ bogies and oval buffers. These were originally 1st/2nd composites.

Fig. 277 No. 7431, of *Diagram E66*, was photographed at Minehead in 1948 with the compartment side facing the camera. **Fig. 278** also shows the same vehicle at the previous location, but illustrates the corridor side of the coach. Painting was executed in the wartime all-over brown with grey roof. **Fig. 279** gives a good close-up view of the Dean pattern of brake cylinder, the 'V' hangers and coach truss rods.

Fig. 278

Fig. 280

DIAGRAM E70
COMPOSITE Corridor Carriage
Clerestory Roof Stock
Lot 982 of 1902
Running numbers 7456–8/61 to *E70*
Running number 7459 to *E66*
Lot 986 of 1902
Running numbers 7462/3/7/8/71 to *E70*
Running numbers 7464–6/9/10 to *E66*
Dimensions: 55′ 0¾″ x 8′ 6¾″
All condemned by May 1952
Passenger accommodation comprised three 1sts, four 3rds, two lavatories. Originally provided with four lavatories. Fitted with Dean 10′ bogies and oval buffers.

DIAGRAM E69
COMPOSITE Corridor Carriage
Clerestory Roof Stock
Lot 928 of 1900
Running numbers 7446–55
Dimensions: 55′ 0¾″ x 8′ 6¾″
All condemned by November 1949
Passenger accommodation comprised four 1sts, three 3rds, 2 lavatories. Provided with Dean 10′ bogies and oval buffers.

Fig. 280 shows the corridor side of No. 7449 at Minehead in 1949. **Fig. 281** In this view, the compartment side of No. 7449 is presented to the camera at the same site and date. At this time it was painted in GWR wartime brown.

Fig. 282 illustrates No. 7467 marshalled into a main line express at Old Oak Common in 1949, still painted chocolate and cream.

Fig. 281

Fig. 282

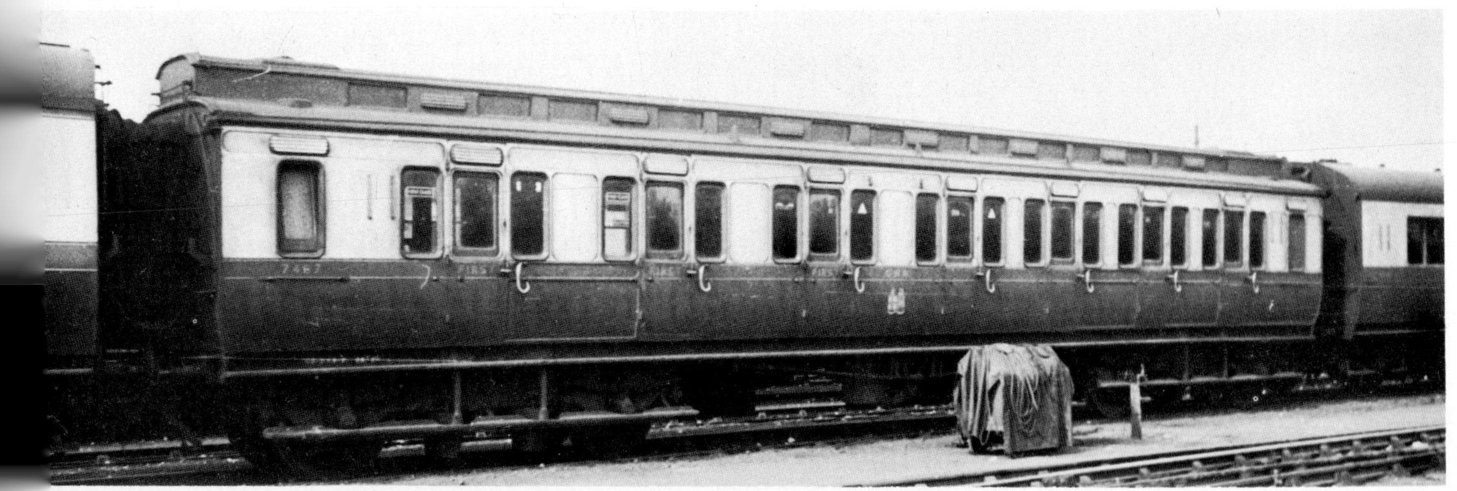

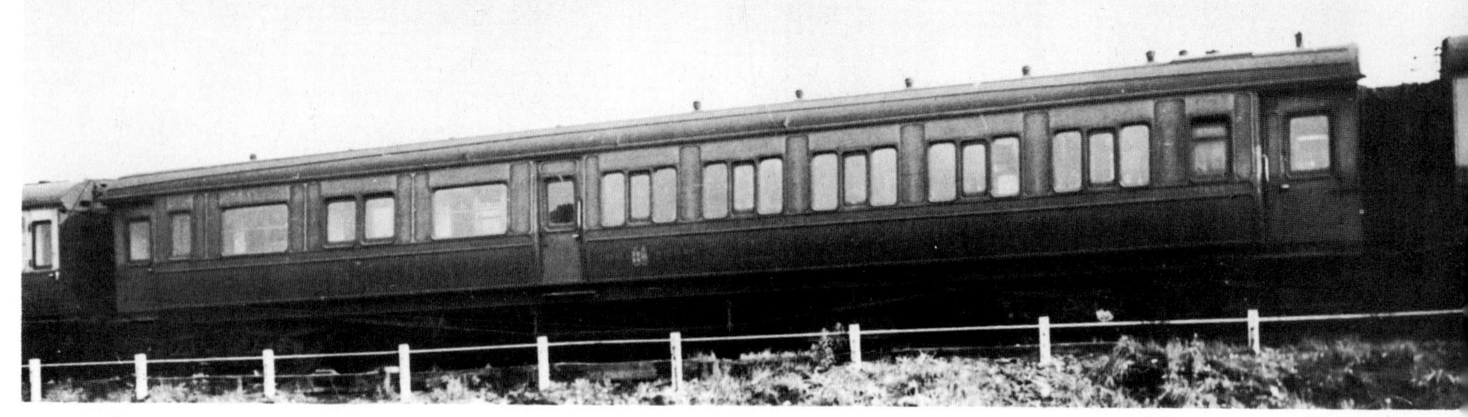

Fig. 283

Fig. 284

DIAGRAM E77
COMPOSITE Corridor Carriage
'Dreadnought' Stock
Lot 1068 of 1905
Running numbers 7639–44
Dimensions: 68′ 0″ x 9′ 6″
All condemned by April 1956
Passenger accommodation comprised three 1sts, five 3rds, totalling 58 seats. This series had staggered corridors and was originally provided with toplights to the windows.

Fig. 283 shows the compartment side of the 40-seat 3rd class section of No. 7644 at Old Oak Common in 1949. **Fig. 284** depicts the same side of No. 7640 at Newton Abbot in 1950. The opposite side of the series is seen in **Fig. 285** where the long corridor is shown nearest the camera. This was No. 7640 at Old Oak Common in 1951. In all three examples the toplights have been plated over.

Fig. 285

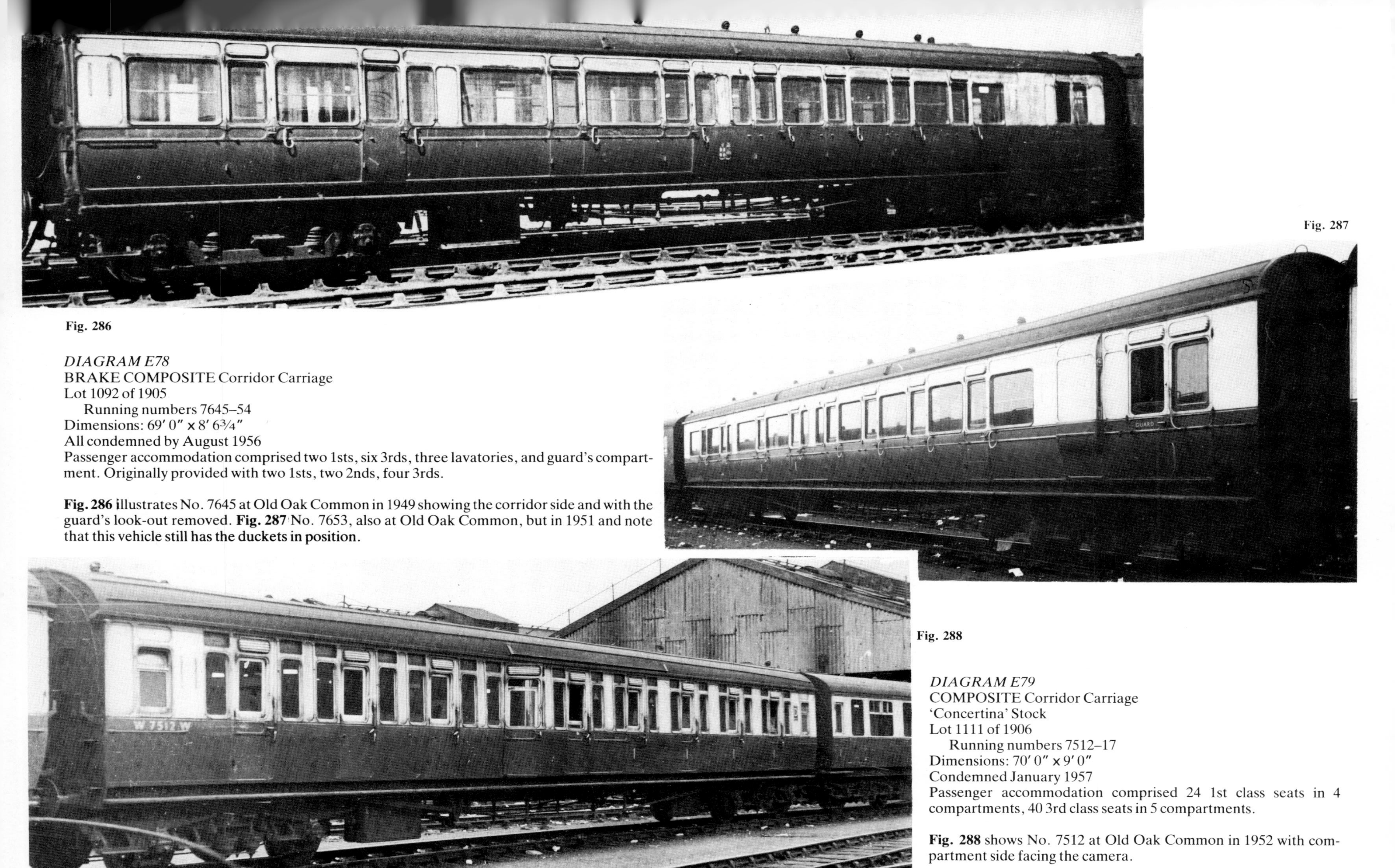

Fig. 286

Fig. 287

DIAGRAM E78
BRAKE COMPOSITE Corridor Carriage
Lot 1092 of 1905
Running numbers 7645–54
Dimensions: 69′ 0″ x 8′ 6¾″
All condemned by August 1956
Passenger accommodation comprised two 1sts, six 3rds, three lavatories, and guard's compartment. Originally provided with two 1sts, two 2nds, four 3rds.

Fig. 286 illustrates No. 7645 at Old Oak Common in 1949 showing the corridor side and with the guard's look-out removed. **Fig. 287** No. 7653, also at Old Oak Common, but in 1951 and note that this vehicle still has the duckets in position.

Fig. 288

DIAGRAM E79
COMPOSITE Corridor Carriage
'Concertina' Stock
Lot 1111 of 1906
Running numbers 7512–17
Dimensions: 70′ 0″ x 9′ 0″
Condemned January 1957
Passenger accommodation comprised 24 1st class seats in 4 compartments, 40 3rd class seats in 5 compartments.

Fig. 288 shows No. 7512 at Old Oak Common in 1952 with compartment side facing the camera.

Fig. 289

DIAGRAM E82
BRAKE COMPOSITE Corridor Carriage
'Toplight' Stock, Bars I
Lot 1137 of 1907
Running numbers 7518–32
Lot 1148 of 1908
Running numbers 7700–11
Dimensions: 56′ 0″ × 9′ 0″
Condemned May 1961

Passenger accommodation comprised two 1sts, four 3rds, two lavatories. These vehicles were fitted with American 8′ bogies.

Fig. 289 shows the compartment side of No. 7711 at Old Oak Common in 1950, with the van end nearest the camera. **Fig. 290** The first class end of No. 7709 in 1951, also at Old Oak Common. **Fig. 291**, taken in 1949, shows the compartment side of No. 7703 with most of the panelling still in place.

Fig. 290

Fig. 291

Fig. 292

DIAGRAM E82
BRAKE COMPOSITE

Fig. 292 illustrates the corridor side of No. 7703 from the first class end; Old Oak Common, 1951. **Fig. 293** depicts No. 7711 in 1949, also taken from the corridor side at Old Oak, but this example is still painted in GWR colours. **Fig. 294** Old Oak Common is again the setting for this view of No. 7709. Notice that there is only one toplight over each end corridor window in this series.

Fig. 293

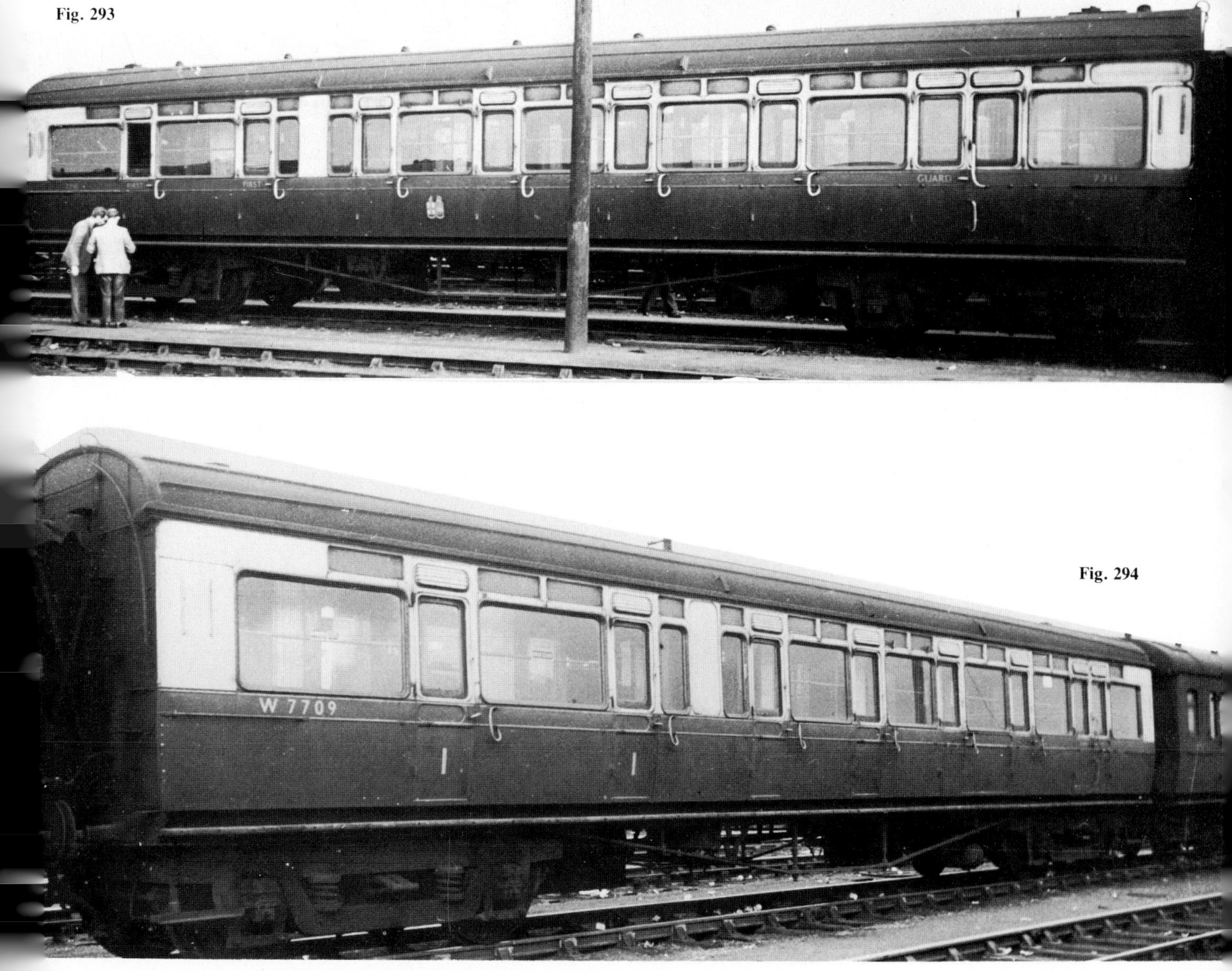

Fig. 294

Fig. 295

Fig. 296

DIAGRAM E83
BRAKE COMPOSITE Corridor Carriage
'Toplight' Stock
Lot 1138 of 1907
Running numbers 7533–47
Dimensions: 57′ 0″ x 9′ 0″
Condemned April 1962

Fig. 297

Passenger accommodation comprised two 3rds, two 1sts, two 3rds, guard's compartment, two lavatories. Originally comprised two 2nds, two 1sts, two 3rds, etc. Provided with 8′ American bogies.

Fig. 295 shows No. 7545 at Old Oak Common in 1950, the compartment side of the vehicle being seen from the ex-2nd class end. **Fig. 296** The van end and compartment side of No. 7540. **Fig. 297** illustrates the corridor side of No. 7540; notice again the peculiar single toplight to the end corridor windows.

Fig. 298

DIAGRAM E85
COMPOSITE Corridor Carriage
'Toplight' Stock, Bars I
Lot 1147 of 1909
Running numbers 7712–27
Lot 1151 of 1908
Running numbers 7728–29
Dimensions: 56′ 0″ x 9′ 0″
Condemned November 1956
Passenger accommodation comprised two 1sts, five 3rds, two lavatories. Series was originally 1st and 2nd class. Fitted with both American 8′ and 7′ 6″ plate bogies.

Fig. 307 depicts the compartment side of No. 7720 at Old Oak Common in 1949, with toplights blanked off.

DIAGRAM E87
BRAKE COMPOSITE Corridor Carriage
'Toplight' Stock, Bars I
Lot 1169 of 1910
Running numbers 7732–37
Dimensions: 56′ 0″ x 9′ 0″
Condemned August 1957
Passenger accommodation comprised two 1sts, four 3rds, guard's compartment,two lavatories. Provided with American 8′ bogies.

The compartment side of this series is seen in **Fig. 299**, which pictures No. 7734 at Banbury in 1952, and the corridor side of No. 7737 can be seen in **Fig. 300** standing outside Old Oak Common carriage shed in 1949. The roof boards read 'Paddington, Leamington Spa & Stratford on Avon'.

Fig. 299

Fig. 300

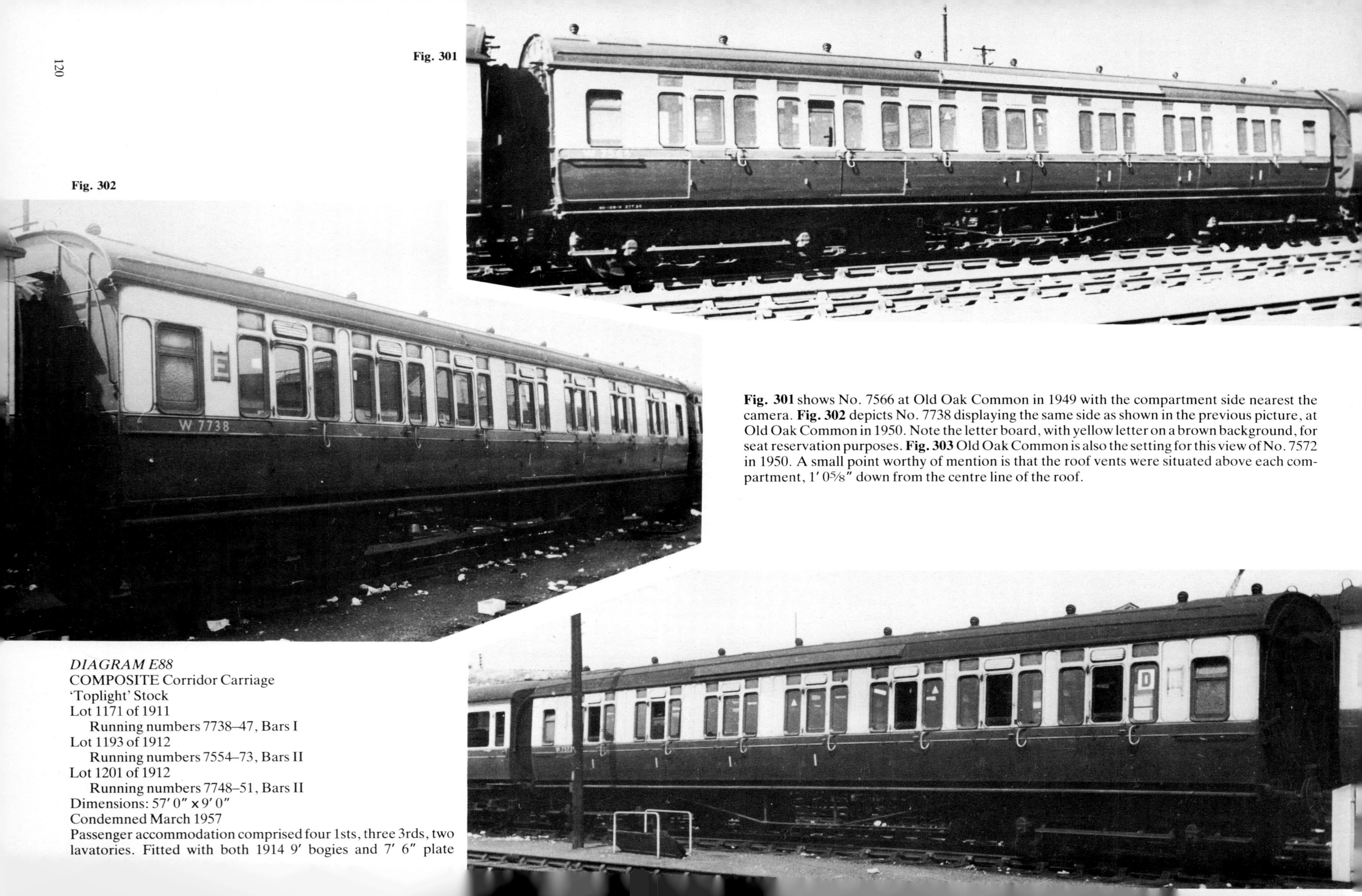

Fig. 301

Fig. 302

Fig. 301 shows No. 7566 at Old Oak Common in 1949 with the compartment side nearest the camera. **Fig. 302** depicts No. 7738 displaying the same side as shown in the previous picture, at Old Oak Common in 1950. Note the letter board, with yellow letter on a brown background, for seat reservation purposes. **Fig. 303** Old Oak Common is also the setting for this view of No. 7572 in 1950. A small point worthy of mention is that the roof vents were situated above each compartment, 1′ 0⅝″ down from the centre line of the roof.

DIAGRAM E88
COMPOSITE Corridor Carriage
'Toplight' Stock
Lot 1171 of 1911
    Running numbers 7738–47, Bars I
Lot 1193 of 1912
    Running numbers 7554–73, Bars II
Lot 1201 of 1912
    Running numbers 7748–51, Bars II
Dimensions: 57′ 0″ x 9′ 0″
Condemned March 1957
Passenger accommodation comprised four 1sts, three 3rds, two lavatories. Fitted with both 1914 9′ bogies and 7′ 6″ plate

Fig. 304

DIAGRAM E88
Three photographs of the *E88* composites, all showing the corridor sides of the vehicles.

Fig. 304 illustrates No. 7567 at Kingsbridge in 1950 in final GWR livery, and fitted with American 8′ bogie. **Fig. 305** shows No. 7747 at Tyseley, sporting BR livery in 1950, and fitted with '1914' type 9′ bogies. **Fig. 306** is a superb picture of No. 7740 at Old Oak Common in 1949, still in GWR livery and with the '1914' type 9′ bogies.

Fig. 305

Fig. 306

Fig. 307

Fig. 308

DIAGRAM E88

This page illustrates an example of how the enthusiast can be confused when researching into railway coach history.

Fig. 307 A corridor side view of No. 7745, a typical *E88* series composite. **Figs. 308** and **309** show a vehicle, No. 7573, which appears to be of post-war vintage. In fact, it comprises an old 'Toplight' underframe and bogies fitted with a new body, to replace the original one destroyed by enemy action. In **Fig. 308** the vehicle was photographed at Kingswear in 1952, and in **Fig. 309** it was seen at Bodmin Road in 1951.

Fig. 309

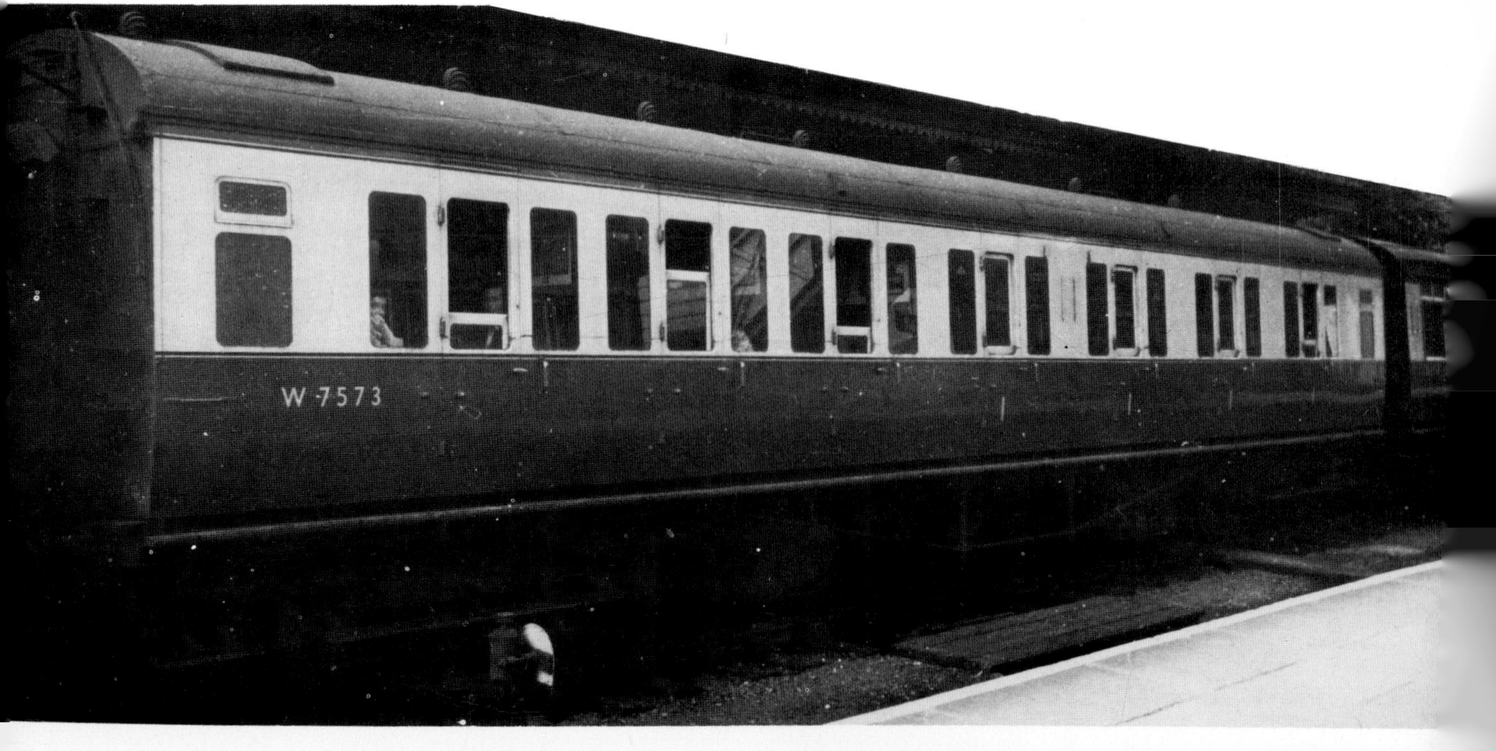

Fig. 310

DIAGRAM E89
COMPOSITE Non-Corridor Carriage
'Toplight' Stock, Bars II
Lot 1187 of 1911
Running numbers 6596–98, 6604/62–65
Dimensions: 57′ 0″ x 9′ 0″
Condemned April 1955
Passenger accommodation comprised four 1sts and five 3rds. Fitted with '1914' type bogies.

DIAGRAM E97
COMPOSITE Non-Corridor Carriage
'Toplight' Series, Multibar
Slightly out of sequence, but placed here for comparison.
Lot 1226 of 1913
Running numbers 6863–70
Dimensions: 69′ 11½″ x 8′ 11¼″
All condemned by June 1957
Passenger accommodation comprised five 1sts and six 3rds. These vehicles were fitted with American 9′ bogies and were branded 'Birmingham Division'.

Fig. 310 is the official Swindon record of No. 6597, painted in the crimson lake livery.

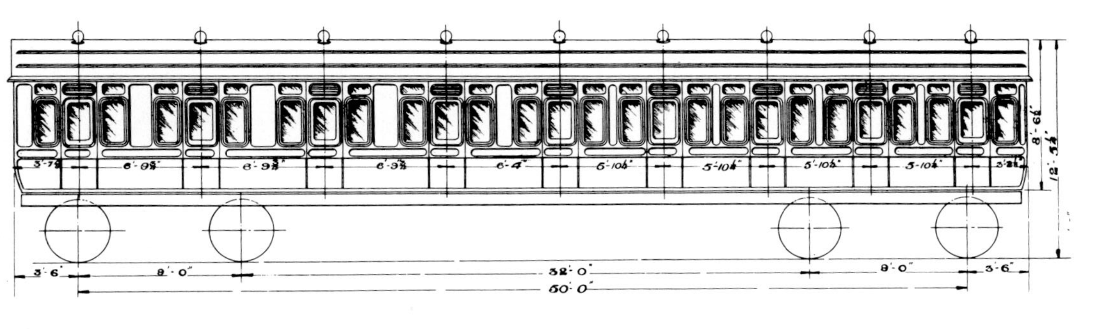

Fig. 311 shows No. 6864 as built at Swindon in 1913 with maroon livery and white roof.

Fig. 311

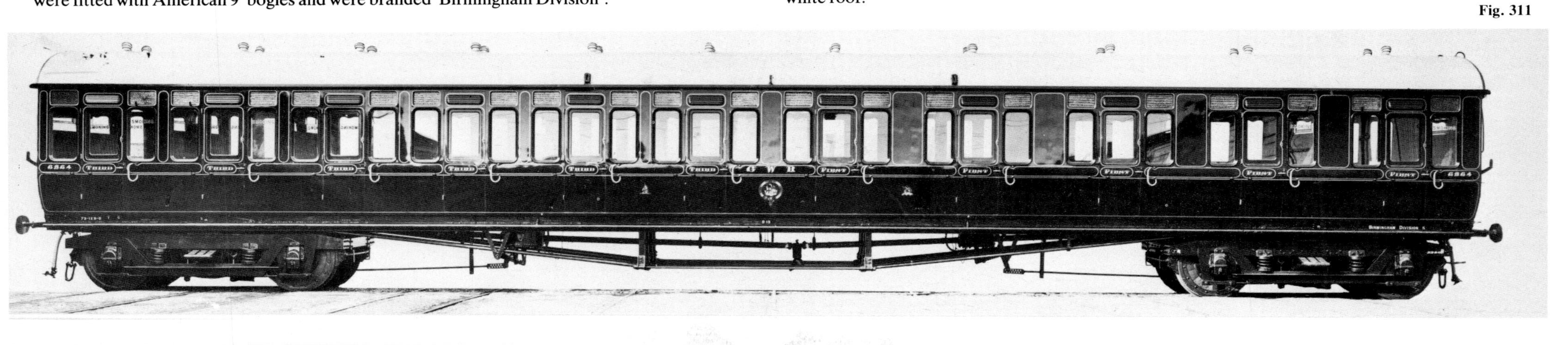

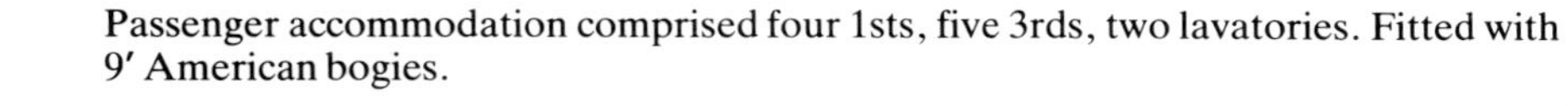

Fig. 312

Passenger accommodation comprised four 1sts, five 3rds, two lavatories. Fitted with 9′ American bogies.

Fig. 312 is the Swindon official photograph of No. 7756, as built, in the crimson lake livery and showing the corridor side. **Fig. 314** No. 7761 at Old Oak in 1952, with the compartment side nearest the camera. The inset picture, **Fig. 313**, illustrates the DC dynamo fitted to this stock for lighting purposes. Note the twist in the truss rods of the vehicle at the top of the photograph.

Fig. 313

DIAGRAM E93
COMPOSITE Corridor Carriage
'Toplight' Stock, Bars II
Lot 1210 of 1912
Running numbers 7752–61
Lot 1213 of 1913
Running numbers 7762–64
Dimensions: 70′ 0″ x 9′ 0″
Condemned August 1958

Passenger accommodation comprised four 1sts, five 3rds, two lavatories. Fitted with 9′ American bogies.

Fig. 314

Fig. 315

Fig. 315 shows No. 7583 at Old Oak Common in 1949 with the compartment side facing the camera. Note the lavatory between 1st and 3rd class compartments. **Fig. 316** The corridor side of the same vehicle, No. 7583, taken at the same time and place as the previous illustration. **Fig. 317** A close-up of the battery box slung underneath these vehicles. The whole front could be lifted out to give access to the batteries, or the cells could be topped up with distilled water through the small hinged trap door.

Fig. 316

DIAGRAM E94
BRAKE COMPOSITE Corridor Carriage
'Toplight' Stock, Bars II
Lot 1200 of 1912
Running numbers 7581–83
Dimensions: 57′ 0″ x 9′ 0″
All condemned in August 1958
Passenger accommodation comprised lavatory, two 1sts, lavatory, four 3rds, guard's compartment. Fitted with '1914' type 9′ bogie.

Fig. 317

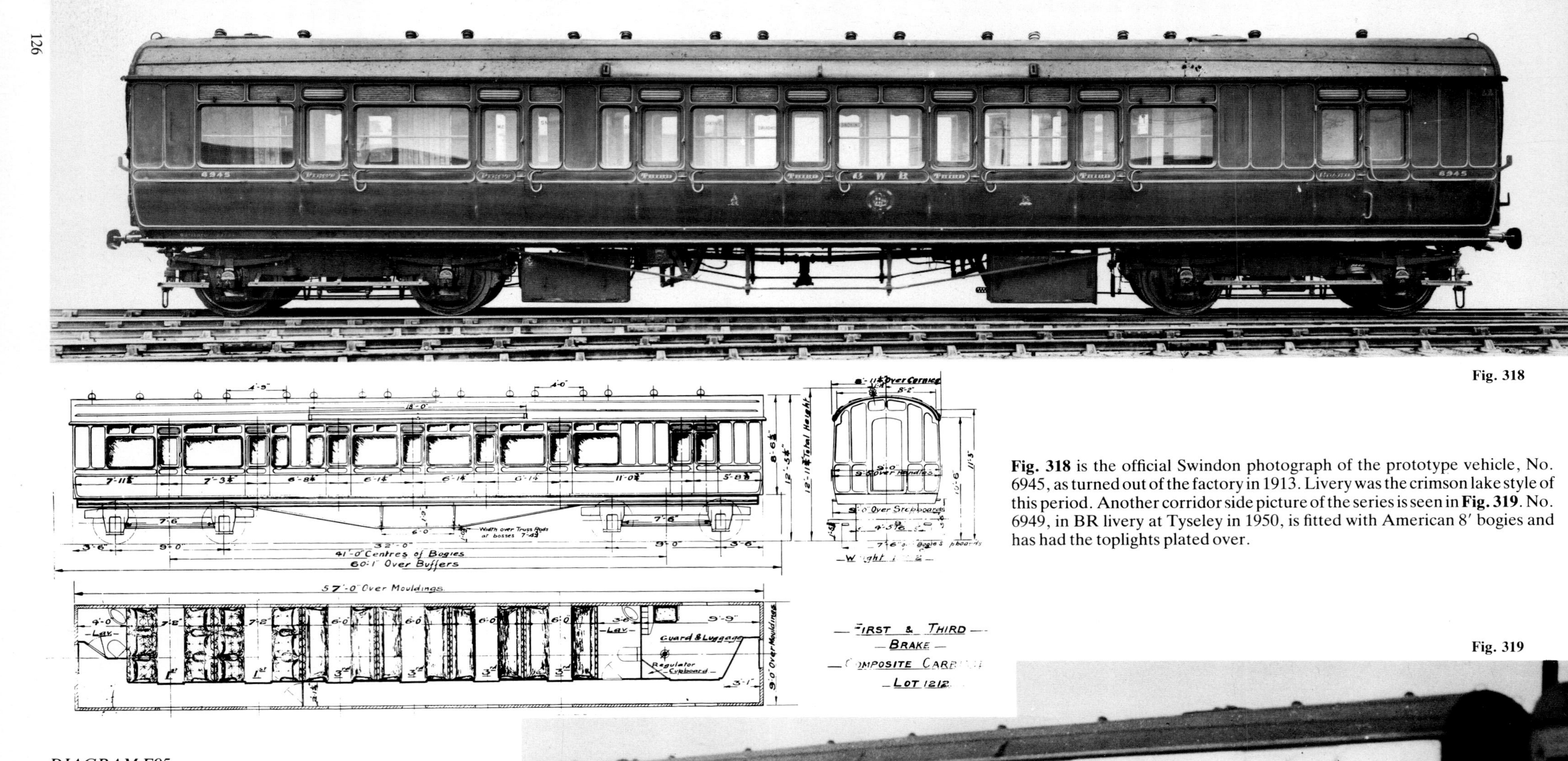

Fig. 318

Fig. 318 is the official Swindon photograph of the prototype vehicle, No. 6945, as turned out of the factory in 1913. Livery was the crimson lake style of this period. Another corridor side picture of the series is seen in **Fig. 319**. No. 6949, in BR livery at Tyseley in 1950, is fitted with American 8′ bogies and has had the toplights plated over.

Fig. 319

DIAGRAM E95
BRAKE COMPOSITE Corridor Carriage
'Toplight' Stock, Bars II
Lot 1212 of 1913
Running numbers 6945–61
Dimensions: 57′ 0″ x 9′ 0″
All condemned by May 1959

These twelve vehicles were almost identical to the *D94* series but had the central lavatory moved to a position next to the guard's compartment. Passenger accommodation comprised lavatory, two 1sts, four 3rds, lavatory, guard's compartment. Provided with '1914' type 9′ bogies.

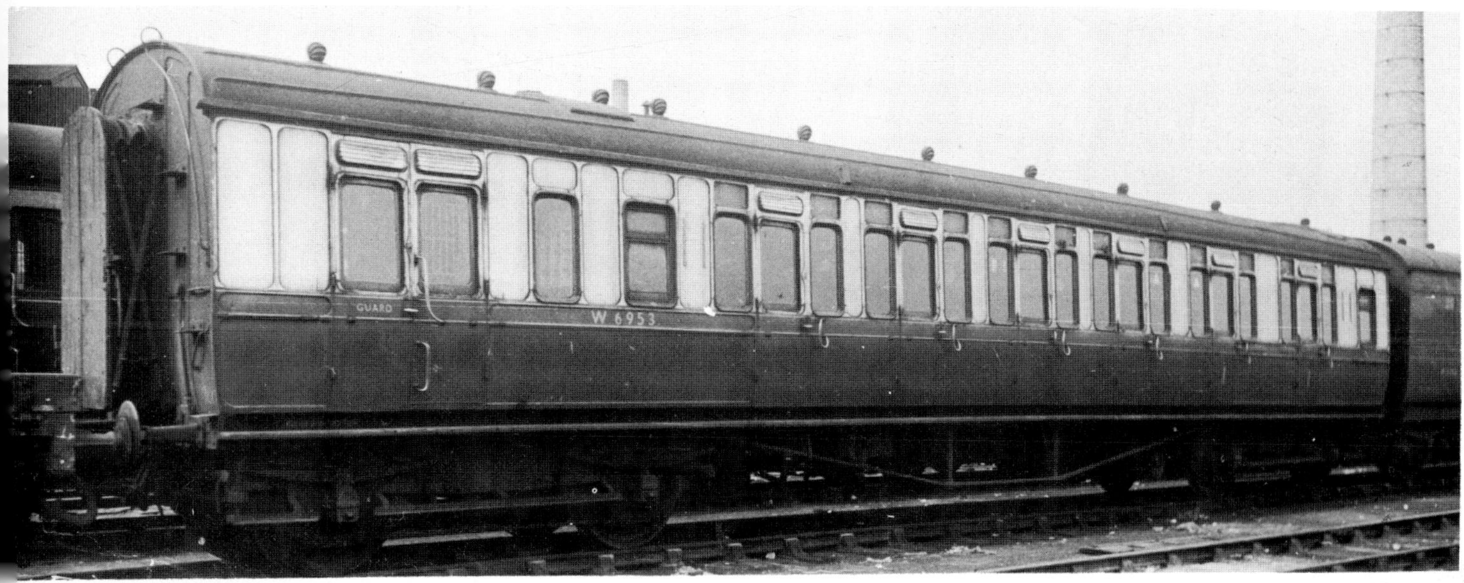

Fig. 320

DIAGRAM E95

Figs. 320 and **322** show the compartment side of No. 6953 at Old Oak Common in 1951. **Fig. 321** No. 6961, photographed at Truro in 1951 from the van end, showing the compartments and divisions quite well. Note that the old sidelamp bracket is still in place.

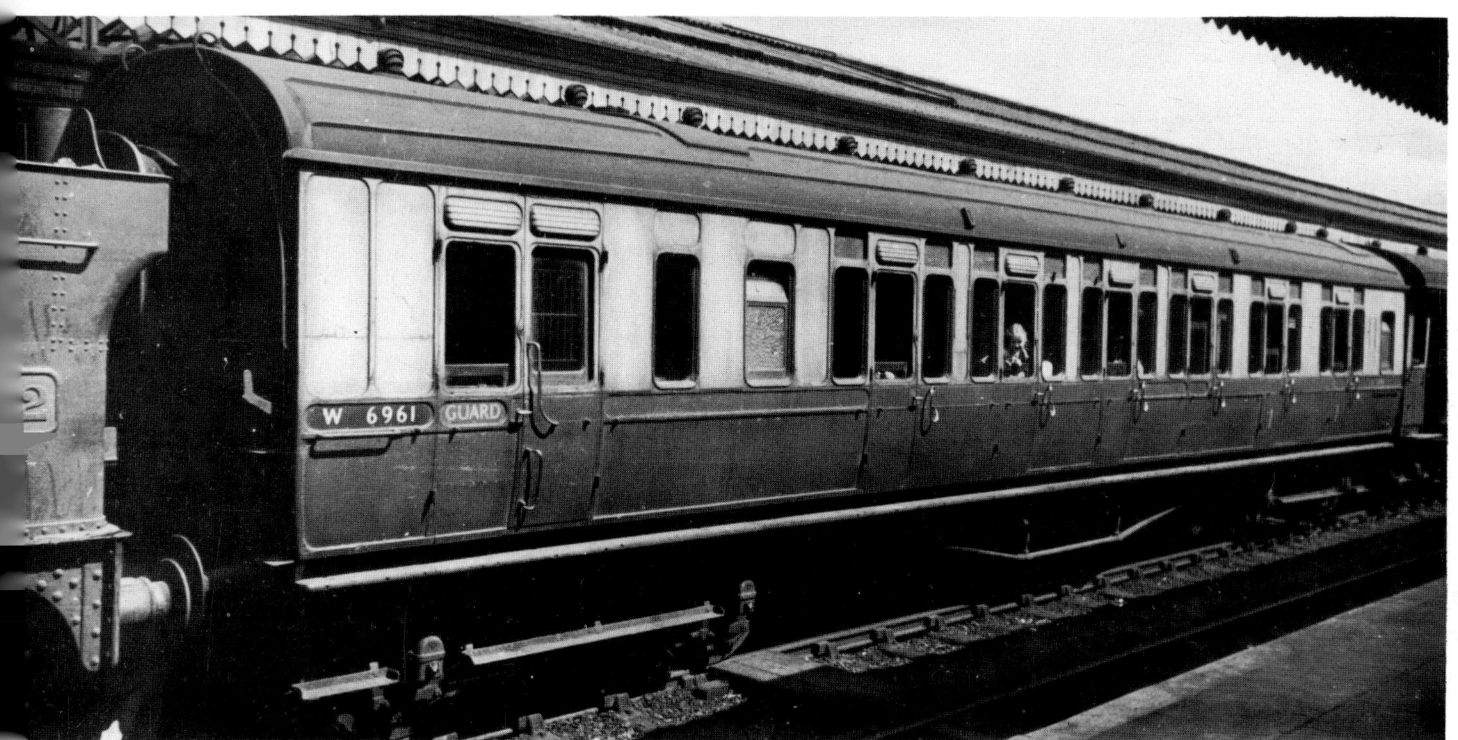

Fig. 321

Fig. 322

Fig. 323

DIAGRAM E96
COMPOSITE Non-Corridor Carriage
'Toplight' Stock, Multibar
Lot 1228 of 1913
Running numbers 6500–11
Dimensions: 56′ 11¼″ x 8′ 11¼″
Condemned June 1956
Passenger accommodation comprised four 1sts and five 3rds.

Fig. 323 depicts No. 6500 as built at Swindon in 1913, wearing the crimson livery with white roof. Note that no battery boxes are shown. This stock was originally branded 'London Suburban Service'. **Fig. 324** No. 6506 painted in BR maroon livery at Tyseley in 1950.

Fig. 324

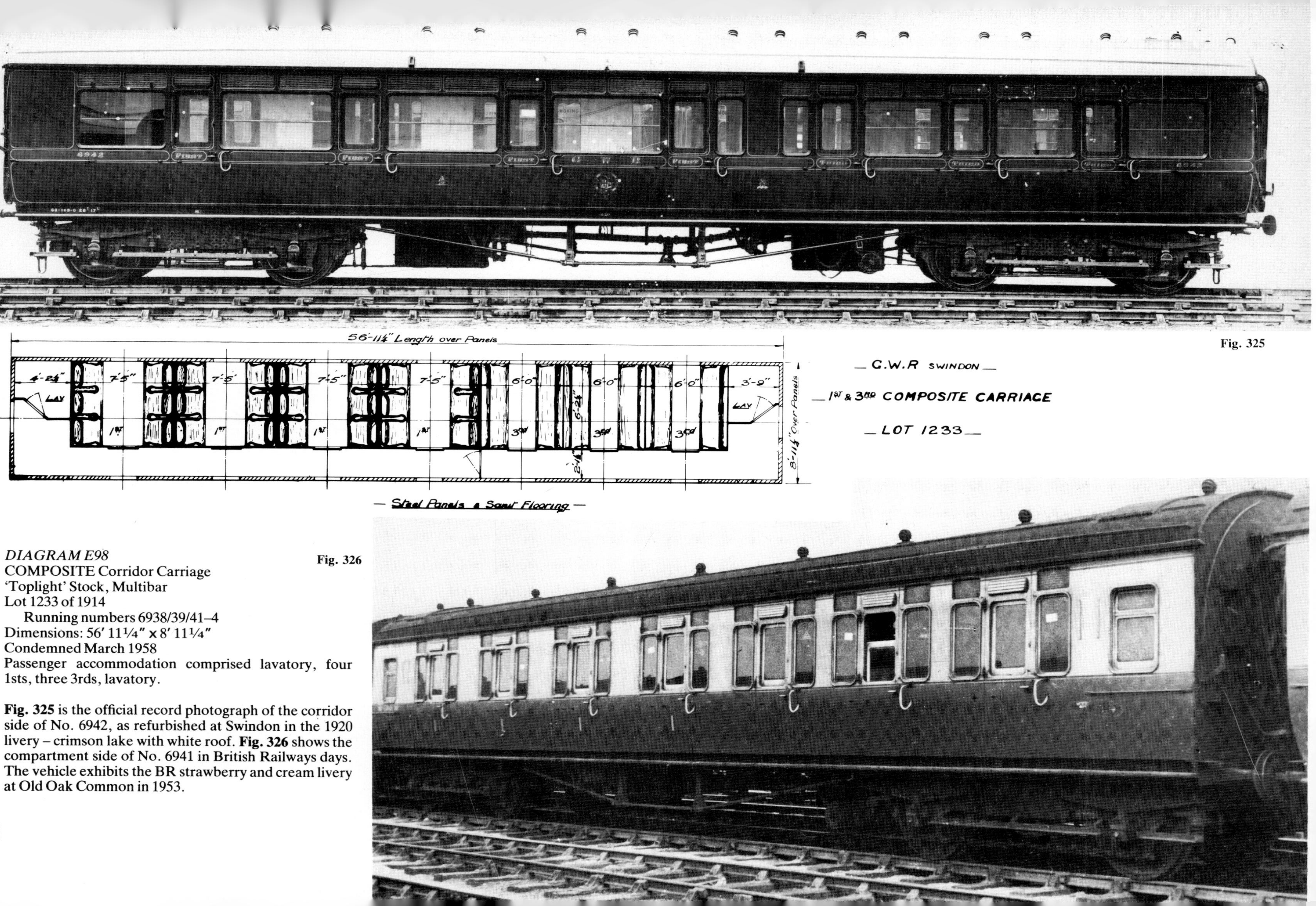

Fig. 325

Fig. 326

DIAGRAM E98
COMPOSITE Corridor Carriage
'Toplight' Stock, Multibar
Lot 1233 of 1914
Running numbers 6938/39/41–4
Dimensions: 56′ 11¼″ x 8′ 11¼″
Condemned March 1958
Passenger accommodation comprised lavatory, four 1sts, three 3rds, lavatory.

Fig. 325 is the official record photograph of the corridor side of No. 6942, as refurbished at Swindon in the 1920 livery – crimson lake with white roof. **Fig. 326** shows the compartment side of No. 6941 in British Railways days. The vehicle exhibits the BR strawberry and cream livery at Old Oak Common in 1953.

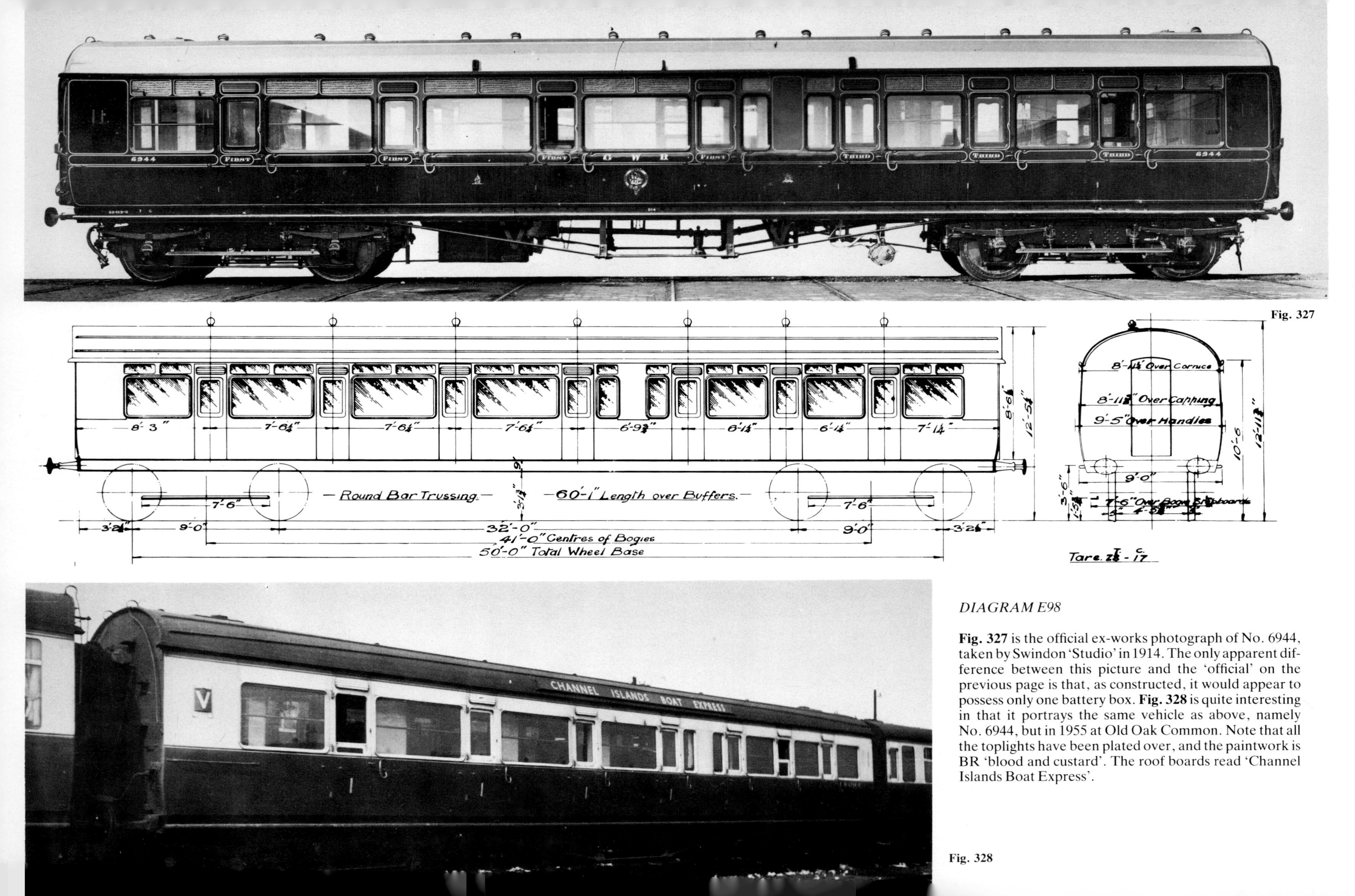

Fig. 327

DIAGRAM E98

Fig. 327 is the official ex-works photograph of No. 6944, taken by Swindon 'Studio' in 1914. The only apparent difference between this picture and the 'official' on the previous page is that, as constructed, it would appear to possess only one battery box. **Fig. 328** is quite interesting in that it portrays the same vehicle as above, namely No. 6944, but in 1955 at Old Oak Common. Note that all the toplights have been plated over, and the paintwork is BR 'blood and custard'. The roof boards read 'Channel Islands Boat Express'.

Fig. 328

Fig. 329

DIAGRAM E99
BRAKE COMPOSITE Corridor Carriage
'Toplight' Stock, Multibar
Lot 1240 of 1914
Running numbers 7766–75
Dimensions: 69′ 11¼″ x 8′ 11¼″
Condemned July 1958
Passenger accommodation comprised lavatory, two 1sts, five 3rds, lavatory. Fitted with American 9′ bogies.

Fig. 330

Fig. 331

Fig. 329 The Swindon official picture of this fine example of Great Western coachwork. No. 7773 stands newly painted in the crimson lake livery outside the Works in 1914, with the corridor side facing the camera. **Fig. 330** shows No. 7768 at Old Oak Common in 1951, painted in the BR colours of strawberry and cream. The bogies had, by this time, been changed for ones of 9′ steel plate pattern. **Fig. 331** shows the same vehicle as above, but depicts the compartment and lavatory side.

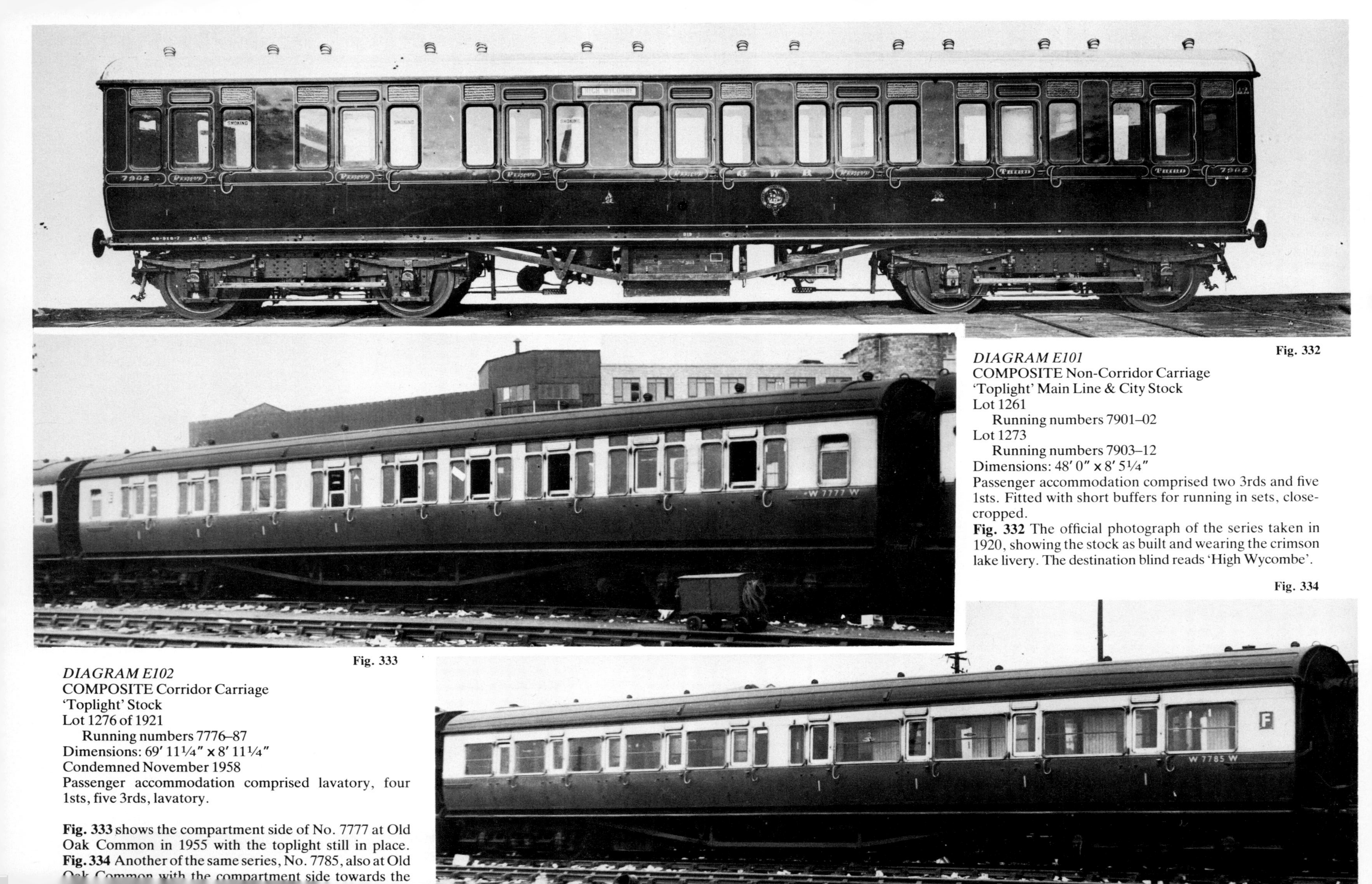

Fig. 332

DIAGRAM E101
COMPOSITE Non-Corridor Carriage
'Toplight' Main Line & City Stock
Lot 1261
Running numbers 7901–02
Lot 1273
Running numbers 7903–12
Dimensions: 48′ 0″ x 8′ 5¼″
Passenger accommodation comprised two 3rds and five 1sts. Fitted with short buffers for running in sets, close-cropped.

Fig. 332 The official photograph of the series taken in 1920, showing the stock as built and wearing the crimson lake livery. The destination blind reads 'High Wycombe'.

Fig. 334

Fig. 333

DIAGRAM E102
COMPOSITE Corridor Carriage
'Toplight' Stock
Lot 1276 of 1921
Running numbers 7776–87
Dimensions: 69′ 11¼″ x 8′ 11¼″
Condemned November 1958
Passenger accommodation comprised lavatory, four 1sts, five 3rds, lavatory.

Fig. 333 shows the compartment side of No. 7777 at Old Oak Common in 1955 with the toplight still in place.
Fig. 334 Another of the same series, No. 7785, also at Old Oak Common with the compartment side towards the

Fig. 335

Fig. 337

DIAGRAM E104
BRAKE COMPOSITE Corridor Carriage
'Toplight' Stock
Lot 1280 of 1922
Running numbers 7788–97
Dimensions: 69′ 11¼″ x 8′ 11¼″
Condemned October 1958
Passenger accommodation comprised guard's and luggage compartment, lavatory, two 1sts, five 3rds, lavatory.

Fig. 336

10′-3½″ 13′-10″ 7′-7¼″ 6′-10½″ 6′-1¼″ 6′-1¼″ 6′-1¼″ 6′-1¼″ 7′-1¼″
8′-6½″ 12′-6¼″
73′-0″ OVER BUFFERS
44′-0″
53′-0″ CENTRES OF BOGIES
62′-0″ TOTAL WHEELBASE
69′-11¼″ OVER PANELS
3′-11⅝″ 9′-0″ 9′-0″ 3′-11⅝″

Fig. 335 No. 7788 at Tyseley in 1950 showing the corridor side of this left-hand van vehicle. **Fig. 336** The compartment side of No. 7790, photographed at Kingsbridge in 1950, with the toplights plated over. **Fig. 337** End details of these 70′ carriages showing the side and tail lamp brackets, roof steps and hand rails, electric connections and gangway.

Fig. 338

Fig. 339

DIAGRAM E108
COMPOSITE Corridor Carriage
Experimental Prototype for 70′ South Wales Stock
From Lot 1276 in 1921
One vehicle only: No. 7782
Dimensions and interior layout identical to *E102* series. This vehicle was built without toplights or bolections around the windows, and with a high waistline, to form a prototype for the later 'South Wales' series.

Fig. 338 The official Swindon picture of No. 7782 as built, with the corridor side facing the camera.

Fig. 340

DIAGRAM E111
COMPOSITE Corridor Carriage
Steel-panelled South Wales Stock
Lot 1319 of 1923
Running numbers 7932/6–42
Dimensions: 70′ 0″ x 9′ 0″
Condemned December 1961
Passenger accommodation comprised lavatory, four 1sts, five 3rds, lavatory. This series had the 1st class compartments at the left-hand end of the corridor side.

Fig. 339 illustrates the compartment side of No. 7941 in the stock shed at Old Oak Common in 1952. **Fig. 340** is the corridor side view of the series, showing No. 7939 at Old Oak Common in 1955.

Fig. 341

DIAGRAM E112
COMPOSITE Corridor Carriage
Steel-panelled South Wales Stock
Lot 1319 of 1923
Running numbers 7931/3–5
Dimensions: 70′ 0″ x 9′ 0″
Condemned February 1961
Identical to *E111*, but the 1st class compartments were located at the right-hand end of the corridor.

Fig. 341 No. 7934 is seen at Old Oak Common in 1952 with the corridor side facing the camera. The compartment side of the same vehicle is illustrated in **Fig. 342**.

Fig. 342

DIAGRAM E113
BRAKE COMPOSITE Corridor Carriage
Steel-panelled Stock
Lot 1322 of 1923
Running numbers 7949–64
Dimensions: 57′ 0″ x 8′ 6″
Condemned July 1962
Passenger accommodation comprised lavatory, two 1sts, four 3rds, lavatory, guard.

Fig. 343 A photograph of No. 7953 as built in 1923 in the restored chocolate and cream livery, with painted pseudo panels, white roof, black underframes and ends.

Fig. 343

Fig. 344

DIAGRAM E115
COMPOSITE Corridor Carriage
Steel-panelled Stock
Lot 1324 of 1923
Running numbers 7605–7/11/3/5/7/9
Running numbers 7621/3
Dimensions: 57′ 0″ x 9′ 0″
Condemned January 1962
Passenger accommodation comprised lavatory, four 1sts, three 3rds, lavatory. Fitted with 9′ plate bogies.

Fig. 344 illustrates the compartment side of No. 7613 at Old Oak Common in 1953.

DIAGRAM E116
BRAKE COMPOSITE Non-Corridor Carriage
Steel-panelled Stock
Lot 1327 of 1924
Running numbers 7169–72, 7510/1
Running numbers 7574–9, 7625/6
Dimensions: 57′ 0″ x 9′ 0″
Condemned November 1961
Passenger accommodation comprised guard's and luggage compartment, six 3rds, one 1st. These vehicles were close-coupled in pairs.

Fig. 345 No. 7579, photographed at Minehead in 1949. Note the single 1st class compartment. **Fig. 346** The opposite side of the series is shown in this view of No. 7578, also present at Minehead in 1949. The small board at the centre of the coach reads 'Taunton'.

Fig. 347

DIAGRAM E118
COMPOSITE Corridor Carriage
Flat-ended Steel-panelled Stock
Lot 1324 of 1924
Running numbers 7608–10/2/4/6/8
Running numbers 7620/2/4
Dimensions: 57′ 0″ x 9′ 0″
Condemned February 1961

Passenger accommodation comprised lavatory, three 3rds, four 1sts, lavatory. These vehicles were similar to *Diagram E115*, but whereas *E115* had the four 1st class compartments on the left-hand side of the corridor, the *E118* series had them on the right-hand side of the corridor.

Fig. 347 No. 7624 as built and painted with the pseudo panels. **Fig. 348** This view of No. 7608 depicts the corridor side of the series in BR days, this example being at Old Oak Common in 1952.

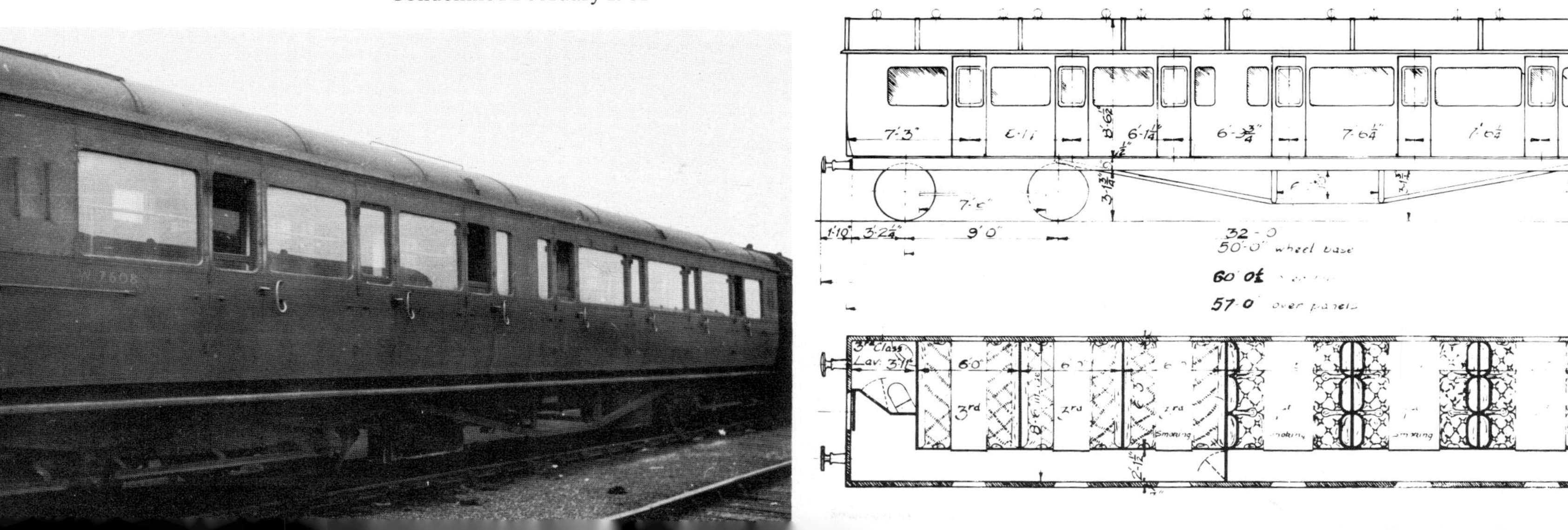

Fig. 348

DIAGRAM E124
COMPOSITE Non-Corridor Carriage
Bow-ended Suburban Stock
Lot 1336 of 1925
Running numbers 6666–91
Dimensions: 58′ 2″ x 9′ 0″
Condemned July 1960.

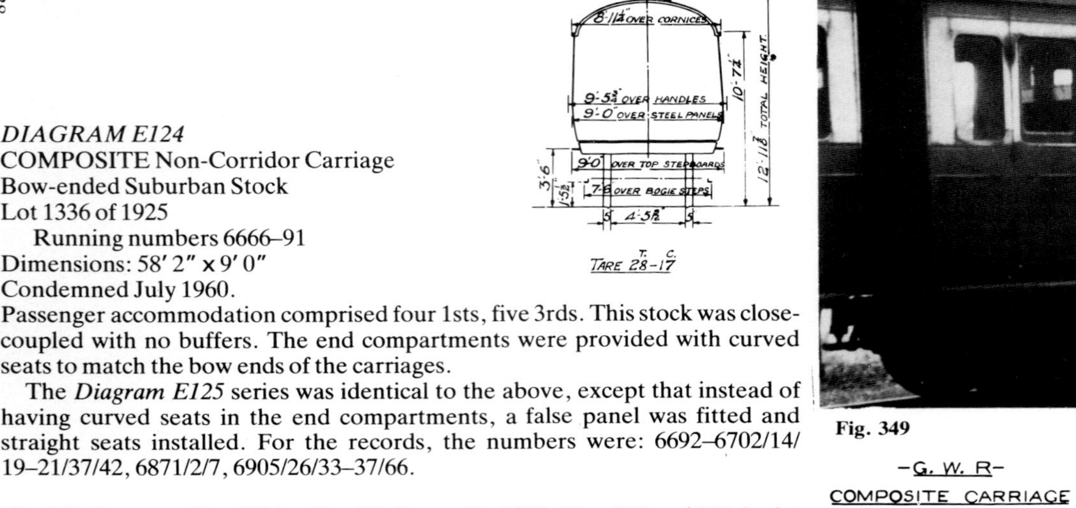

Passenger accommodation comprised four 1sts, five 3rds. This stock was close-coupled with no buffers. The end compartments were provided with curved seats to match the bow ends of the carriages.

The *Diagram E125* series was identical to the above, except that instead of having curved seats in the end compartments, a false panel was fitted and straight seats installed. For the records, the numbers were: 6692–6702/14/19–21/37/42, 6871/2/7, 6905/26/33–37/66.

Fig. 349 illustrates No. 6684 at Cardiff General in 1952. **Figs. 350** and **351** depict No. 6680 and 6668 in British Railways maroon livery at Cardiff, also in 1952.

Fig. 349

–G. W. R–
COMPOSITE CARRIAGE
-SUBURBAN SERVICE-
-SWINDON- –MARCH 1924-
–LOT 1336–

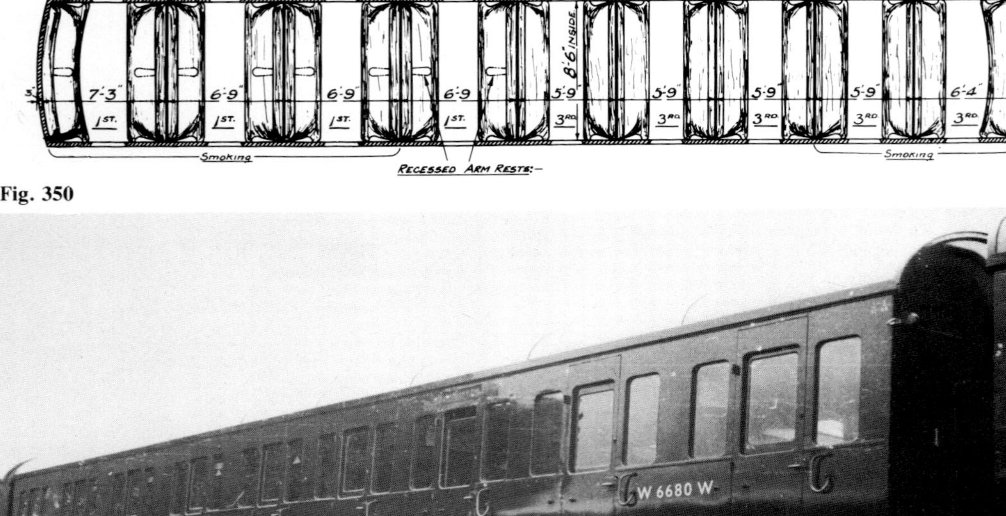

Fig. 350

Fig. 351

Fig. 352

DIAGRAM E127
COMPOSITE Corridor Carriage
Bow-ended Stock
Lot 1351 of 1925
Running numbers 6519–25–8/30–2/36
Lot 1373 of 1927
Running numbers 6024/6/9/30/4/7/50/68/99, 6105/35/7/8/45/6/9/50/5/6/8/60/7/81/7/92/4/7/8, 6201/3/9/11
Dimensions: 58′ 4½″ x 9′ 0″
Condemned February 1962
Passenger accommodation comprised lavatory, four 1sts, three 3rds, lavatory.
Fitted with 7′ plate bogies.

Fig. 352 The official picture of No. 6029 as built in 1925, showing the corridor side and the mock-panelling livery. **Fig. 353** shows No. 6181 inside the stock shed at Old Oak Common in 1955, with the compartment side nearest the camera. The roof boards read 'Paddington, Newport, Cardiff and Swansea'.

Fig. 353

Fig. 354 depicts No. 6203 at Old Oak in 1953 with the double waist line livery of BR. 'Paddington, Gloucester & Cheltenham' is the route displayed on the roof boards.

Fig. 354

Fig. 355

DIAGRAM E128
BRAKE COMPOSITE Corridor Carriage
Bow-ended Stock
Lot 1350 of 1926
Running numbers 6475–81/3/91–5/7/8, 6512–8
Dimensions: 58′ 4½″ x 9′ 0″
Condemned January 1963
Passenger accommodation comprised lavatory, four 3rds, two 1sts, lavatory, guard. Fitted with 7′ bogies.

Fig. 355 shows the compartment side of No. 6517 at Tavistock in 1953, seen from the van end. **Fig. 356** No. 6481 at Kingswear in 1952 with the corridor side on view.

▼ **Fig. 356**

DIAGRAM E129
BRAKE COMPOSITE Non-Corridor Carriage
Bow-ended, Close-coupled Stock
Lot 1355 of 1926
Running numbers 6545/7/51/3/6/60/1/3/5/6
Dimensions: 58′ 2″ x 9′ 0″
Condemned December 1961
Passenger accommodation comprised four 3rds, one 1st, two 3rds, guard's and luggage compartment. Fitted with 9′ bogies. Two of these vehicles formed a 'B' set, which was the combination of any two brake composites, forming a train.

Fig. 357 depicts an example of the series, No. 6565, as built in 1926, painted in the mock-panel style. The close-coupling is on the left.

▼

Fig. 357

DIAGRAM E129

Fig. 358

Fig. 358 This full page study shows the centre coupling between brake composites Nos. 6565 and 6566, thus forming a 'B' set, a permanently coupled two-coach train for working on the smaller branches. Note the mock-panel painting, all the details of the panelling being faithfully painted in! Photograph dated 1926.

DIAGRAM E131
COMPOSITE Non-Corridor Carriage
Bow-ended Suburban Stock
Lot 1376 of 1927
Running numbers 6231/3/5–7/42/8/9/50/2/5/6/8/9/60/4/72, 6329/31/44–6/9/50/4/7, 6360/2/4/9/70/6/87/8/90, 6416/35/58/68/9
Lot 1388 of 1929
Running numbers 6624 -39
Dimensions: 58′ 2″ x 9′ 0″
Passenger accommodation comprised four 1sts and five 3rds.
Fitted with 7′ plate bogies.

Fig. 359

Fig. 360

Fig. 359 No. 6362 in British Railways maroon livery with yellow lining. The location is Windsor in 1951.
Fig. 360 No. 6390 at Old Oak Common in 1951. Notice that the 'First' class markings have been removed.

DIAGRAM E132
COMPOSITE Corridor Carriage
Bow-ended Main Line Stock
Lot 1382 of 1928
Running numbers 6011–6/18–23/5/7/31/2/5/8–45/51/4/5/65–7/70/2–4/6–83/5/9–94/6
Dimensions: 57′ 4½″ x 9′ 0″
Condemned December 1962
Passenger accommodation comprised lavatory, four 1sts, three 3rds, lavatory. Fitted with 7′ plate bogies.

Fig. 361 No. 6096 is shown in this official Swindon picture, illustrating an example of the series as built in the new GW livery of 1928.

Fig. 361

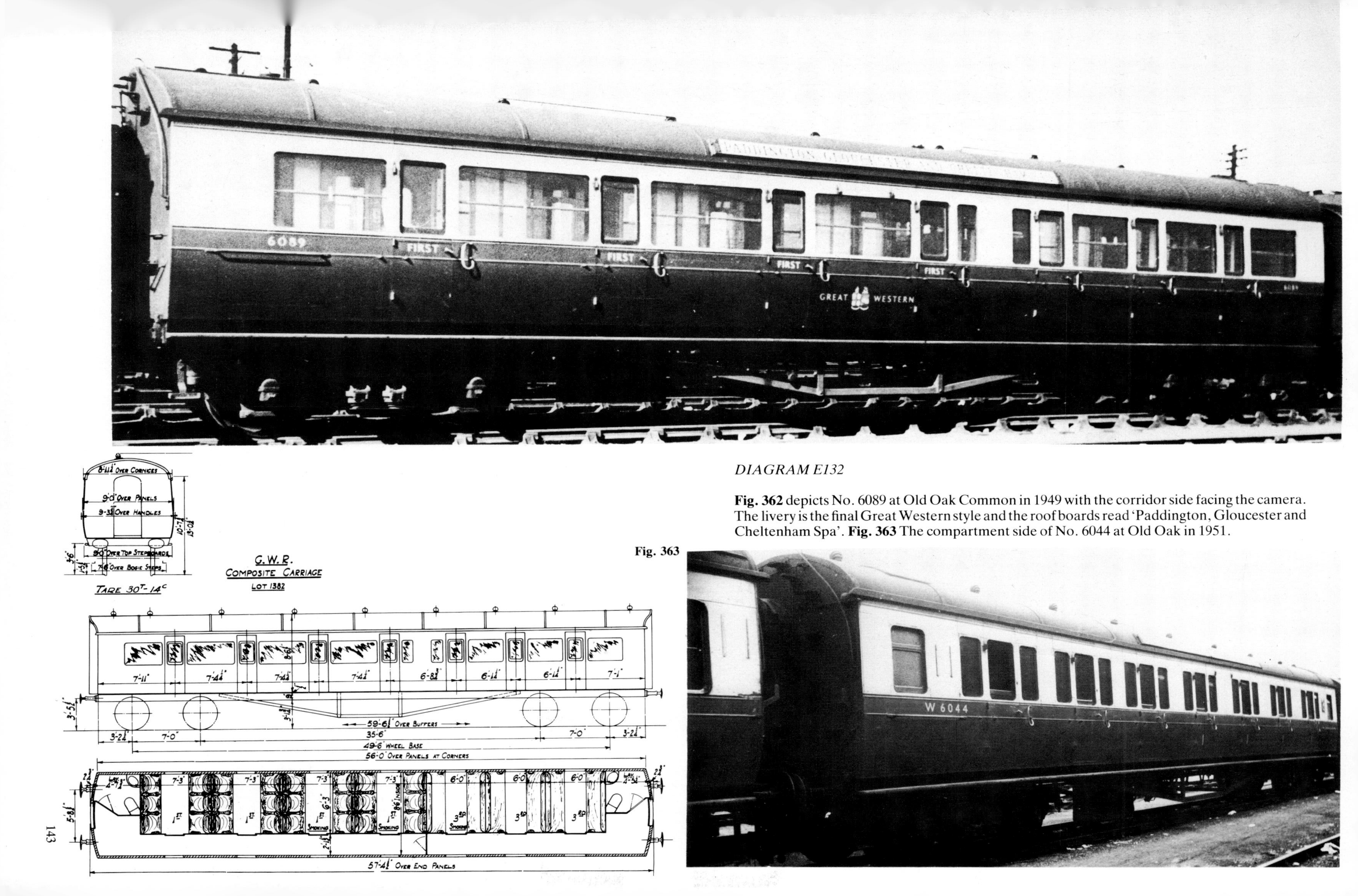

DIAGRAM E132

Fig. 362 depicts No. 6089 at Old Oak Common in 1949 with the corridor side facing the camera. The livery is the final Great Western style and the roof boards read 'Paddington, Gloucester and Cheltenham Spa'. **Fig. 363** The compartment side of No. 6044 at Old Oak in 1951.

Fig. 363

DIAGRAM E132

Fig. 364 Another full page picture, showing superb detail of the doors and windows on the corridor side of composite No. 6069. The photograph was taken at Swindon to illustrate the new style flush windows. The small gold numeral transfers on the top right-hand corner of the vehicle indicated the seating capacity of the coach; in this case, 24 first class and 24 third class.

Fig. 365

Fig. 366

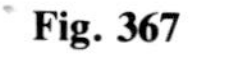
Fig. 367

DIAGRAM E134
COMPOSITE Non-Corridor Carriage
Bow-ended Stock for Newport and Cardiff Service
Lot 1390 of 1928
Running numbers 6567–78
Dimensions: 58′ 2″ x 9′ 0″
Condemned March 1961
Passenger accommodation comprised two 3rds, five 1sts, two 3rds. Fitted with 7′ plate bogies.

Fig. 365 No. 6572 is seen as built in this official Swindon picture of 1928. Note the two boxes, one large and one small. Large for batteries, small for regulator gear.

DIAGRAM E136
COMPOSITE Corridor Carriage
Bow-ended Stock
Lot 1398 of 1929
Running numbers 6101–4
Dimensions: 57′ 4½″ x 8′ 10¼″
Condemned December 1962
Passenger accommodation comprised lavatory, four 1sts, three 3rds, lavatory. Fitted with 7′ plate bogies.

Fig. 366 No. 6101 at Swindon in 1929 as built, with the corridor side facing the camera. **Fig. 367** The same vehicle in 1954 at Old Oak Common with the compartment side displayed. The roof boards read 'Channel Islands Boat Express'.

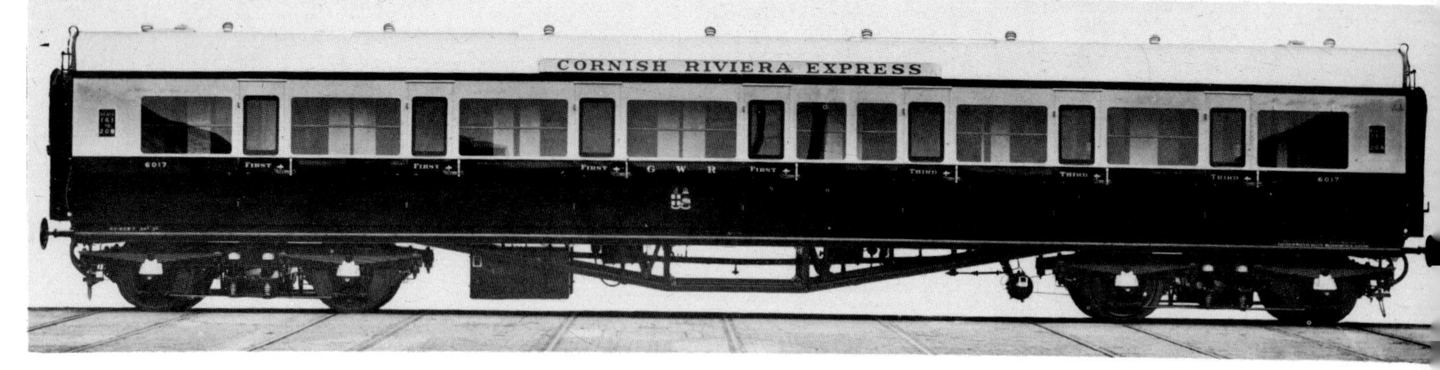

Fig. 368

Fig. 369

DIAGRAM E137
COMPOSITE Corridor Carriage
Bow-ended 'Cornish Riviera' Stock
Lot 1424 of 1929
Running numbers 6017/28/33/46/8/52/8/60/3/4/9/71/86
Lot 1433 of 1930
Running numbers 6163–6
Dimensions: 61′ 4½″ x 9′ 5¾″
Condemned December 1962
These vehicles were identical in layout to *E136* but all the compartments were larger, i.e. lavatories were 5′ 0½″ against 4′ 5¼″, 1sts were 7′ 6″ instead of 7′ 3″, and 3rds were 6′ 8″ compared with 6′ 0″ on the smaller vehicles; also the *E137* carriages were 7½″ wider. They were fitted with 9′ plate bogies and provided with chromium-plated door handles.

Fig. 368 shows No. 6017 as built in 1929 with the corridor side in view, and complete with roof boards. **Fig. 369** The same vehicle in British Railways days inside Old Oak Common carriage shed in 1955, exhibiting the compartment side. In **Fig. 370** we see another of the series, No. 6069, also at Old Oak Common but in 1951. Note that when viewed from the corridor side, the first class compartments are right-handed in this example, the opposite design to No. 6017 above.

Fig. 370

Fig. 371

DIAGRAM E138
BRAKE COMPOSITE Corridor Stock
Bow-ended 'Cornish Riviera' Stock
Lot 1425 of 1929
Running numbers 6087/8/95/7/8, 6100/7/8/18/20/1/4/34/47/8/51/2/3
Dimensions: 61′ 4½″ x 9′ 5¾″
Condemned January 1962
Passenger accommodation comprised lavatory, four 3rds, two 1sts, lavatory, guard's and luggage compartment. Fitted with 9′ plate bogies.

Fig. 371 The official photograph of No. 6088 as turned out of the carriage shop in 1929, displaying roof boards reading 'Paddington and Falmouth'. **Fig. 372** depicts No. 6087 at Kingsbridge in 1950 and shows the same side as No. 6088 above but, being slightly at an angle, the door handle recesses and flat doors to the guard's compartment are seen to better advantage.

Fig. 372

Fig. 373 The compartment side of the series is shown in this picture, taken at Old Oak Common in 1951; the vehicle number is 6151.

Fig. 373

Fig. 374

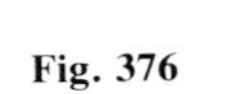

Fig. 375

DIAGRAM E140
BRAKE COMPOSITE Non-Corridor Carriage
Bow-ended Bristol Suburban Service Stock
Lot 1407 of 1930
Running numbers 6445–57/9–65
Lot 1445 of 1930
Running numbers 6523/4, 6656/7, 6703/4/22/3, 6894/5, 6995/6/9–7000
Running numbers 6381/2, 6409/10–4/70/1/3/4, 6534/5/7/8/41/2/8/9/54/5/7/8/89/90
Lot 1455 of 1931
Running numbers 6240/1/61/2, 6365/6/71/2/4/5, 6656/7, 6968/9/75/8/83/4/9/90
Dimensions: 61′ 2″ x 9′ 3″
Condemned March 1962
Passenger accommodation comprised four 3rds, one 1st, one 3rd, guard's and luggage compartment. This series was fitted with 7′ plate bogies and short buffers at the compartment ends. Two carriages would be coupled together to form a 'B' set.

No. 6969 is seen in **Fig. 374** at Brent in 1952, while **Fig. 375** illustrates No. 6265 at Liskeard in 1951.

DIAGRAM E141
COMPOSITE Non-Corridor Carriage
Bow-ended Suburban Service Stock
Lot 1405 of 1930
Running numbers 6431–4/6–43
Lot 1449 of 1930
Running numbers 6336/7/9–43/7/53/8
Lot 1456 of 1931
Running numbers 6724/31/4/44/7/50/2/4/8/61/6/8/75/80/95, 6802/4/86/92, 6929
Dimensions: 61′ 2″ x 9′ 3″
Condemned May 1962
Passenger accommodation comprised three 3rds, four 1sts, two 3rds. Fitted with 7′ bogies.

Fig. 376 shows No. 6432 resplendent in the GWR double waist line livery of 1930. Note that the coat of arms transfer is placed off-centre to avoid the door panel and jamb.

Fig. 376

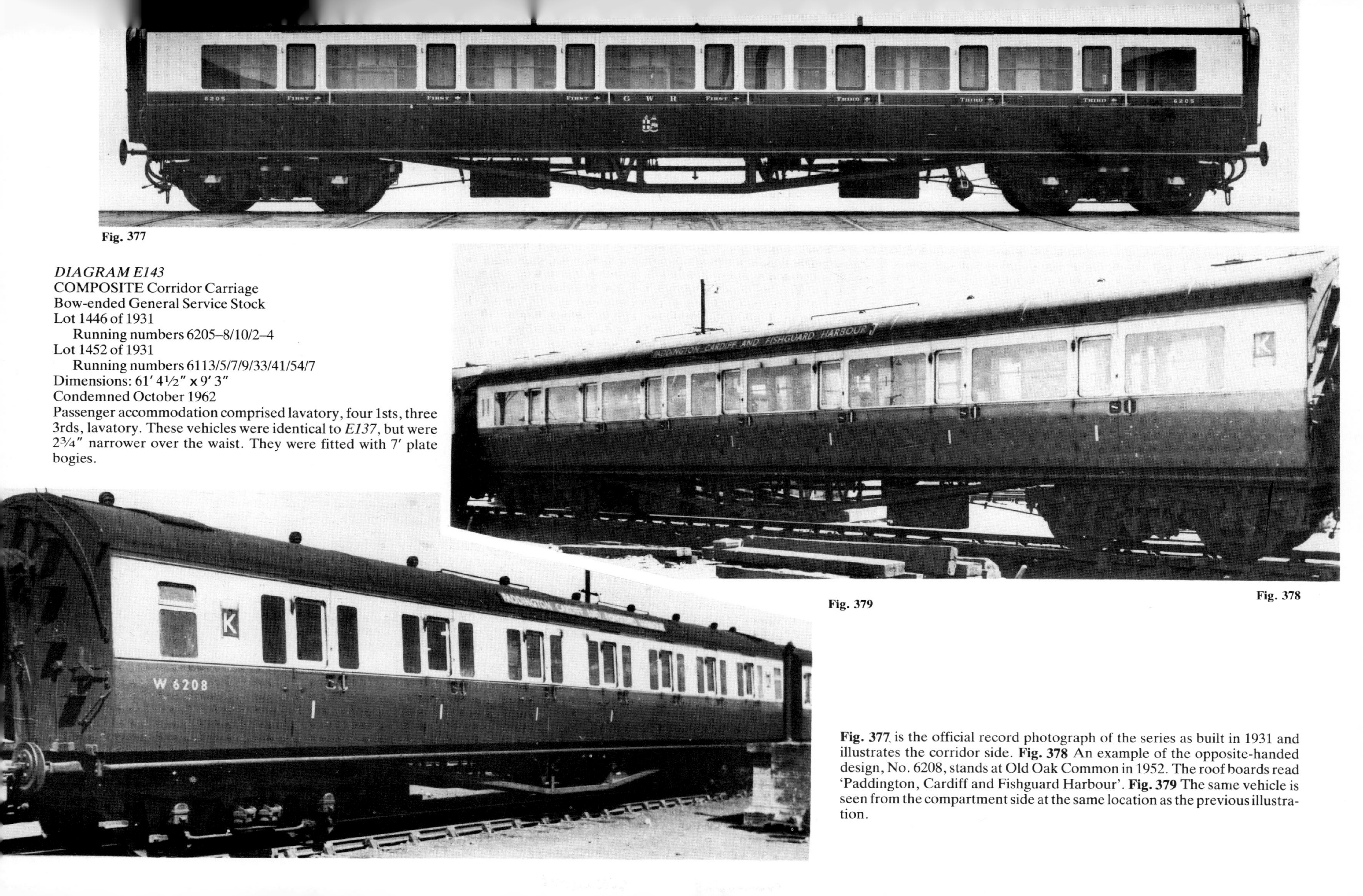

Fig. 377

DIAGRAM E143
COMPOSITE Corridor Carriage
Bow-ended General Service Stock
Lot 1446 of 1931
Running numbers 6205–8/10/2–4
Lot 1452 of 1931
Running numbers 6113/5/7/9/33/41/54/7
Dimensions: 61′ 4½″ x 9′ 3″
Condemned October 1962
Passenger accommodation comprised lavatory, four 1sts, three 3rds, lavatory. These vehicles were identical to *E137*, but were 2¾″ narrower over the waist. They were fitted with 7′ plate bogies.

Fig. 379

Fig. 378

Fig. 377 is the official record photograph of the series as built in 1931 and illustrates the corridor side. **Fig. 378** An example of the opposite-handed design, No. 6208, stands at Old Oak Common in 1952. The roof boards read 'Paddington, Cardiff and Fishguard Harbour'. **Fig. 379** The same vehicle is seen from the compartment side at the same location as the previous illustration.

Fig. 380

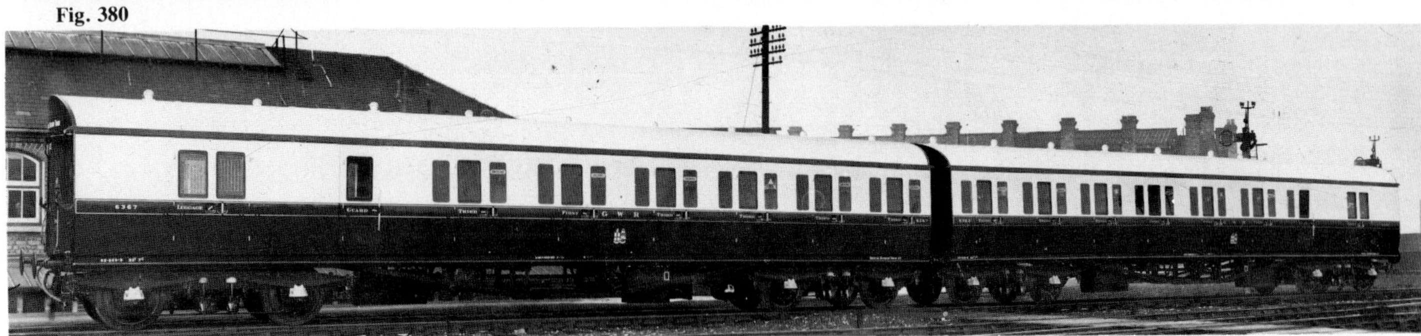

Fig. 381

DIAGRAM E145
COMPOSITE Non-Corridor Carriage
Bow-ended Stock
Lot 1479 of 1933
Running numbers 6061/75, 6122/3/59/61/8/75/80/6/8/91/3/9, 6200/2/4/15–7/9–22/4/5
Lot 1479 of 1933
Running numbers 6228/9/32/4/8/9/46/51/3/4/7/63/8/97, 6316/35/ 8/48/59/61/3/7/8/73
Dimensions: 61′ 2″ × 9′ 3″
Condemned December 1962
Passenger accommodation comprised four 3rds, one 1st, one 3rd, guard. Fitted with 9′ bogies, and short buffers at one end. These vehicles were close-coupled, and formed in pairs as 'B' sets. The series was identical to *E140*, the only variation being the provision of the 9′ bogies.

Fig. 380 illustrates the series as built in 1933. No. 6368 is seen newly painted and highly polished outside the Swindon factory, branded 'Bristol Division Train 36'. **Fig. 381** Taken at the same time and place as the previous photograph, this view shows two vehicles, Nos. 6363 and 6367, formed into a 'B' set and branded 'Bristol Division Train 21'. **Figs. 382** and **383** show the two vehicles of another 'B' set of the *E145* configuration; these were Nos. 6216 and 6217 in BR livery and photographed at Swindon.

DIAGRAM E146
BRAKE COMPOSITE Corridor Carriage
Flat-ended, High-waisted Stock
Lot 1491 of 1933
Running numbers 6579–88
Dimensions: 57′ 0″ × 9′ 0″
Condemned May 1963
Passenger accommodation comprised lavatory, four 3rds, two 1sts, lavatory, guard's and luggage compartment. Fitted with 9′ plate bogies. These had only four doors on the compartment side and were provided with narrow windows. Both battery boxes were located underneath the corridor side of the carriage.

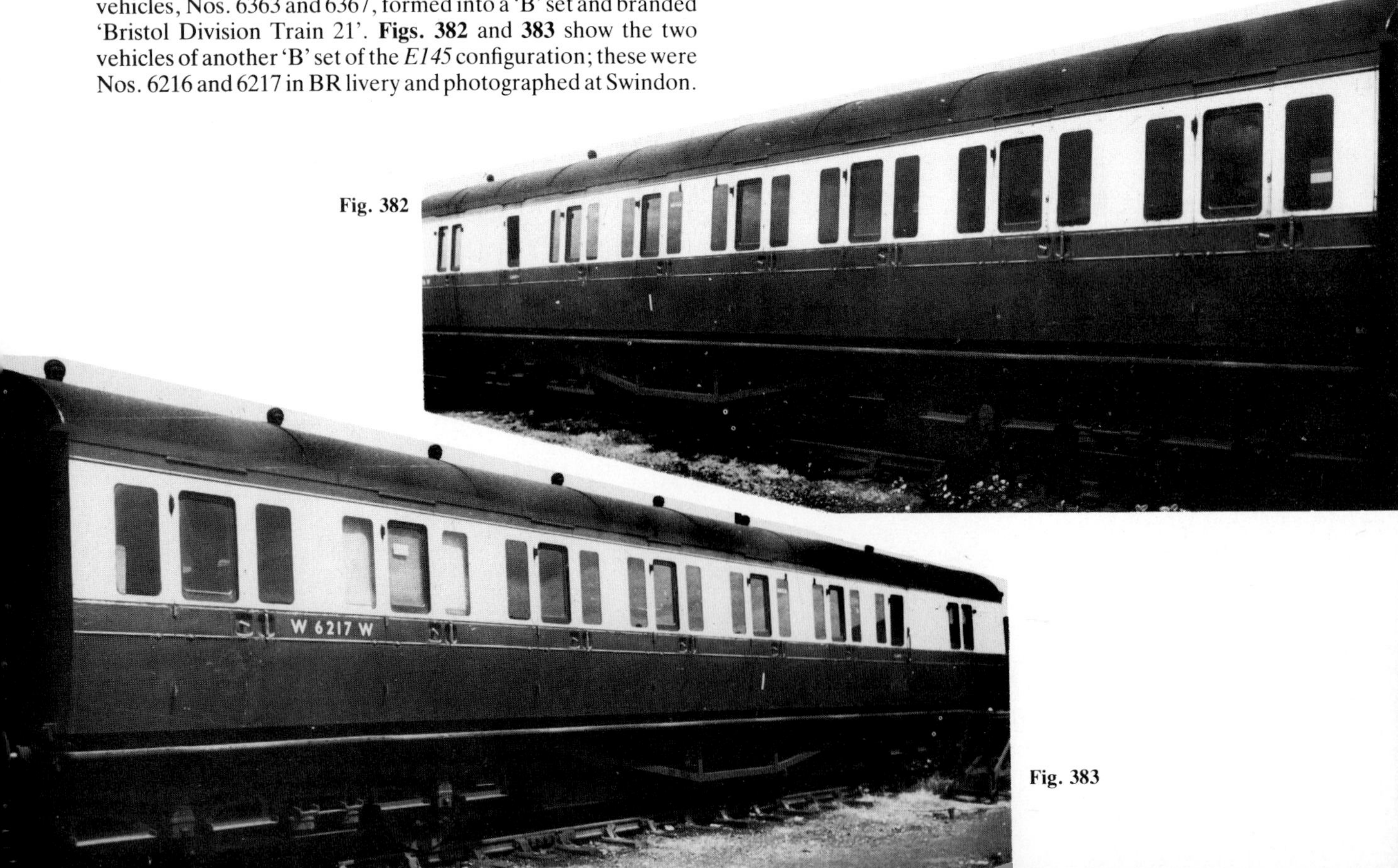

Fig. 382

Fig. 383

Fig. 384

Fig. 385

Fig. 384 shows the corridor side of No. 6583, as built with a right-hand van. **Fig. 385** The compartment side of the same vehicle.

Fig. 386 depicts No. 6793 as built in 1933. Note the short buffers at the compartment end.

DIAGRAM E147

BRAKE COMPOSITE Non-Corridor Carriage
Flat-ended Stock

Lot 1494 of 1933
Lot 1505 of 1934
Lot 1523 of 1935
Lot 1550 of 1936

see page 153 for running numbers

Dimensions: 57′ 0″ x 9′ 0″
Condemned December 1963
Passenger accommodation comprised four 3rds, one 1st, one 3rd, guard's and luggage compartment. Fitted with 9′ bogies and formed into 2-coach 'B' sets.

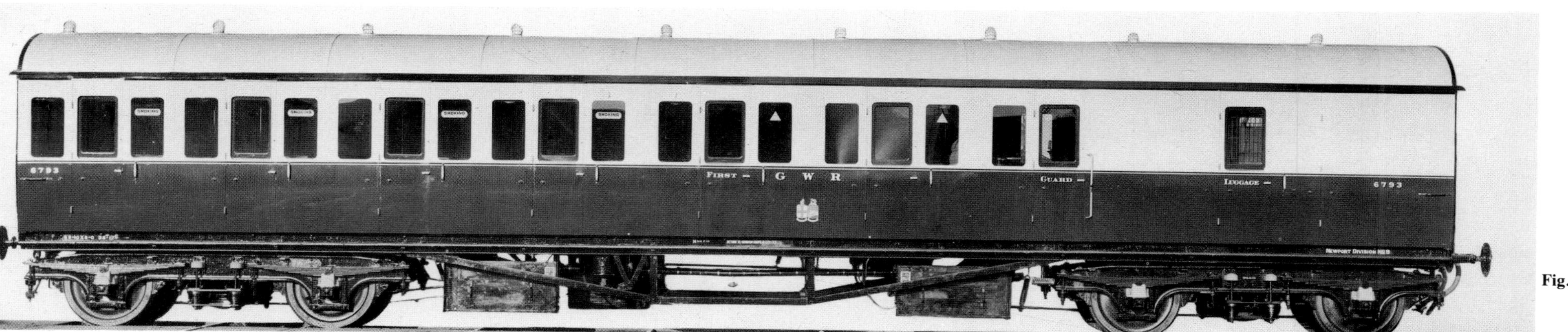

Fig. 386

Fig. 387 is the official photograph of two vehicles formed into a 'B' set for 'Llanelly No. 4'; these were Nos. 6785/6 of Lot 1494. **Fig. 388** shows two more vehicles of the series close-coupled into a 'B' set, recorded by the camera in 1936 and wearing the livery of that period. These were Nos. 6755 and 6756, branded 'Truro No. 1'.

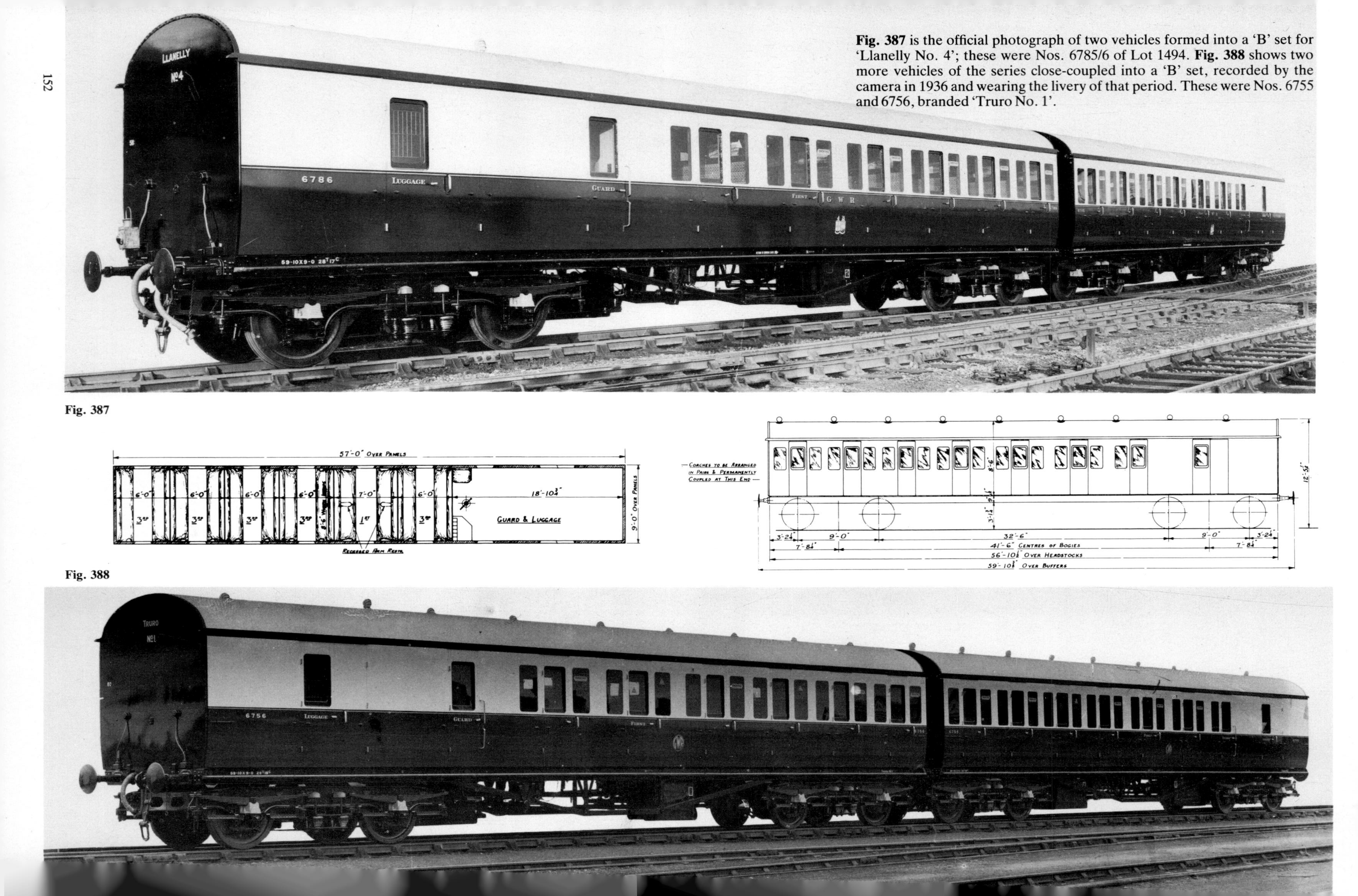

Fig. 387

Fig. 388

Fig. 389

Fig. 390

DIAGRAM E147
BRAKE COMPOSITE 'B' Set Carriages
Flat-ended Series of 1933–36
Lot 1494 of 1933
Running numbers 6762–5/9–74/6-9/81–94/6/7, 6800–1
Lot 1505 of 1934
Running numbers 6873–6/8–85/7–91/3/6–9, 6900–4/6–8
Lot 1523 of 1935
Running numbers 6803/5–17/9/21
Lot 1550 of 1936
Running numbers 6707–11/5/25–7/9/30/2/6/ 8–40/1/3/5
Running numbers 6746/8/9/51/3/5–7/9/60/7/ 98/9, 6818/20/2/3/7
Note: a few of these vehicles ran as individual coaches – 6207–10, 6822/3/7/37/8/50. Nos. 6812 and 6820 were trailer cars.

DIAGRAM E148
BRAKE COMPOSITE Corridor Carriage
Flat-ended General Service Stock
Lot 1508 of 1934
Running numbers 6909–24/7/8/30/1
Lot 1526 of 1935
Running numbers 6824–6/8/32–6/40/2–9/51/2
Dimensions: 57′ 0″ x 9′ 0″
Condemned December 1963
Passenger accommodation comprised lavatory, four 3rds, two 1sts, lavatory, guard's and luggage compartment. Fitted with 9′ pressed-steel bogies. The only apparent difference between *E148* and *E146* was that the guard's door was only fitted with a single light.

Fig. 389 illustrates the compartment side of No. 6909 as built at Swindon in 1934 and **Fig. 390** shows the corridor side of the same vehicle. In **Fig. 391**, No. 6836 is seen at Old Oak Common in 1951 in BR strawberry and cream livery.

Fig. 391

Fig. 392

8'-6"
12'-5⅜"
3'-1¾" 9¼"
3'-2¼" 9'-0" 35'-6" 9'-0" 3'-2¼"
7'-8¼" 44'-6" BOGIE CENTRES 7'-8¼"
59'-10½" OVER HEADSTOCKS
63'-6½" OVER BUFFERS.

DIAGRAM E149
COMPOSITE Corridor Carriage
'Centenary' Stock
Lot 1538 of 1935
Running number 6658–61
Dimensions: 61′ 4½″ x 9′ 7″
Condemned January 1965
Passenger accommodation comprised lavatory, four 1sts, three 3rds. Fitted with 9′ pressed-steel bogies and provided with doors at the ends only.

This stock was built in 1935 to commemorate the 100 years existence of the GWR, 1835–1935, and two complete sets were eventually constructed for use in the 'Limited' (the 'Cornish Riviera Express'). Fuller details can be found in *A Pictorial Record of the Great Western Coaches, Part 2*, published by OPC.

Fig. 392 shows the compartment side of No. 6659 at Old Oak Common in 1951 in BR livery. **Fig. 393** No. 6660 was also at Old Oak in 1951, but this time with the corridor side towards the camera.

Fig. 393

Fig. 394

DIAGRAM E151
COMPOSITE Corridor Carriage
Flat-ended 'Sunshine' Stock
Lot 1553 of 1936
Running numbers 6853–8
Lot 1560 of 1936
Running numbers 6606/7/11/2/4/7/8/20/2/3
Dimensions: 58′ 7″ x 9′ 0″
Passenger accommodation comprised lavatory, three 1sts, four 3rds, lavatory. Fitted with 9′ pressed-steel bogies.

Fig. 394 illustrates the compartment side of No. 6858 at Old Oak in 1952.

DIAGRAM E152
BRAKE COMPOSITE Corridor Carriage
Flat-ended Large-window Stock
Lot 1557 of 1936
Running numbers 6859–62, 6925/32/40/65/7/71/3/81/2/5/8/91–4/7
Dimensions: 60′ 11¼″ x 9′ 0″
Passenger accommodation comprised lavatory, four 3rds, two 1sts, lavatory, guard's and luggage compartment. Fitted with 9′ pressed-steel bogies.

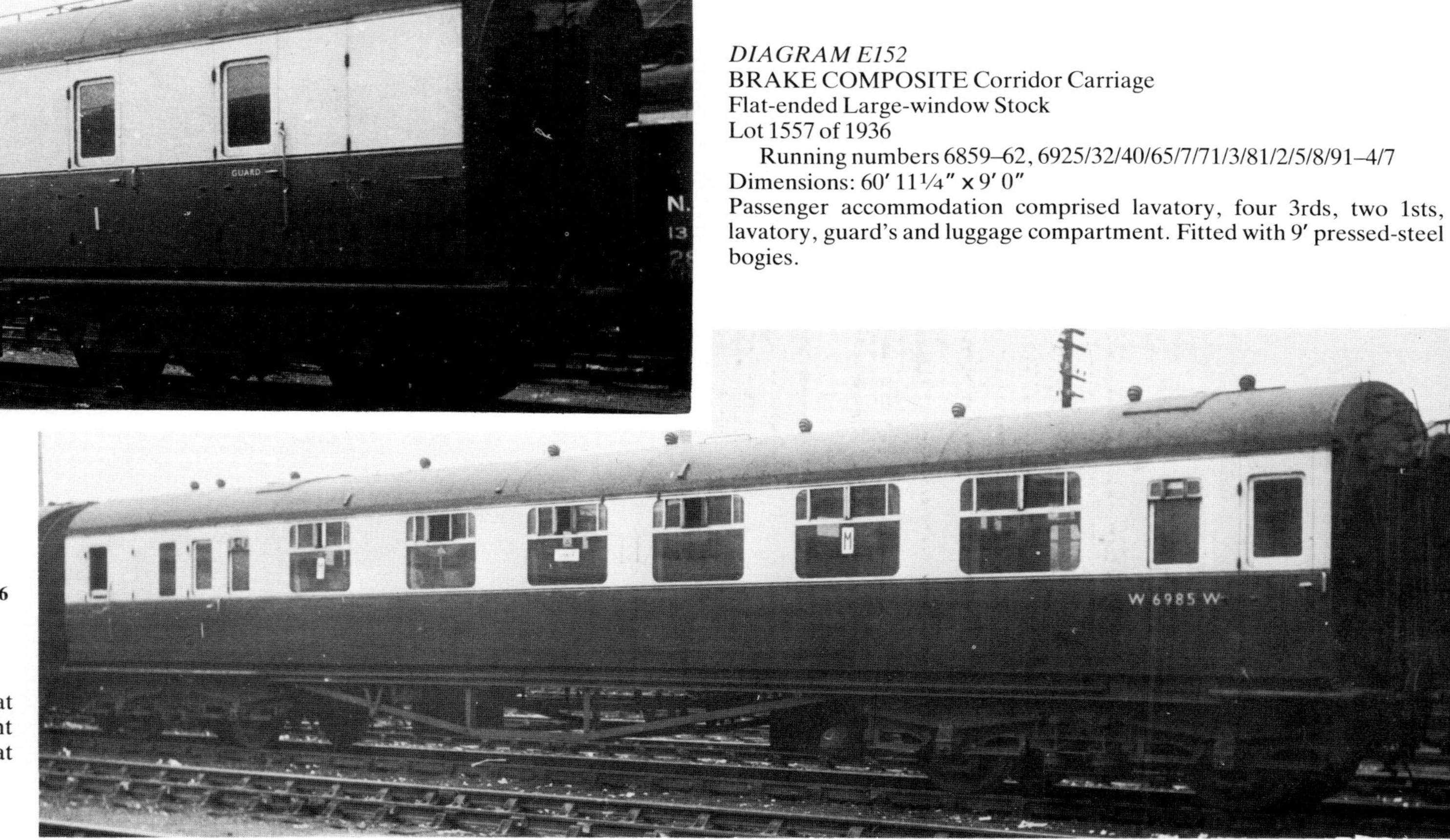

Fig. 395

Fig. 396

Fig. 395 depicts the van end and corridor side of No. 6992 at Old Oak in 1951. The third class end and the compartment side can be seen in this view (**Fig. 396**) of No. 6985 at Old Oak in 1956.

Fig. 397

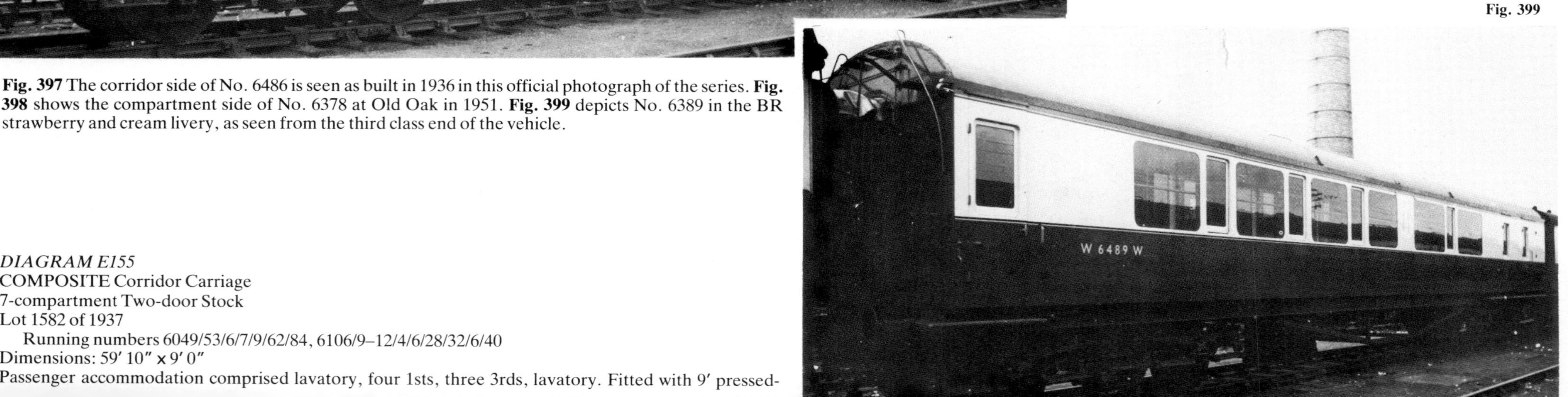

Fig. 398

Fig. 399

DIAGRAM E153
BRAKE COMPOSITE Corridor Carriage
Large-window Four-door Stock
Lot 1572 of 1936
Running numbers 6378/9/84/5/97, 6400/6/7/66/7/72–4/84/6/9/90/6/9, 6529
Dimensions: 60′ 11¼″ x 9′ 0″
Passenger accommodation comprised lavatory, four 3rds, two 1sts, guard's and luggage compartment. This series was almost identical to *E152*, the difference being 1¼″ in width over the handles.

Fig. 397 The corridor side of No. 6486 is seen as built in 1936 in this official photograph of the series. **Fig. 398** shows the compartment side of No. 6378 at Old Oak in 1951. **Fig. 399** depicts No. 6389 in the BR strawberry and cream livery, as seen from the third class end of the vehicle.

DIAGRAM E155
COMPOSITE Corridor Carriage
7-compartment Two-door Stock
Lot 1582 of 1937
Running numbers 6049/53/6/7/9/62/84, 6106/9–12/4/6/28/32/6/40
Dimensions: 59′ 10″ x 9′ 0″
Passenger accommodation comprised lavatory, four 1sts, three 3rds, lavatory. Fitted with 9′ pressed-

Fig. 400

Fig. 401

Fig. 400 shows No. 6059 as built in 1937, with the corridor side on view. **Fig. 401** illustrates No. 6111 at Swindon in 1942. The photograph illustrates the wartime livery of milk chocolate brown with straw coloured lining on the compartment side. **Fig. 402** The corridor side of No. 6059 at Old Oak Common in 1952. **Fig. 403** illustrates the compartment side of the same vehicle at the same location.

Fig. 402

Fig. 403

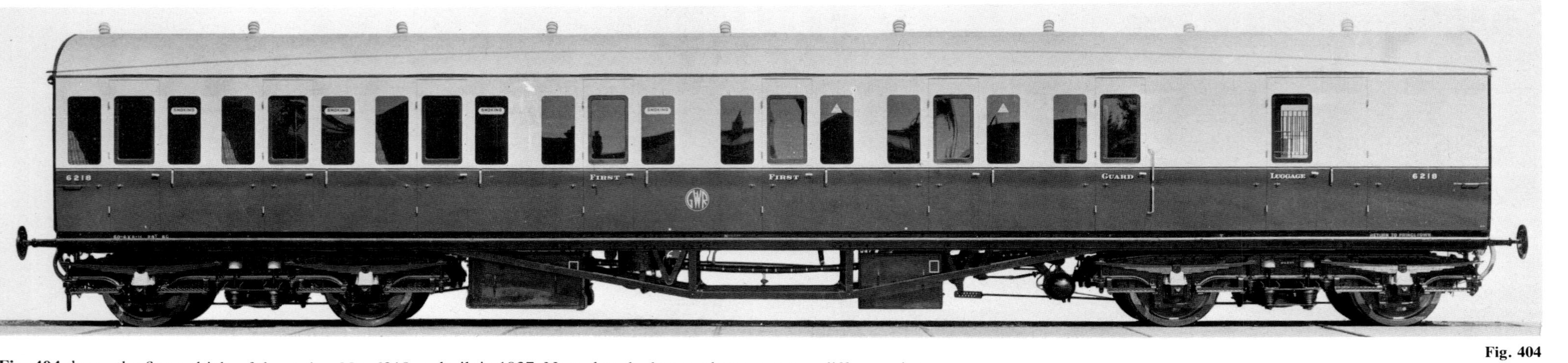

Fig. 404

Fig. 404 shows the first vehicle of the series, No. 6218, as built in 1937. Note that the battery boxes are two different sizes.

Fig. 405

Fig. 405 is the official Swindon photograph of the series as built in 1938, with corridor side of No. 7022 nearest the camera.

Fig. 406 shows one of the same series in 1949 in the then-new BR livery with grey roof.

Fig. 406

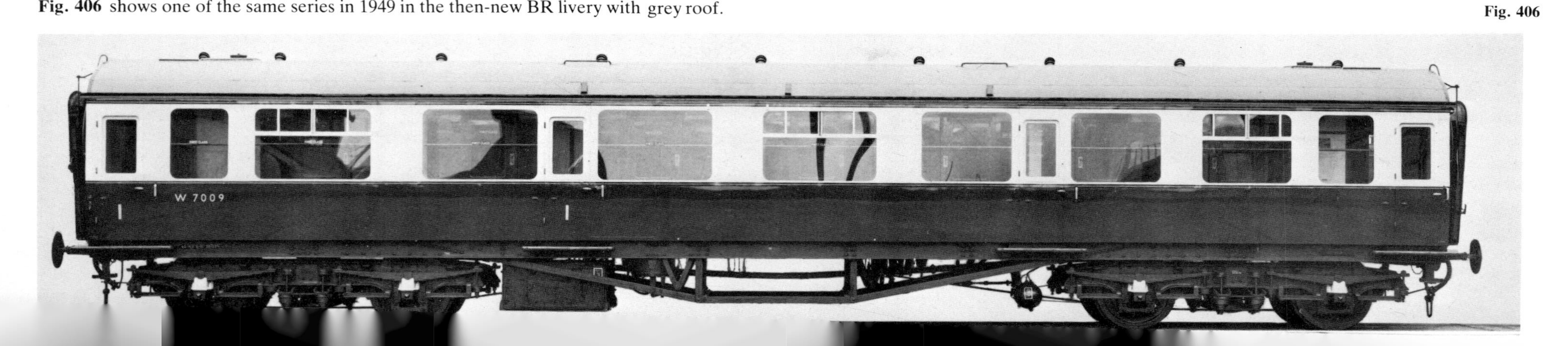

◁ *DIAGRAM E157*
BRAKE COMPOSITE Non-Corridor Carriage
Suburban Service Stock

Lot 1568 of 1937
Running numbers 6218/23/6/7/30/43–5/65/96, 6300/3/5/7/9/12/3/4/7/8
Dimensions: 57′ 0″ x 8′ 11″
Condemned November 1963

Passenger accommodation comprised three 3rds, two 1sts, one 3rd, guard's and luggage compartment. These vehicles therefore differed from the *E147* series in having an additional first class compartment in place of a third class compartment. They were fitted with 9′ pressed-steel bogies.

DIAGRAM E158
COMPOSITE Corridor Carriage
Lot 1587 of 1938
Running numbers 7001–56

Lot 1621 of 1940
Running numbers 7301–40
Dimensions: 59′ 10″ x 8′ 11″

Passenger accommodation comprised lavatory, four 1sts, three 3rds, lavatory. Fitted with 9′ pressed-steel bogies and provided with four doors on the corridor side and two doors on the compartment side.

Fig. 407

Fig. 408

DIAGRAM E158

Fig. 407 No. 7028 at Old Oak Common in 1951, with the compartment side nearest the viewer. **Fig. 408** Taken at the same site and date as the previous photograph, this depicts the opposite end of No. 7026. This coach was formed in the 'Bristolian', hence the 'Paddington and Bristol' roof boards. **Fig. 409** is inserted so that liveries may be compared. This 1947 picture of No. 7318 shows the GWR's last style of coat of arms, etc. Painting was chocolate and cream (although it would be more realistic to describe this as milk chocolate and daffodil yellow!). The carriage had double black and gold waist lining and the tops of the axleboxes were sky blue.

Fig. 409

Fig. 410

DIAGRAM E159
BRAKE COMPOSITE Corridor Carriage
Main Line Stock
Lot 1589 of 1938
Running numbers 6355/6, 6408/21/85/7, 6533/9/40/3/4/6/50/2/9/62/4/95/9, 6600/3/5/8–10/9, 6705/6/13, 6829
Lot 1590 of 1938
Running numbers 7060–4
Lot 1622 of 1939
Running numbers 7341–6, specially fitted for coupling to Pullman gangways
Lot 1640 of 1941
Running numbers 7357–71

Dimensions: 60′ 11¼″ x 8′ 11″
Passenger accommodation comprised lavatory, four 3rds, two 1sts, lavatory, guard's and luggage compartment. Fitted with 9′ pressed-steel bogies.

Fig. 410 is the official picture of the series, taken at Swindon in 1938. No. 6487 is seen with the corridor side facing the camera. **Fig. 411** Old Oak Common is the location for this picture of the van end and corridor side of No. 7062 in 1952. **Fig. 412** The compartment side of No. 7062 at the same place and time as the previous photograph.

Fig. 411

Fig. 412

DIAGRAM E159

Fig. 413 is the official photograph of No. 7061, taken expressly to illustrate the special gangway fitted to five vehicles of this series to enable the stock to connect up with Pullman gangways. The photograph also shows several other details, such as the end steps and handrail to the roof; note that the latter has a straight section and does not follow the curve of the roof. Also of interest is the small feature handed down of the first left-hand step being fixed upside down to all its fellows. This was to clear the tail lamp when being placed on or off the bracket immediately below.

Fig. 414

DIAGRAM E162
COMPOSITE Corridor Carriage
Main Line Stock
Lot 1639 of 1941
Running numbers 7271–90
Dimensions: 59′ 10″ x 8′ 11″
Passenger accommodation comprised lavatory, four 1sts, three 3rds, lavatory. Provided with four doors on the corridor side and three doors on the compartment side, and fitted with 9′ pressed-steel bogies.

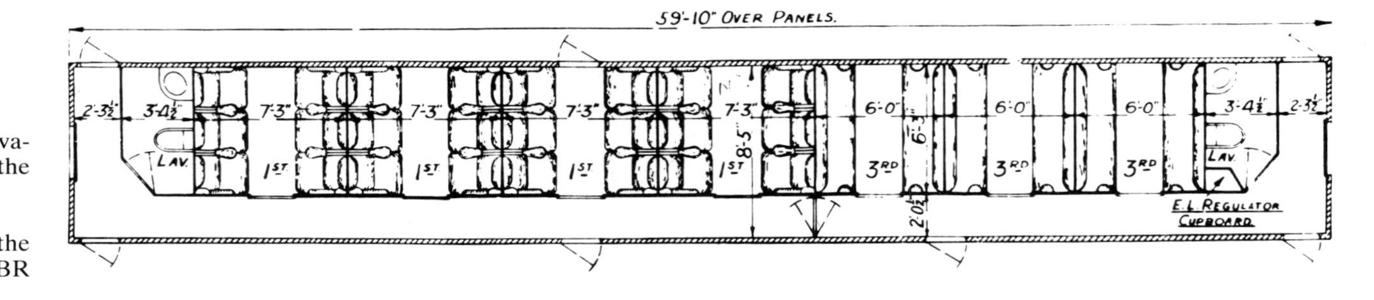

Fig. 414 shows No. 7276 as built in 1941, with the corridor side nearest the camera. **Fig. 415** No. 7283, photographed in 1947, but already painted in BR livery.

Fig. 415

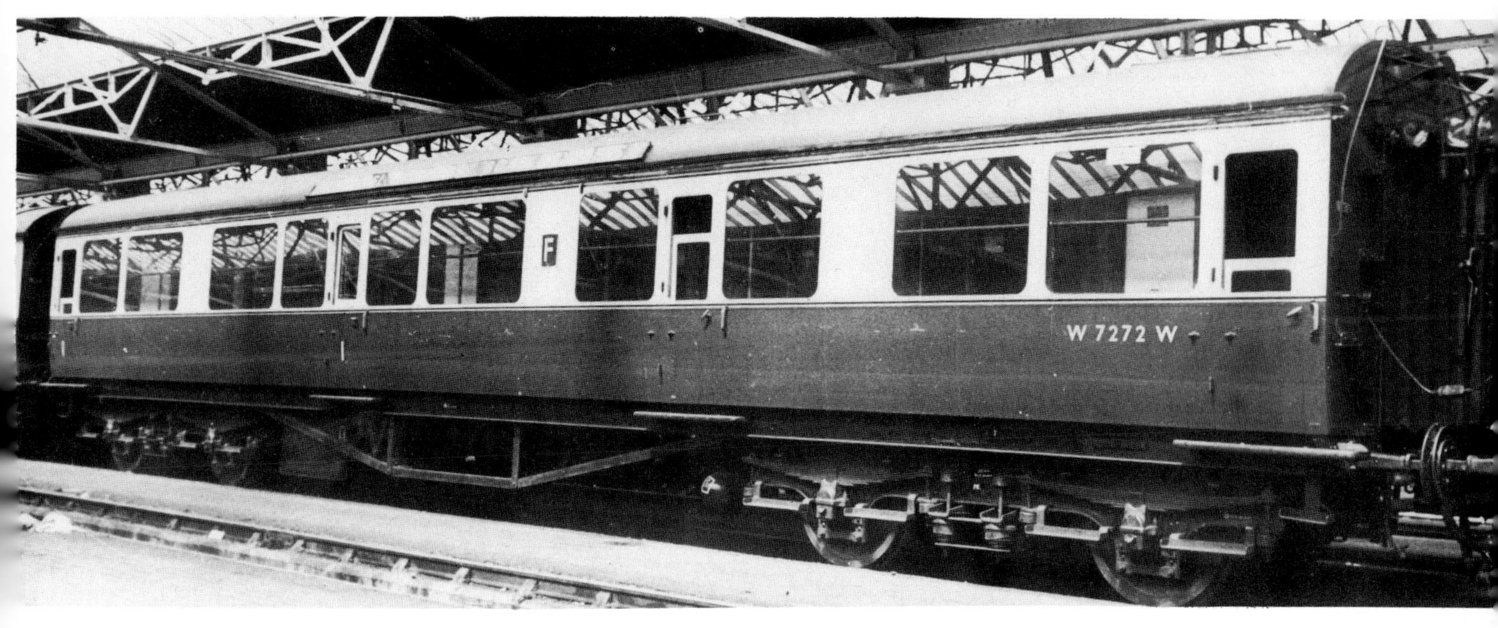

Fig. 416

DIAGRAM E162

Fig. 416 depicts the corridor side of No. 7272 inside the carriage shed at Old Oak Common in 1951. The wording on the roof boards is 'Channel Islands Boat Express'. **Fig. 417** shows the compartment side of No. 7282 and illustrates well the three-door pattern on this side of the series. The legend 'Paddington and Bristol' is carried on the roof boards.

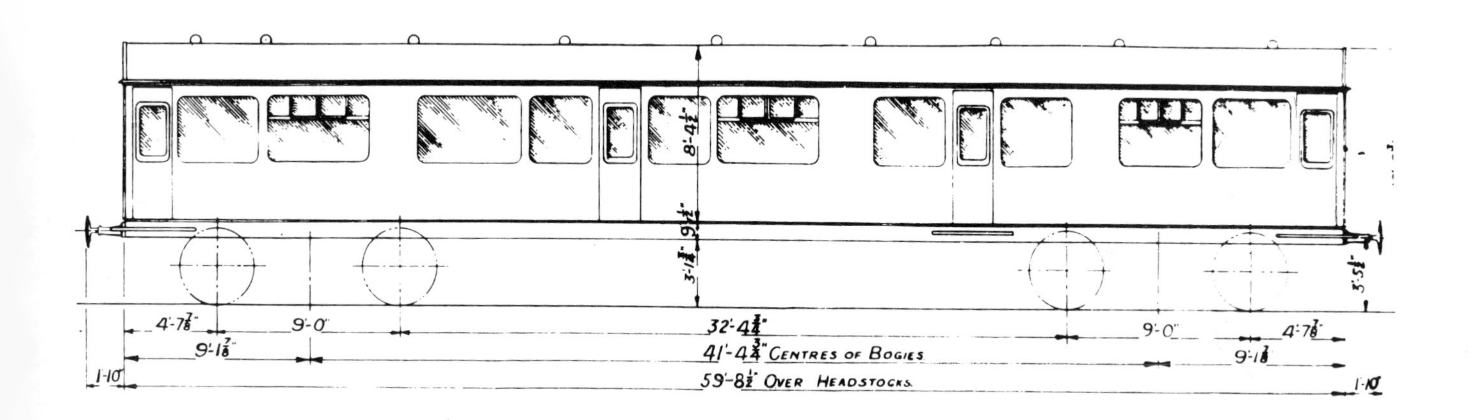

Fig. 417

Fig. 418

DIAGRAM E163
COMPOSITE Corridor Carriage
Angle-ended, Dome-roofed 'Hawksworth' Stock
Lot 1689 of 1947
Running numbers 7252–62
Dimensions: 64′ 0″ x 8′ 11″
Passenger accommodation comprised lavatory, four 1sts, three 3rds, lavatory. Fitted with 9′ pressed-steel bogies.

Fig. 418 illustrates the corridor side of No. 7252 as built in 1947, and wearing the last GWR livery. Note that the battery boxes were mounted centrally, one on each side. **Fig. 419** gives a good view of the compartment side of No. 7252 at Old Oak Common in 1952. The cantrail boards read 'Paddington, Cardiff and Fishguard Harbour'.

Fig. 419

The corridor side of the same vehicle is seen in **Fig. 420**, taken at the same location and date as the previous picture.

Fig. 420

Fig. 421

DIAGRAM E164
BRAKE COMPOSITE Corridor Carriage
Angle-ended, Dome-roofed 'Hawksworth' Stock
Lot 1690 of 1948
Running numbers 7372–85
Lot 1705 of 1948
Running numbers 7838–47
Lot 1738 of 1950
Running numbers 7848–67
Dimensions: 64′ 0″ x 8′ 11″
Passenger accommodation comprised lavatory, four 3rds, two 1sts, lavatory, vestibule, guard's and luggage compartment. Fitted with 9′ pressed-steel bogies.

Fig. 422

Fig. 421 The compartment side is seen in this view of No. 7372 standing on the carriage turntable at Old Oak Common in 1951. **Fig. 422** is the Swindon official picture of No. 7383 as built in 1948, showing the corridor side in the first BR livery. **Fig. 423** depicts the van end and compartment side of No. 7844, also at Old Oak Common in 1951.

Fig. 423

Fig. 424

DIAGRAM E165
COMPOSITE Corridor Carriage
Angle-ended, Dome-roofed 'Hawksworth' Stock
Lot 1704 of 1949
Running numbers 7798–7816
Lot 1737 of 1950
Running numbers 7818–7822
This series was identical to *E163*.

66'-8" OVER BUFFERS
63'-0" OVER CORNERS
64'-0" OVER PANELS AT ENDS
E.L. REGULATOR CUPBOARD
LAV

Fig. 424 illustrates No. 7799 in the first style of painting for Western Region coaches, namely chocolate and cream with double waist line and lead grey roof. The photograph is dated 1949. **Fig. 425** shows No. 7804 of the same series but painted in the BR crimson lake and cream livery with single waist line, irreverently known as 'blood and custard'.

Fig. 425

Fig. 426

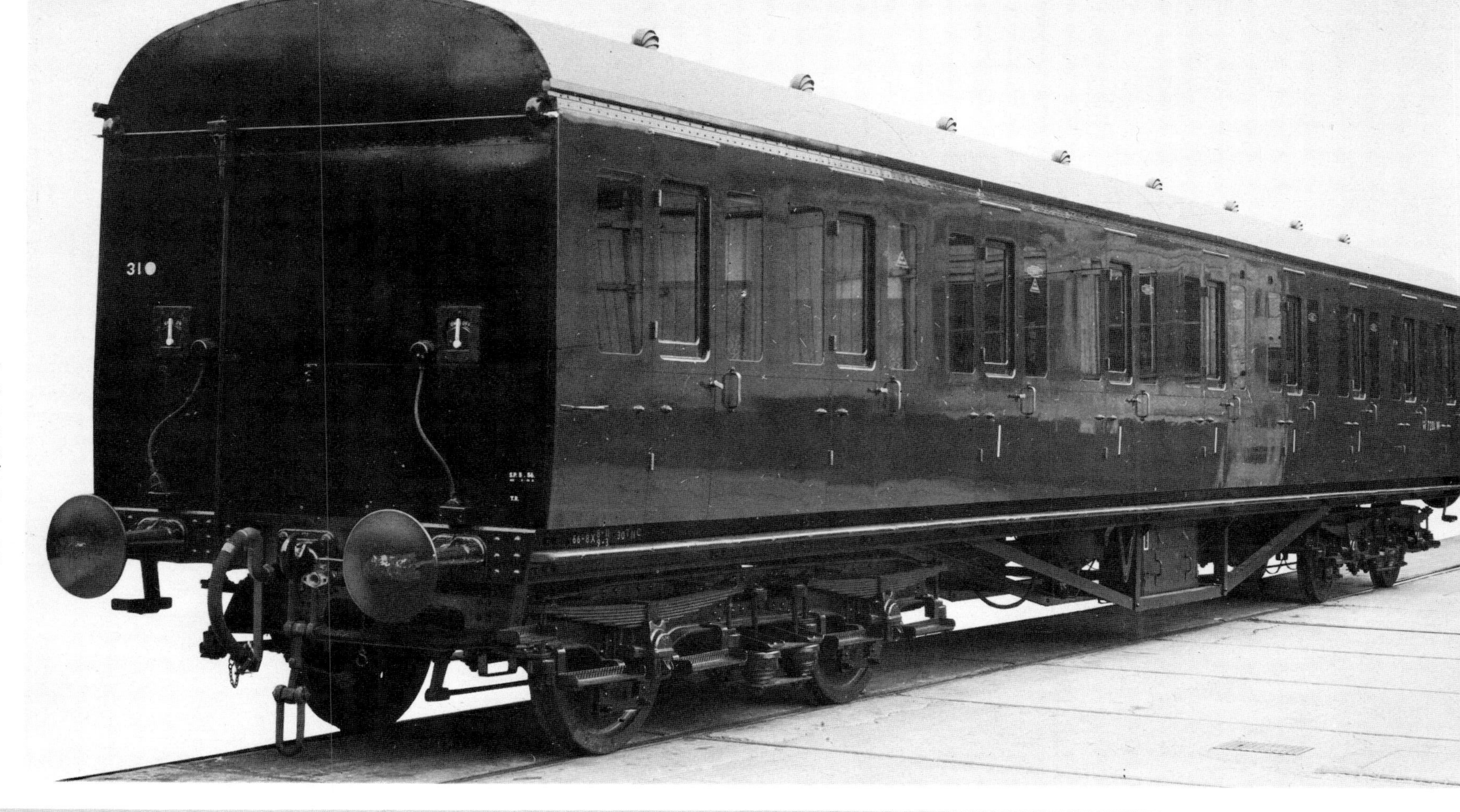

DIAGRAM E166
COMPOSITE Non-Corridor Carriage
Flat-ended 9-compartment Stock
Lot 1762 of 1952
Running numbers 7173–82
Lot 1767 of 1953
Running numbers 7183–7208
Dimensions: 63′ 0¾″ x 8′ 11″
Passenger accommodation comprised two 3rds, five 1sts, two 3rds.

Fig. 426 The official three-quarter view of the series, which shows the end details of No. 7201 well, including the electric lighting switches. **Fig. 427** A broadside view of the same vehicle. Note that one battery box is positioned in the centre of the carriage and one is off-set. At this time, the coach was painted in BR maroon with straw-coloured lettering, lead grey roof, and black underframes and ends.

Fig. 427

BR DIAGRAM B
COMPOSITE Corridor Carriage
BR Standard Mk1 Stock of 1951

Fig. 428 The compartment side of vehicle No. W15059, built at Eastleigh for the Western Region to Lot 30022, and photographed in strawberry and cream livery with lead grey roof. Note the hinged automatic coupling. **Fig. 429** A broadside view of BR Standard Mk1 coach No. W15425, an example of the series built under Lot 30076, and showing the corridor side.

Fig. 428

Fig. 429

Fig. 430

Swindon-built for LM Region to pre-war diagram.
COMPOSITE Non-Corridor Carriage
9-compartment Stock

Lot 1479 of 1953
Running numbers M16797–16841
Lot 1772 of 1953
Running numbers M16842–16876
Dimensions: 59′ 3½″ x 8′ 11″
Fitted with 9′ pressed-steel bogies.

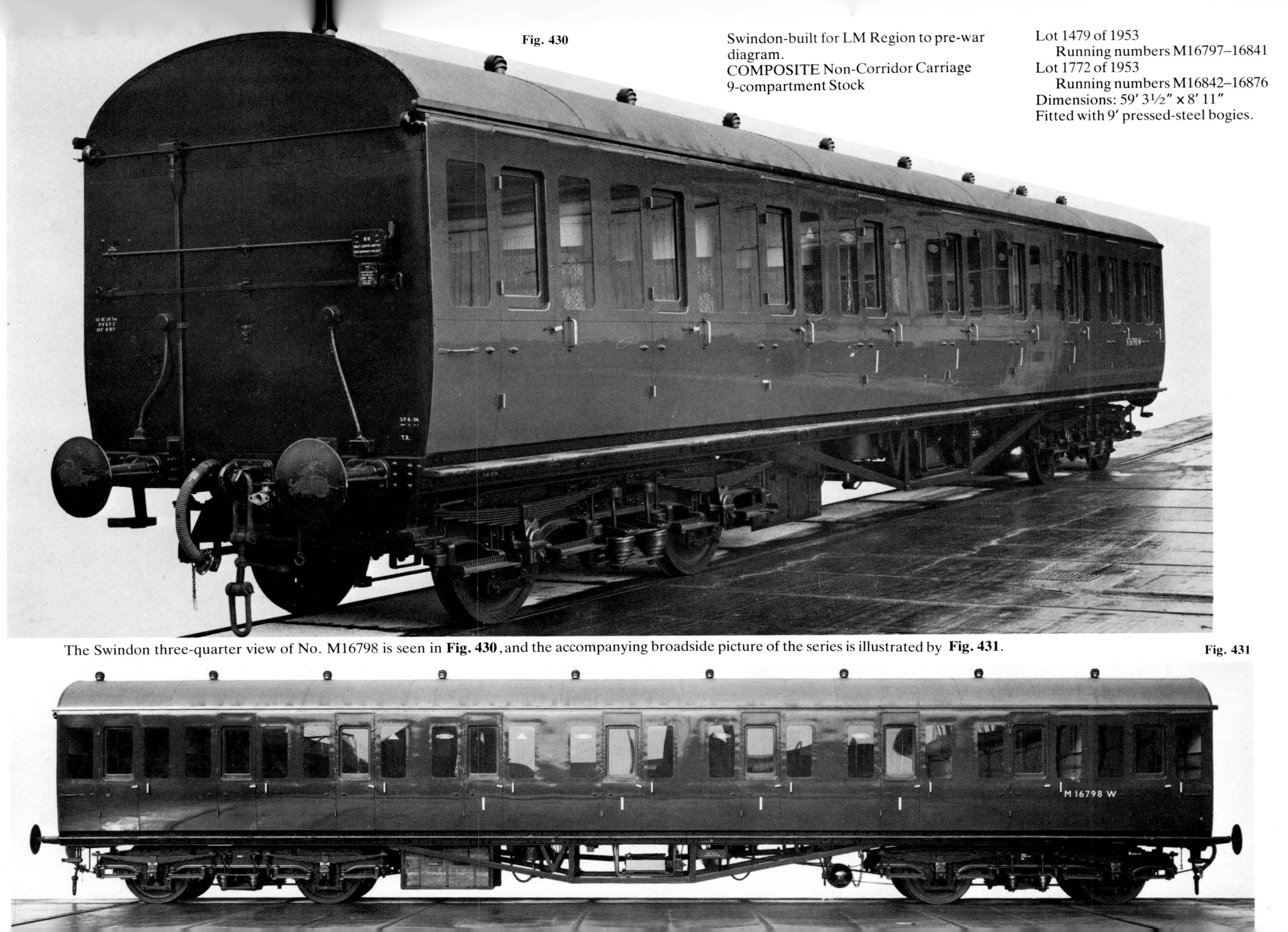

The Swindon three-quarter view of No. M16798 is seen in **Fig. 430**, and the accompanying broadside picture of the series is illustrated by **Fig. 431**.

Fig. 431

Fig. 432

DIAGRAM BR 126
COMPOSITE Corridor Carriage
Swindon-built BR Standard Mk1 Stock of 1953 BR Lot 30005

Fig. 432 The corridor side of No. W15086 is seen in this photograph carrying BR strawberry and cream livery. **Fig. 433** A fine three-quarter view of the same vehicle.

Fig. 433

BRAKE COMPOSITE
Narrow Gauge Stock

Welshpool & Llanfair/Cambrian Railways stock, later absorbed by the Great Western Railway. Bogie carriage No. 1 is illustrated in **Fig. 434**, showing first and third class saloons, guard's compartment, and verandahs at each end.

Fig. 434

Fig. 435

COACH INTERIORS

1890/91

Two early pictures of the seating arrangements inside bogie clerestory stock. **Fig. 435** shows the interior of the first corridor train's 3rd class vehicle No. 255 of 1890. Although the quality of the negative is very poor, it was thought of sufficient interest to be included. **Fig. 436** gives a good view of the normal internal seating of a standard clerestory carriage. The actual vehicle concerned is No. 7067, a slip coach of *Diagram F5*, Lot 601 of 1891. However, I must add that this photograph was not taken until 1932 when the vehicle was completely renovated. Note that the clerestory glass panels in the roof have been painted over, also the ventilator in the clerestory is non-functional.

Fig. 436

Fig. 437

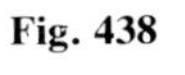

Fig. 438

1900

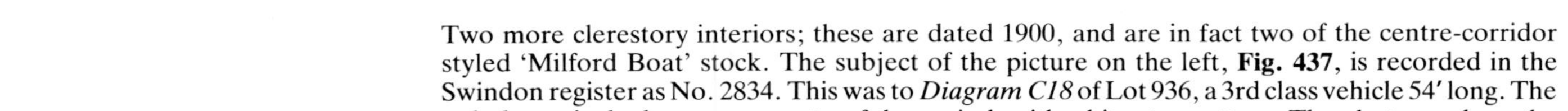

Two more clerestory interiors; these are dated 1900, and are in fact two of the centre-corridor styled 'Milford Boat' stock. The subject of the picture on the left, **Fig. 437**, is recorded in the Swindon register as No. 2834. This was to *Diagram C18* of Lot 936, a 3rd class vehicle 54′ long. The upholstery is the brown moquette of the period, with white star pattern. The photograph on the right, **Fig. 438**, portrays one of the Brake 3rds of the same series for the Irish boat service from Milford Haven. These were to the *D32 Diagram* of Lot 935.

1911

Fig. 439

These two pictures illustrate the seating and upholstery in one of the non-corridor composites, constructed for the Birmingham service in 1911. The carriage concerned was No. 6597, one of the *E89* series, built in 1911 under Lot 1187. **Fig. 439** shows the 3rd class compartment in which the trim was dark blue rep with a pattern of red triangles. Note that at this period the 3 indicating third class was transferred on to the door. **Fig. 440** depicts the 1st class accommodation of the same series. The upholstery was of a dark green cloth with walnut woodwork and a floral patterned carpet.

Fig. 440

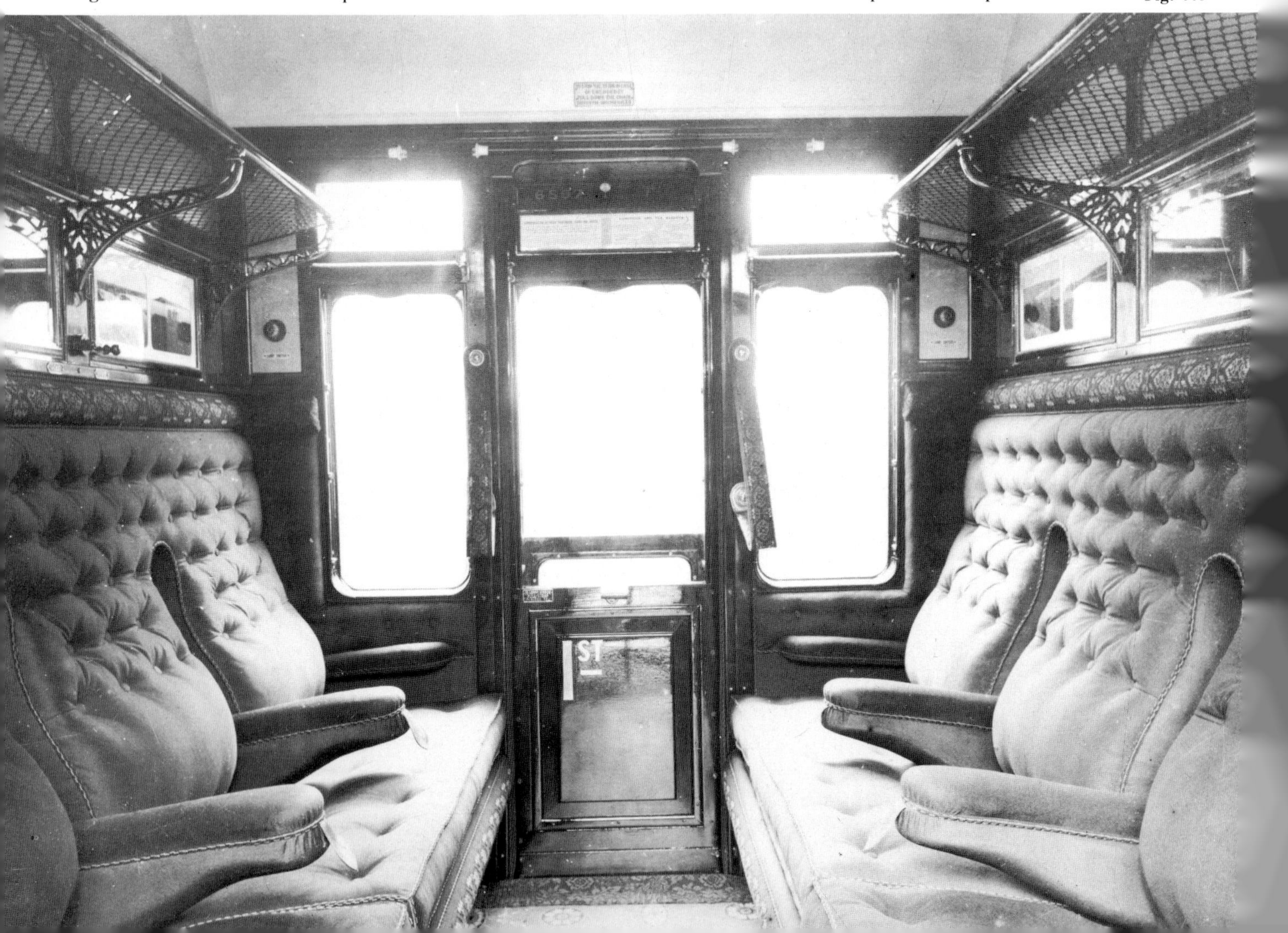

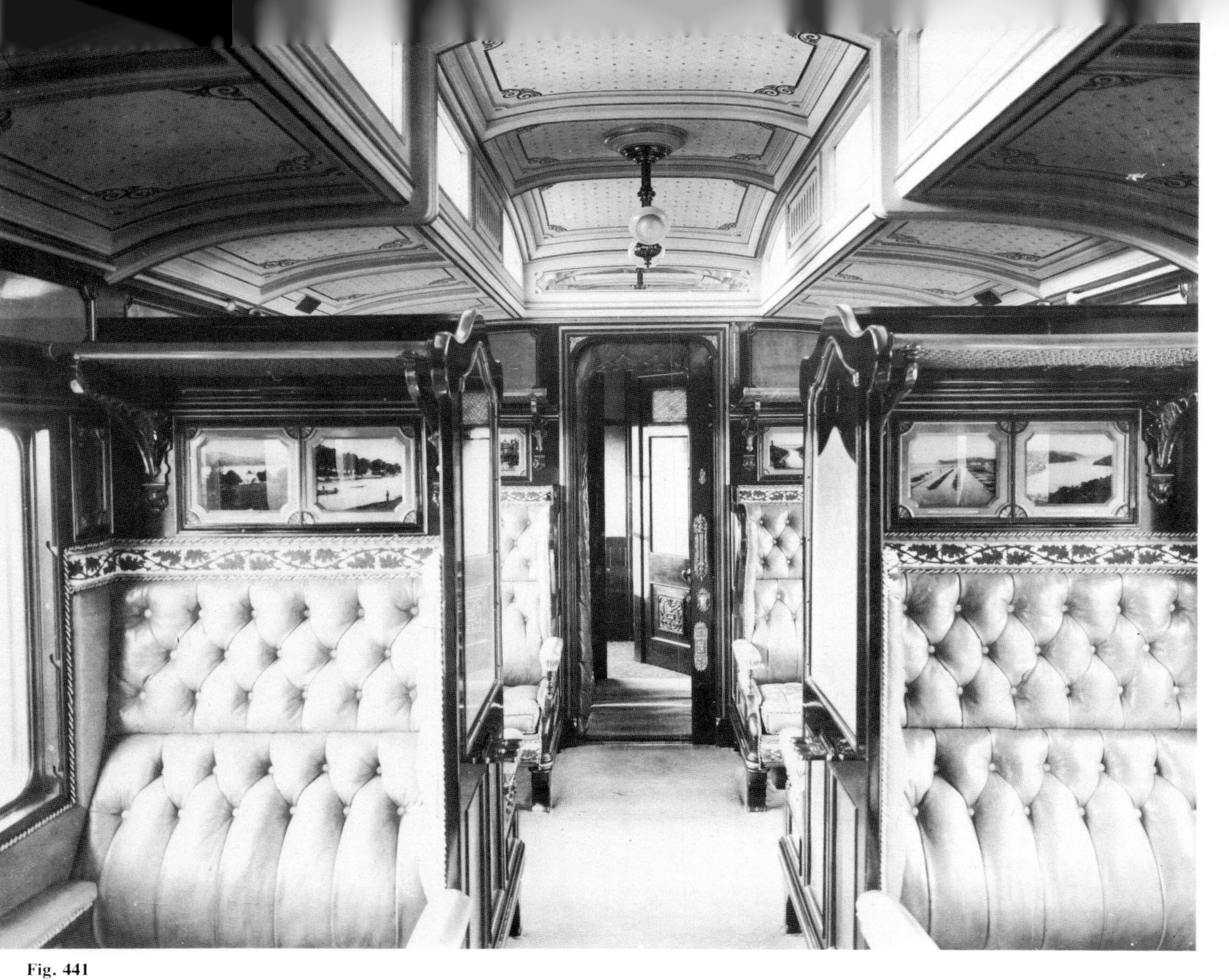

Fig. 441

Although slightly out of sequence, I considered readers would be interested in these two pictures of the Royal carriages of the GWR as they do show the magnificent coachwork which was built into these vehicles. **Fig. 441** illustrates the interior of No. 8283, the single carriage which was constructed to *Diagram A5*. Just note that superb decor on the clerestory roof. **Fig. 442** is an unusual view of the side corridor of No. 234, another of the 'Royal' series, with a lavish use of mahogany and gold filigree.

Fig. 442

Fig. 443

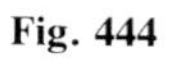

Fig. 444

1923

These two pictures show the interior design of the main line stock in the 1923 period. **Fig. 443** The 1st class compartment of No. 7958, one of the *E133 Diagram* Brake composites. The trim was of a dark chocolate with gold piping and white linen antimacassars.

Note the soft leather arm slings on each side of the sliding corridor door. **Fig. 444** shows the 3rd class interior of the same series of vehicles, the upholstery being a black-patterned red rep with light brown linoleum as a floor covering.

Fig. 445

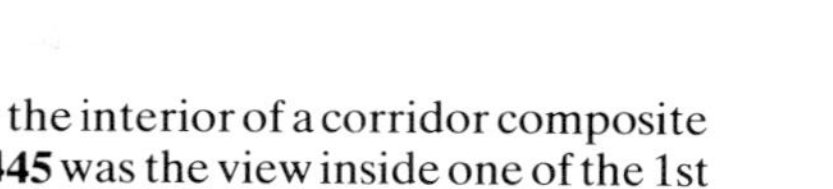

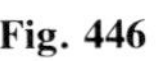

Fig. 446

1928

Jumping ahead five more years, the next four illustrations show the interior of a corridor composite carriage, No. 6076 of the *E132 Diagram* built to Lot 1382. **Fig. 445** was the view inside one of the 1st class compartments looking in towards the corridor side. The seat covering here was in a dark brown unpatterned cloth with yellow and brown piping. The carpet was a lighter shade of brown, marked 'GWR' and with edges in a darker chocolate. **Fig. 446** shows the same compartment, but looking out towards the compartment outer door. Note the scenes through the windows. These were, of course, stripped on to the negative afterwards, but were, nevertheless, very well executed.

Fig. 447

Fig. 448

1928

Two photographs of the interior furnishing of the 3rd class accommodation of the corridor composite No. 6076. **Fig. 447** depicts the outer side and door of the compartment with the upholstery in rep having a pattern of black, yellow and red. Above the door, on either side, can be seen the emergency cord and note that at this time, blinds were fitted to all windows and doors within the compartments, neatly rolled up in hidden cavities at the top of the lights. **Fig. 448** illustrates the same compartment but looking out towards the corridor. Immediately above the sliding door were the two switches for the electric lighting. The door straps were of course for lowering the windows.

Fig. 449

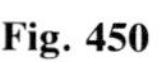

Fig. 450

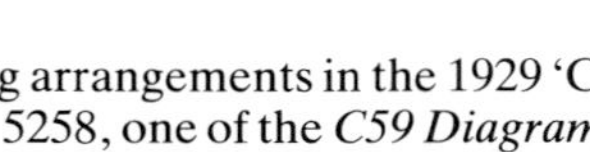

1929

These two illustrations give a good idea of the 3rd class seating arrangements in the 1929 'Cornish Riviera' stock. **Fig. 449** shows the corridor side of vehicle No. 5258, one of the *C59 Diagram* series under Lot 1426. With the exception of a slightly different pattern in the seating trim, the layout was identical to that of the previous page. **Fig. 450** shows the side looking towards the compartment door. Note the blank windows resulting from the lack of 'scenery' treatment.

Fig. 451

Fig. 452

1929

First class interiors of the 1929 'Cornish Riviera' series. These two pictures were taken inside one of the corridor composites, No. 6063 of the *Diagram E137* built under Lot 1424. Both pictures are looking outwards towards the outer compartment doors. **Fig. 451** shows the usual layout, with the fold away arm-rests and with light switches in each corner. **Fig. 452** taken inside No. 6017 illustrates the collapsible table in position. This fitment was normally stowed away in the vestibules, but by means of its one leg and two wall hooks, could be fixed into any compartment.

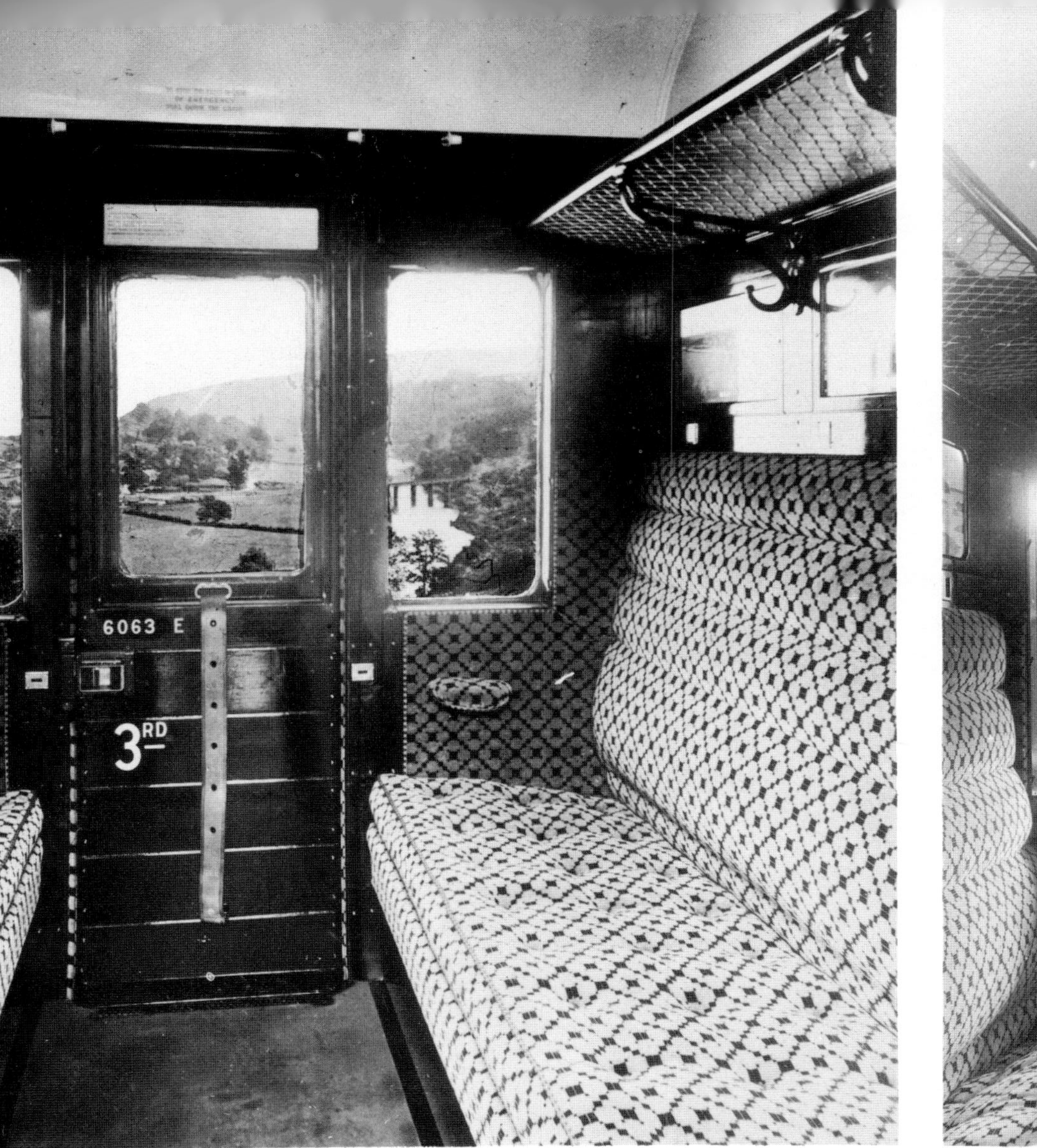

Fig. 453

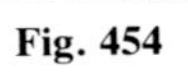
Fig. 454

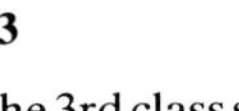
1933

Another change in materials for the upholstery of the 3rd class seating took place in the early 1930s. This was again a rep, having a warm pinky-grey base and a pronounced pattern of black, yellow and red. **Fig. 453** shows this new trim well, with the camera pointing towards the outer door. Note also the provision made to take the collapsible tables, previously used only in the 1st class compartments. **Fig. 454** was taken inside the same vehicle, but this time in one of the smoking compartments and looking towards the corridor side. The round object in the roof is the ventilator, which could be opened or shut by means of a sliding vane.

Fig. 455

Fig. 456

1933

A comparison here between a main line corridor carriage interior, and a non-corridor branch-line vehicle. **Fig. 455** is the inside of a 1st class corridor composite No. 6579 built to *Diagram E146* under Lot 1491 in 1933; the brown cloth three-a-side seating is clearly seen. Compare this interior with that of **Fig. 456** taken inside the 1st class compartment of No. 6707, *Diagram E147*, one of the 'B' set vehicles of Lot 1550 built in 1936. Note that the carpet bears the then new 'GWR' roundel in black pile, and the seating is only a spacious four with one folding armrest in the centre.

Fig. 457

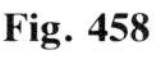
Fig. 458

1935

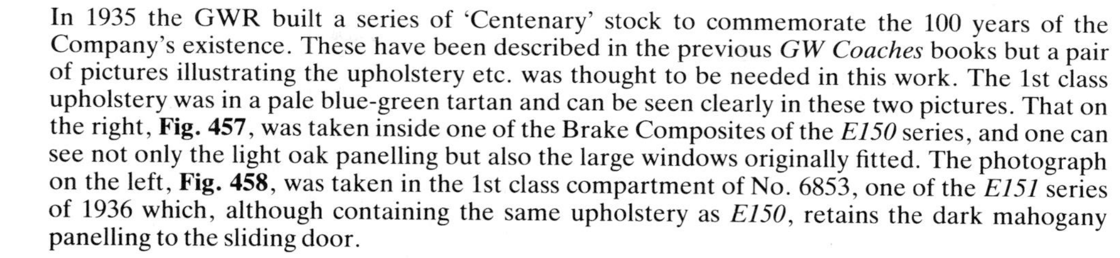
In 1935 the GWR built a series of 'Centenary' stock to commemorate the 100 years of the Company's existence. These have been described in the previous *GW Coaches* books but a pair of pictures illustrating the upholstery etc. was thought to be needed in this work. The 1st class upholstery was in a pale blue-green tartan and can be seen clearly in these two pictures. That on the right, **Fig. 457**, was taken inside one of the Brake Composites of the *E150* series, and one can see not only the light oak panelling but also the large windows originally fitted. The photograph on the left, **Fig. 458**, was taken in the 1st class compartment of No. 6853, one of the *E151* series of 1936 which, although containing the same upholstery as *E150*, retains the dark mahogany panelling to the sliding door.

Fig. 459

1936

Whilst still considering the 1935/6 internal decor of the *E151* series of composites it was thought that illustrations showing the layout of the corridor might be of interest to modellers and for reference. Therefore these two photographs are inserted for just that purpose. **Fig. 459** shows the view straight down the corridor from the 1st class end towards the dividing swing door which separated the 1st from 3rd class travellers. **Fig. 460** is inside the 3rd class side looking towards the same door, but from the other side.

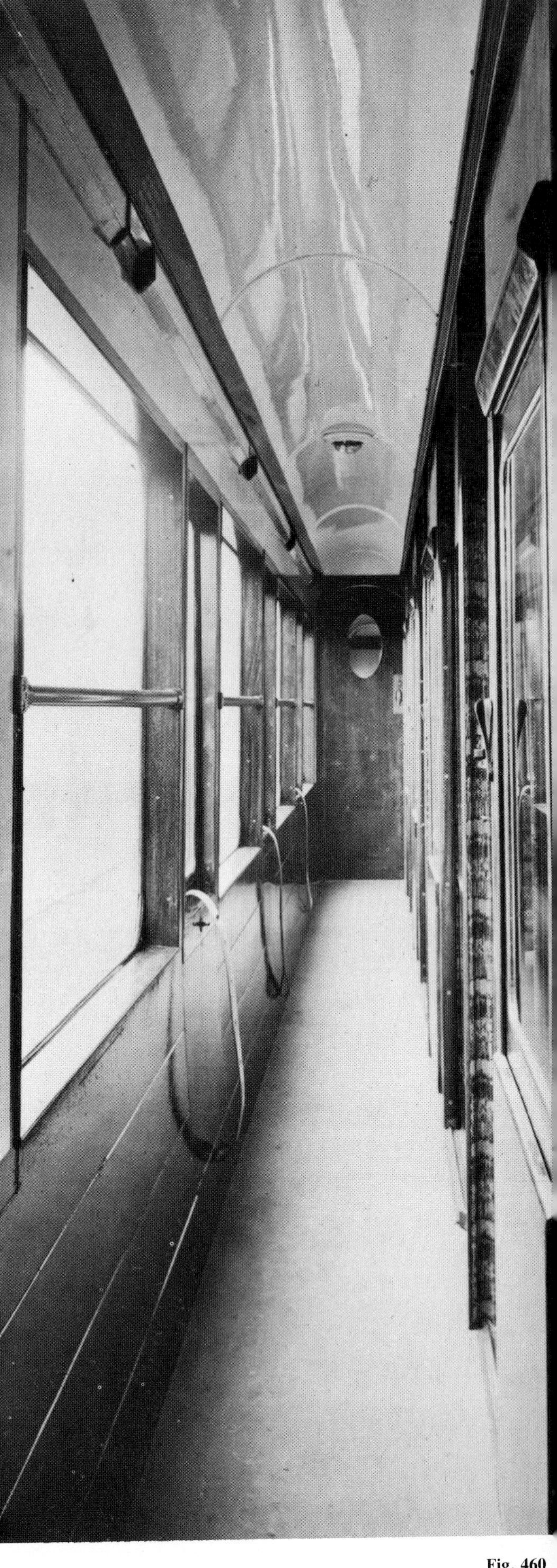

Fig. 460

Fig. 462

1936

The year 1936 saw the inception of so-called 'modernity' in the coach design on the Great Western Railway, and these two pictures show the new style well. **Fig. 461** is a 3rd class interior of a Composite, No. 6001 of the *E153* series. Note that the wood panels are in lighter birchwood veneers, and the upholstery is in the 'fan' design of orange and brown moquette. The large windows do not lower, but have sliding panels in the top halves and curtains have taken the place of roller blinds. **Fig. 462** shows the same materials for the trim, but this interior is one of the excursion stock series of *Diagram C71* under Lot 1558. This is a complete 3rd class vehicle with three semi-partitions without doors, dividing the seating up into three sections.

Fig. 461

Fig. 463

Fig. 464

Fig. 465

1937

Fig. 463 shows the internal decor of a 1st class compartment in 1937. The upholstery is still dark brown cloth, with veneer woodwork, in place of the heavy mahogany. This vehicle was a sixty-four seater non-corridor 1st and had a single retractable arm rest on each side of every compartment. Built to Lot 1566, its *Diagram* was *A21* and this vehicle was No. 8033. **Fig. 464** illustrates the van interior of one of the excursion Brake 3rds, *D123* vehicle No. 1298 and the guard's vestibule is seen in the centre. **Fig. 465** is of the combined van and guard's compartment in one of the non-corridor Brake 3rds, No. 1419 to be precise, of Lot 1570 to *Diagram D125*. The hand brake stands in the centre. The First Aid cabinet and fire extinguisher are on the left, steam radiator, seat, and letter rack are on the right.

Fig. 466

1938

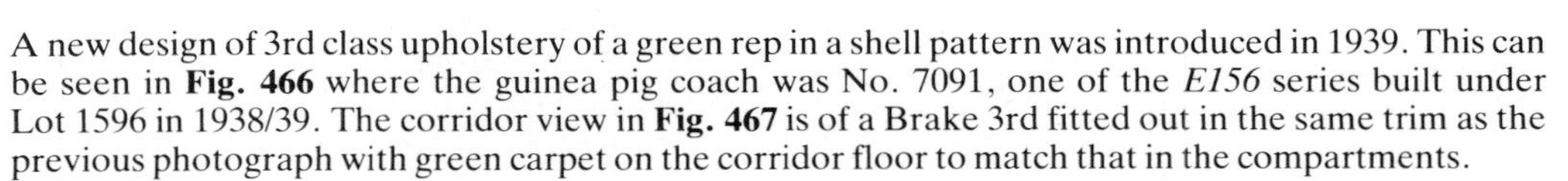

A new design of 3rd class upholstery of a green rep in a shell pattern was introduced in 1939. This can be seen in **Fig. 466** where the guinea pig coach was No. 7091, one of the *E156* series built under Lot 1596 in 1938/39. The corridor view in **Fig. 467** is of a Brake 3rd fitted out in the same trim as the previous photograph with green carpet on the corridor floor to match that in the compartments.

Fig. 467

Fig. 468

Fig. 469

1939

To show the 1st class interiors of this period, two pictures of the same vehicle are displayed here. **Fig. 468** is the view from the corridor sliding door looking towards the compartment window. The trim here is the same 1935 style of blue and green tartan with green-blue carpet, and curtains in box pelmets. **Fig. 469** is the same compartment, but looking in towards the corridor. Note the 'SMOKING' sign and ashtrays on the door pillars, with the roof ventilator just above the door. The carriage concerned was No. 7341 of Lot 1622 to *Diagram E159*.

Fig. 470

Fig. 471

1941

War-time in Britain called for some emergency measures inside passenger carriages. Firstly the windows were restricted in size by the addition of black strip around the edges. This can be seen in the illustration in **Fig. 470**. The notice reads 'Please keep blinds drawn during the blackout'. Secondly, all the interior light bulbs were exchanged for low wattage blue lamps, all designed of course to avoid giving away the movements of a train at night to enemy aircraft. These blue bulbs can be seen in the corridor side view of the *E159 Diagram* vehicle shown in **Fig. 471**.

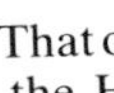

Fig. 472

Fig. 473

1945

Two 1st class compartments are shown here, both dated 1945. That on the left, **Fig. 472**, is the interior of four-a-side accommodation in a Brake Composite built especially for the Highworth Branch. The coach is No. 6831 of *Diagram E161*, Lot 1608. Note that the trim is still the chocolate cloth with gold piping. The notice reads 'Safety First. Before alighting, be sure the coach is at the platform'. **Fig. 473** on the right illustrates the new upholstery of the post-war period. This 1st class compartment in No. 7022, one of the *E158* series, has just been re-fitted with the updated trim, a fawn pattern floral design on a dark blue background, with fawn carpet to match.

The photograph on the left, **Fig. 474**, is also of No. 7022, the re-fitted *E158* design, and this shows the 3rd class decor, which was in the 1939 green rep with carpet and curtains to match. The wood panels were oak veneer with darker inlaid motif. **Fig. 475** shows the corridor of No. 796, one of the corridor 3rd carriages of the *C82 Diagram*. Note the rather stark simplicity of the design, the sliding panel in the window, and the single door in the corridor side.

Fig. 474

Fig. 475

Fig. 476

Fig. 477

Fig. 478

1947

In 1947/8 several passenger vehicles of the GWR were overhauled at Swindon and the re-furnishing and decor handed over to Messrs Hamdens. One of these vehicles was No. 6302, a corridor composite built in 1938 under Lot 1588 to *Diagram E160*. The three photographs shown here are from the left, **Fig. 476**, the lavatory compartment, **Fig. 477**, the corridor view and, on the right, **Fig. 478**, one of the 1st class compartments.

Fig. 480

1948

On the left of this page, **Fig. 479**, is the 3rd class compartment design of Messrs Hamdens, as applied to coach No. 6302. It serves as a good comparison with the Swindon fitted 3rd compartment of No. 398, shown on the right, **Fig. 480**. This was one of the *C83 Diagram* series, built under Lot 1693 of 1948. Personally, I think the GWR made a better job of it, but then of course I'm an old 'Western' man!

Fig. 481

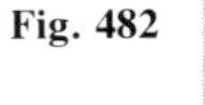

Fig. 482

1949

Two views, one in each direction, inside a post-war 1st class compartment of a corridor composite. **Fig. 481** shows the corridor side of No. 7252 of Lot 1689 built in 1948 to *Diagram E163.* For the opposite view, i.e. towards the compartment window, see **Fig. 482**. This was inside vehicle No. 7799 of *Diagram E165* built to Lot 1704 in 1949. Note the map of the system over the centre seat, which shows BR(WR) before Dr. Beeching wielded his axe.

Fig. 483

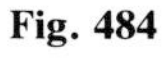

Fig. 484

1949

New stock built in 1948/49 bore the marks of a severe change of design in internal decoration, which heralded the change of ownership from GWR to British Railways. These two pictures illustrate this point fairly well. **Fig. 483** shows the outer door side of Corridor Brake 3rd No. 833, built in 1948 to *Diagram D131*, under Lot 1692. The view down the corridor seen in **Fig. 484** is of vehicle No. 7252, one of the *E163* series, built at the same time as the previous illustration. Note the severity of the corridor windows.

Fig. 485

Fig. 486

1950

Nevertheless, some carriage stock, built during the change-over from GWR to BR(WR) still bore the traditional coach-building standards of the old company and here we show examples of the 3rd class accommodation as at 1950. **Fig. 485** is of the corridor side of a 3rd compartment in No. 7799, one of the corridor composites of the *E165* series built under Lot 1704. The opposite view looking outwards is seen in **Fig. 486** taken inside No. 2646 of the *C83* series, a non-corridor 3rd constructed under Lot 1745.

Moving on into 1952, these two pictures show the interiors of, on the left, **Fig. 487**, a 3rd class compartment and, on the right, **Fig. 488**, a 1st class compartment. Both illustrations are of non-corridor vehicles, the 3rd class belonging to No. 7081 of the *E167 Diagram*, built under Lot 1750, and the 1st class is No. 7197, a composite of *E166* classification built under Lot 1762.

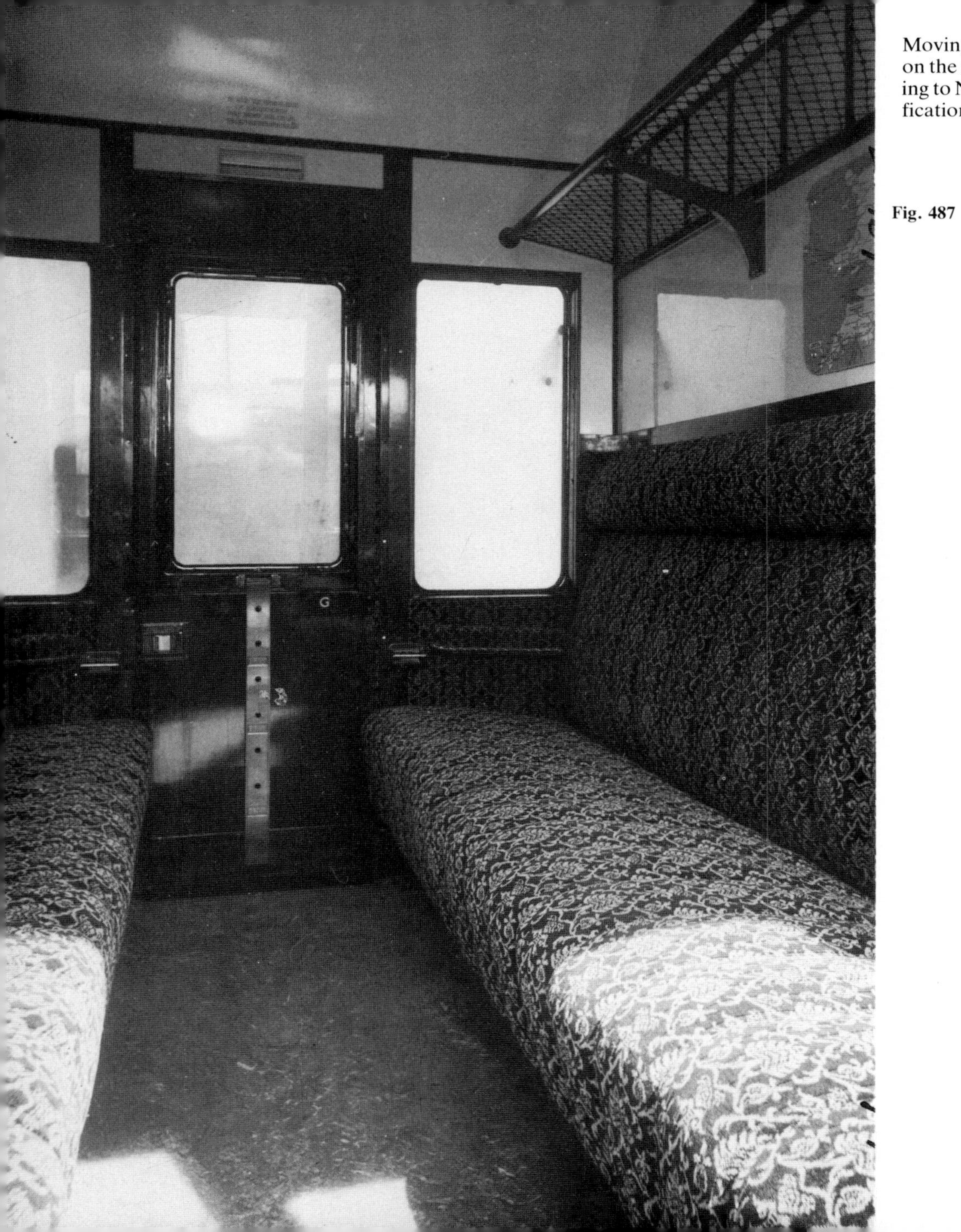

Fig. 487

Fig. 488

1953

Three different upholstery designs in British Railways stock circa 1953, that in **Fig. 489** being 1st class in vehicle No. 7389, one of the last 'B' sets built to GWR designs, to *Diagram E167*, Lot 1775. **Fig. 490** shows the 3rd class accommodation in the same series, and **Fig. 491** illustrates a different design of trim, but in the same series of *E167*.

Fig. 489

Fig. 490

Fig. 491

Fig. 492

1954

Finally, two pictures of British Railways floral design upholstery: **Fig. 492** shows a 3rd class compartment in the *D132* series, built under Lot 1764 and **Fig. 493**, the open 3rd series of Type J carriages built in 1954 under Lot 30079 by BR at York.

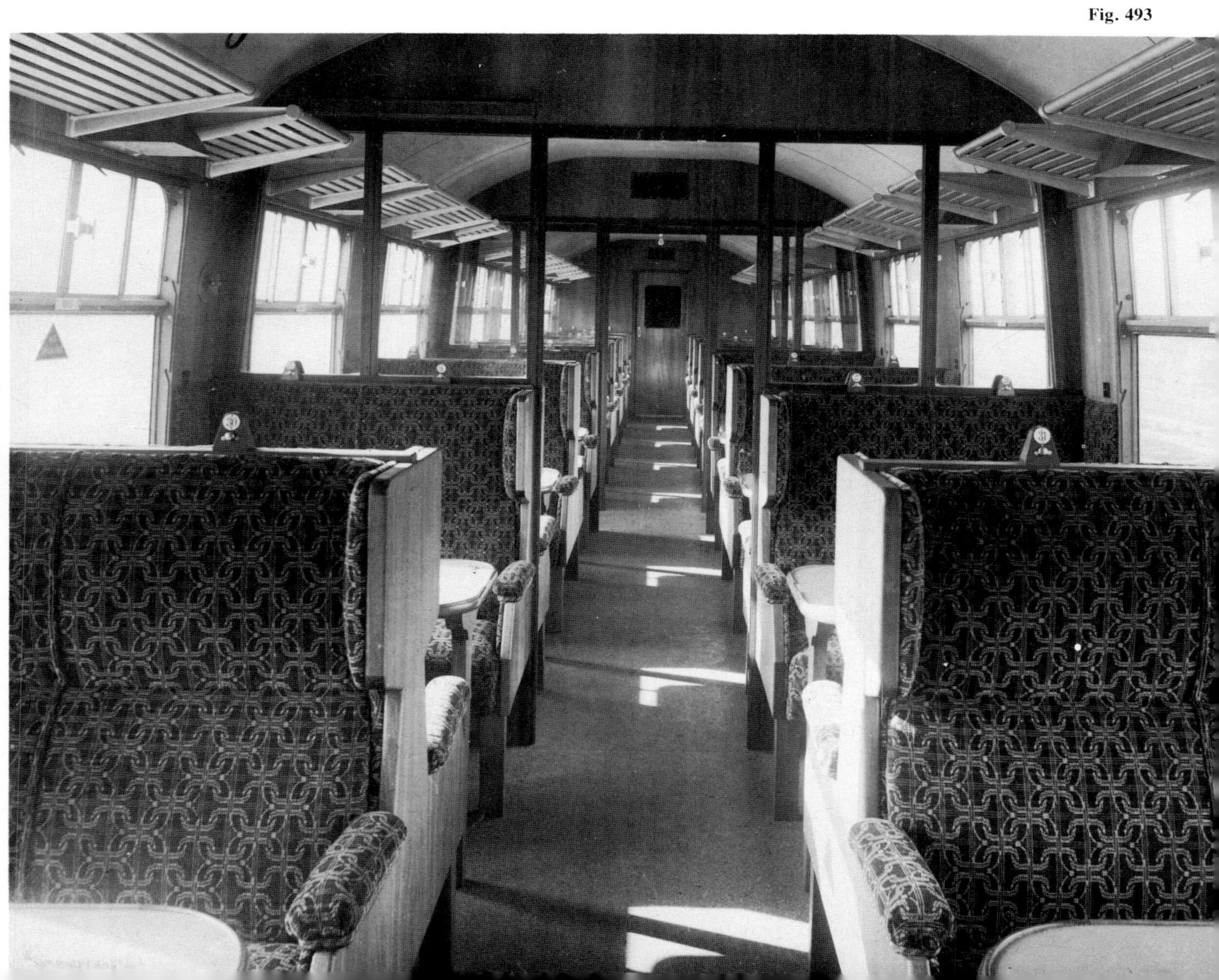

Fig. 493

As the great majority of the photographs in this work have been produced to illustrate specifically the variety of, and changes in, carriage body designs it was thought that some pages showing close-up detail of the standard fittings would round off this *Part 1* conveniently. On this page are two illustrations of the GWR standard suspended corridor connections. One view, **Fig. 494**, shows the gangways properly connected up, whilst **Fig. 495** depicts the detached condition.

Fig. 494

Fig. 495

Fig. 496

The two pictures here show clearly the vacuum brake cylinder, its mounting and part of the brake rigging, **Fig. 496**, whilst in the upper illustration, **Fig. 497**, the position of the cylinder on the underframe can be seen, just behind the truss angles queen posts. Note also the siting of the dynamo being driven via a large pulley wheel on the bogie axle.

Fig. 497

Fig. 498

Fig. 498 at the top of this page shows an example of the 'heavy duty' 9′ wheel-base plate carriage stock bogie. This type was often used on vehicles carrying parcels, mail, and milk etc. such as the 'Siphons', 'Monsters' and Passenger Brake Vans. In the lower illustration, **Fig. 499**, is the lighter duty 9′ plate bogie for carriages. It can be seen that this example is fitted with volute springs and Mansell wooden-centred wheels.

Fig. 499

Fig. 500

Two good, detailed pictures of the standard 9′ plate bogie are provided on this page. **Fig. 500** is the underneath view as the truck is being transported along the carriage shop, whilst in **Fig. 501** we see the same bogie being lowered on to the tracks. Note that the top halves of the axleboxes and the spring anchors are painted bright sky blue to indicate to carriage examiners the use of special bearings.

Fig. 501

Fig. 502

Fig. 503

These pictures show three stages in the fitting of wheels to the standard underframe. In **Fig. 502** the chassis is being lowered on to the 9′ bogie; **Fig. 503** shows one end completed, and in **Fig. 504** the finished underframe is seen outside the Swindon carriage shop, awaiting its body.

Fig. 504

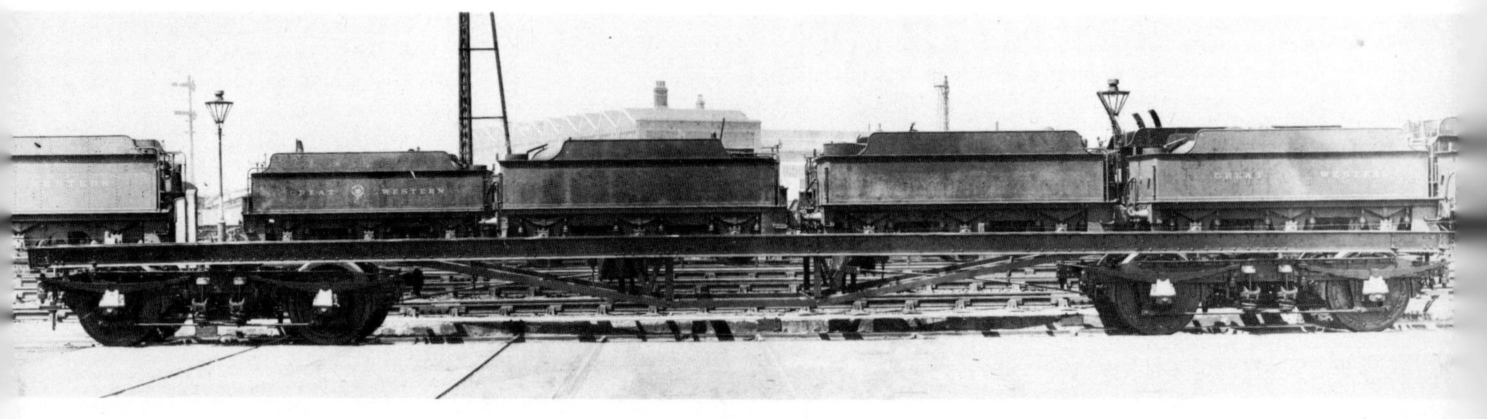

Fig. 505

Three angled views of the GWR 9′ wheel-base, pressed-steel bogie. **Fig. 505** shows the end view, and the dynamo pulley can be seen through the holes in the end stretcher. **Fig. 506** is an excellent view looking down on to the top of the bogie, showing the centre boss and the side bearers, as well as the brake rigging. Finally, a three-quarter view at ground level, **Fig. 507**, showing both side and end of this well known Swindon product.

Fig. 506

Fig. 507

Fig. 508

Fig. 509

During the construction of the Hawksworth series of carriage stock in 1948, an experimental chassis was constructed of light alloy and the upper illustration shows this underframe before undergoing trials, **Fig. 508.**

Figs. 509 and **510** are two more views of the Swindon 9′ pressed-steel bogie; full side view and top three-quarter.

Fig. 510

Fig. 511

Fig. 512

Finally, three photographs illustrating the standard GWR carriage underframe, fitted with the 9′ pressed-steel bogies, **Figs. 511**, **512** and **513**. All the details are clearly visible, and the only point I would draw attention to, is the pronounced upward bow of the channel section solebars. This would of course be cancelled out upon receiving the weight of the carriage body.

Fig. 513

COPIES OF ORIGINAL GWR COACH DIAGRAM DRAWINGS AVAILABLE FROM BRITISH RAIL/OXFORD PUBLISHING CO. JOINT VENTURE

Diagram	Drawing Order No.	Type
A7	14723/C	First
A8	14724/C	First
A9	14725/C	First
A10	14726/C	First
A11	14727/C	First
A12	14728/C	First
A13	14729/C	First
A15	14731/C	First
A16	14732/C	First
A17	14733/C	First
A18	14734/C	First
A19	14735/C	First
A20	14736/C	First
A22	14738/C	First
A23	14739/C	First
C19	14757/C	Third
C23	14761/C	Third
C24	14762/C	Third
C25	14763/C	Third
C29	14767/C	Third
C30	14768/C	Third
C31	14770/C	Third
C32	14771/C	Third
C33	14772/C	Third
C35	14774/C	Third
C38	14778/C	Third
C39	14779/C	Third
C45	14785/C	Third
C46	14786/C	Third
C49	14789/C	Third
C50	14791/C	Third
C52	14793/C	Third
C53	14794/C	Third
C54	14795/C	Third
C58	14799/C	Third
C59	14800/C	Third
C60	14801/C	Third
C62	14803/C	Third
C63	14804/C	Third
C64	14805/C	Third
C65	14807/C	Third
C66	14808/C	Third
C67	14809/C	Third
C68	14811/C	Third
C69	14812/C	Third
C70	14814/C	Third
C71	14815/C	Third
C72	14816/C	Third
C73	14818/C	Third
C74	14819/C	Third
C76	14822/C	Third
C77	14823/C	Third
C81	14828/C	Third
C82	14829/C	Third
C83	14830/C	Third
C84	14831/C	Third
C85	14832/C	Third
D8	15427/C	Brake Third
D10	15429/C	Brake Third
D27	15446/C	Brake Third
D29	15448/C	Brake Third
D30	15449/C	Brake Third
D32	15451/C	Brake Third
D42	15464/C	Brake Third
D43	15465/C	Brake Third
D44	15466/C	Brake Third
D45	15467/C	Brake Third
D46	15468/C	Brake Third
D47	15469/C	Brake Third
D48	15470/C	Brake Third
D49	15472/C	Brake Third
D51	15474/C	Brake Third
D52	15475/C	Brake Third
D53	15476A/C	Brake Third
D55	15477/C	Brake Third
D56	15478/C	Brake Third
D57	15479/C	Brake Third
D62	15484/C	Brake Third
D67	15489/C	Brake Third
D69	15491/C	Brake Third
D80	15503/C	Brake Third
D82	15505/C	Brake Third
D83	15506/C	Brake Third
D84	15507/C	Brake Third
D85	15508/C	Brake Third
D86	15509/C	Brake Third
D87	15510/C	Brake Third
D88	15511/C	Brake Third

Diagram	Drawing Order No.	Type
D90	15513/C	Brake Third
D91	15514/C	Brake Third
D92	15515/C	Brake Third
D93	15516/C	Brake Third
D94	15517/C	Brake Third
D95	15518/C	Brake Third
D98	15521/C	Brake Third
D101	15524/C	Brake Third
D104	15527/C	Brake Third
D105	15528/C	Brake Third
D106	15529/C	Brake Third
D107	15530/C	Brake Third
D109	15532/C	Brake Third
D111	15534/C	Brake Third
D115	15538/C	Brake Third
D116	15539/C	Brake Third
D117	15540/C	Brake Third
D118	15541/C	Brake Third
D119	15542/C	Brake Third
D120	15544/C	Brake Third
D121	15546/C	Brake Third
D122	15547/C	Brake Third
D123	15548/C	Brake Third
D124	15549/C	Brake Third
D127	15552/C	Brake Third
D130	15555/C	Brake Third
D132	15557/C	Brake Third
D133	15558/C	Brake Third
E66	14922/C	Composite
E69	14923/C	Composite
E70	14924/C	Composite
E77	14930/C	Composite
E78	14932/C	Composite
E79	14933/C	Composite
E82	14936/C	Brake Composite
E83	14937/C	Brake Composite
E85	14939/C	Composite
E87	14941/C	Brake Composite
E88	14942/C	Composite
E89	14943/C	Composite
E97	14951/C	Composite
E93	14947/C	Composite
E94	14948/C	Brake Composite
E95	14949/C	Brake Composite
E96	14950/C	Composite
E98	14952/C	Composite
E99	14953/C	Brake Composite
E101	14955/C	Composite
E102	14956/C	Composite
E104	14958/C	Brake Composite
E108	14962/C	Composite
E111	14965/C	Composite
E112	14966/C	Composite
E113	14967/C	Brake Composite
E115	14969/C	Composite
E116	14970/C	Brake Composite
E118	14972/C	Composite
E124	14978/C	Composite
E127	14981/C	Composite
E128	14982/C	Brake Composite
E129	14983/C	Brake Composite
E131	14985/C	Composite
E132	14986/C	Composite
E134	14988/C	Composite
E136	14990/C	Composite
E137	14991/C	Composite
E138	14992/C	Brake Composite
E140	14994/C	Brake Composite
E141	14995/C	Composite
E143	14997/C	Composite
E145	14999/C	Composite
E146	15000/C	Brake Composite
E147	15001/C	Brake Composite
E148	15002/C	Brake Composite
E149	15003/C	Composite
E151	15007/C	Composite
E152	15008/C	Brake Composite
E153	15009/C	Brake Composite
E155	15011/C	Composite
E157	15014/C	Brake Composite
E158	15015/C	Composite
E159	15016/C	Brake Composite
E162	15019/C	Composite
E163	15020/C	Composite
E164	15021/C	Brake Composite
E165	15023/C	Composite
E166	15024/C	Composite
E156	15012/C	Composite